W9-AOQ-543

The Arabesque Table

The Arabesque Table

Contemporary Recipes from the Arab World

Reem Kassis

Legend

Vegan

Vegetarian

Dairy-free

Gluten-free

30 minutes or less

5 ingredients or less

Introduction

The Tastes of Home

My father's two favorite dishes are *hareeseh* (a stew of wheat with lamb and chicken) and *kubbeh nìyeh* (a lamb and bulgur tartare). He always eats them with such zest, the smile on his face wider than any we are used to seeing. It's usually on the occasions of such meals that he speaks openly of his childhood in the hills of the Galilee and of how delicious his mother's food was, his elaborate tales ending along with the meal.

Hareeseh and *kubbeh nìyeh* were never my preferred dishes growing up, they were too rustic and lacking excitement. Then again, I found fault in almost every dish my mother made, not just those two. It was only once I left Jerusalem at age seventeen that I started to appreciate her cooking and realize how exceptional it was, ultimately writing *The Palestìnìan Table* as an ode to my family and the foods I had grown up with.

While I was working on *The Arabesque Table* in Philadelphia, the world was in the grip of a viral outbreak that wreaked havoc on everyone's lives. The photo shoot was set to start in March at my childhood home in Jerusalem. Two days before traveling, a blanket quarantine was issued and I had to cancel our flights. My daughters were disappointed to not see their grandparents, and while my heart ached for them, it shattered at the distance and lack of control we have to be close to those we love. I put on a brave face for my parents, but the minute I hung up the phone with them, tears streamed against my strongest efforts to hold them in. It would be the first time in my life I would go for more than a year without seeing my aging parents.

I remembered then my father telling us about the many years he spent abroad in the United States, where he would write letters to his parents to schedule a time to call twice a year on the only phone in the village. Maybe I am being a little unreasonable and overly emotional, I thought. In this day and age, I FaceTimed every day. But in that instant, all I craved was the warmth of my mother's embrace, the scent of our home, and the flavors of the stuffed chicken and rolled grape leaves she had promised to prepare on the day we were supposed to land. Suddenly, I understood why my father loved those two dishes so much. It wasn't the dishes themselves, it was the memories they kept alive for him. It was the connection to a past that had started to slip away. I was now the parent whose strongest tie to her family and past were the humble dishes of a childhood, which in spite of having been spent in the midst of war, conflict, and uncertainty, was nonetheless a warm and happy one.

Over the following weeks, recollections of my childhood flickered in and out of focus, as they often do on the days I am most nostalgic. After so many years spent living abroad, I still crave the warmth of our family kitchen, the smells wafting through our door when I arrive, and the pleasure on my parents' faces when they see me and my own family now enjoying something they have prepared. I crave the things that say welcome home.

What Is Home?

By the time this book reaches your hands, I will have spent more years living abroad than I did growing up in Jerusalem. Still, I refer to Jerusalem as home. I'm writing this final part in the middle of June, in Jerusalem, where the smells of grape leaves and apricot blossoms mingle in the air. I tread the smooth cobblestone steps leading to Damascus gate and into the belly of a city as old as history itself. I breathe in the perfumed summer breeze, ignoring the exhaust fumes and honks coming from the road above, and I realize this is where I feel most at home, but also where I feel most out of place. My years abroad have changed me, just as this holy city shrouded in mystery and spirituality has also changed.

Home is such an elusive notion, and I catch myself wondering, what will my daughters call home? Yasmeen and Hala were born in London where we spent five years. We then relocated to Philadelphia where our closest friends are Korean, Indian, Jewish, and Arab. My daughters spend their summers back in Jerusalem and are proud to be Palestinian. They eat *maqlubeh* and *maftool* (with some coaxing), but their nightly dinner table is as likely to have hummus as it is to have sushi, schnitzel, or pizza—the preferred foods of most four- and six-year olds I imagine?

I compare my childhood to theirs. I grew up between three kitchens where my mother's and grandmothers' pantries smelled of nutmeg and allspice, their cupboards of za'atar and pickled olives, and their storage rooms of freekeh and bulgur. I look at my pantry and refrigerator today, and wedged against my bottle of pomegranate molasses is a jar of kimchee, and next to a bag of za'atar is a bag of kasuri methi, and beneath the Arabic script on the leafy-green tahini jar are block English letters on a can of Italian tomatoes. This is symbolic not only of my kitchen, but of life as we know it today.

When I first set out to write this book, I wanted to capture this evolving and cross-cultural Arab table. I quickly realized, though, that to truly understand this modern life and way of eating, one had to understand the entire culinary history of the Arab World and the journey that brought us to this point. We spend so much time celebrating certain dishes or debating the origins of others without paying heed to just how rich and complicated the culinary past of our region is. History leaves its marks through a region's architecture, music, markets, literary arts . . . and most of all, through its cuisine. Cuisine holds memory and history, and in the case of the Arab World, it speaks of occupations and cultural migrations as it charts the fluctuating face of our region and its shifting borders.

To the extent that one can capture these details in a 256-page cookbook, I have slipped in snippets of this history whenever and wherever possible. From the elaborate banquets of the caliphs and the wars waged over rare spices, to the historic recipes reimagined for today's cook and the cutting-edge chefs inspired by multiple culinary traditions, *The Arabesque Table* is more than just a compilation of modern Arabic recipes. It is a book that celebrates the evolution of our cuisine and the stories of cross-cultural connection it recounts while paying tribute to the history and journey that have led us to this point.

What Is National Cuisine?

Since leaving Jerusalem, I have lived in five different countries. At every turn, I have wondered where our sense of rootedness comes from. Does it come from a land that houses and feeds a family for generations, or is it family and shared history that give meaning and value to the land? I don't pretend to have the full answer, but my personal experience tells me that what binds us to a place and to others is more than political borders and artificial constructs. It is our collective memories: the shared stories, foods, smells, and music that we attach meaning to. It is the tales told around a fire under the sky of a land handed down for generations. It is the sound of a *ka'ak* vendor pushing his wooden cart through a thronged street, and the smell of garlic frying in olive oil before being splashed into a bubbling stew. It is the image of blossoming olive groves, the taste of their freshly pressed liquid gold. It is the feel of a young grape leaf between our fingers, perfectly ripe for picking. It is the meals our mothers made for us when we were sick or sad, and the ones they prepared when we were celebrating too. It is these most taken-for-granted details that over time become the collective memories of a family, and of a population, forming our broader shared identities.

What I believe humans share above all else, however, is the desire for connection and belonging. And at the end of the day, that's what food is about. Inviting someone to eat at your table is a very intimate act, an expression of love. You are welcoming them into your life and sharing with them not only a meal, but the history and stories the meal holds. That was exactly what I attempted to do with my first book, *The Palestinian Table*. In it, I wove a very personal narrative of my family's recipes and stories through which I invited others to explore the history of Palestinian cuisine and the often-overlooked narrative of its people.

In the process of writing and promoting the book, I became immersed in the world of food and food history. I started to see how interconnected that history was, how difficult it is to delineate the exact origins of every dish we eat, and how many ingredients are not native to the lands that use them most.

Take a moment and think of Italian food. Many of the first dishes we think of today as Italian are heavily tomato based. When we think Belgian or Swiss, chocolate is one of the first things that come to mind. Go to a Thai restaurant, and it's hard to fathom eating a curry that doesn't use chili peppers. Yet, none of these foods is native to those nations. Tomatoes, cacao, and chilies are all native to Mexico and South America and only reached Europe and Asia after the Spanish colonization of the Americas. The same applies to Spanish food itself. Tapas, some of the most recognized components of Spanish cuisine today, rely heavily on frying—think croquetas, patatas bravas, and fried seafood. The very use of oil for deep-frying, however, was only introduced to Spain by the Moors in the Middle Ages. We may think of shawarma and falafel as unique to the Middle East, but can you find one culture across the world that does not take a kind of meat or vegetable and wrap it in some form of bread? From Mexican tacos and Chinese baos to Italian strombolis and Indian kati rolls, cultures across the world are more similar than we care to admit.

Today, there is a big trend toward highlighting the nuances that set different national cuisines apart. We think of ourselves as cultured and sophisticated the more we know about the unique culinary traditions of individual nations. But the very idea of a national cuisine is a relatively recent construct, rising only in the late eighteenth and early nineteenth centuries with the rise of the nation state. At its core, food is a regional and ethnic artifact, often more closely tied to language and religion than it is to an arbitrary political boundary. Think of religious or ethnic groups, such as Armenians, who live across the world but share the same cuisine regardless of where they are. Compare this to people living in the same country, such as India, where the population enjoys vastly different culinary practices and cuisines across the nation. It quickly becomes obvious that religion, language, and landscape, as well as geography, climate, and socio-economic factors, are the vital components in defining food culture.

National cuisine is a beautiful way to forge a unique collective identity in the face of a rapidly globalizing world. But rather than focus on what differentiates the various cuisines of the Arab world, I take a step back in *The Arabesque Table* to show the commonality across the many Arab nations, celebrate the beauty of learning from one another, and recognize the impact of our interaction with outside culinary traditions. While reading this, the word *fusion* may come to mind, but fusion is not new to the Arab world. Centuries of migration, occupation, and trade have left their mark on our cuisine. The kind of cultural integration we see happening in our cuisine today has been visible throughout history, and an honest account of any culinary landscape admits and celebrates the positive angles of this history, recognizing that no cuisine is stagnant, but rather a dynamic force that changes through circumstance, integrates with other cultures, and evolves with the times.

A Word on History

The Fertile Crescent—the Cradle of Civilization where agriculture originated, or more recently—the Middle East, has long been a major center of world affairs, its important role in trade, geopolitics, and religion recognized for millennia. But alongside this privileged position comes a tumultuous history of fallen empires, occupations, and centuries of migration stretching from the start of civilization to the present day. The ingredients, cooking methods, and dishes enjoyed throughout this history have evolved and changed just like the region itself.

The first strokes of writing—the cuneiform script—were taken in this region and then used to record, on stone tablets, the oldest recipes known to man around the seventeenth century BCE. From there, it's a period of silence until about the eighth or ninth century AD after which several Arabic recipe collections were recorded. At the height of medieval Arab civilization between the seventh and thirteenth centuries AD, Arabs were the only people in the world even writing cookbooks. It was also during this period that the Arabs conquered Persia, incorporating many of their culinary practices, and the Moors occupied Spain and ended up influencing the entirety of European cuisine.

Following this period, the Ottoman Turks became the predominant power in the region, their cuisine taking cue from *Kitab al-Tabìkh* and *Kitab Wasf al-At'ima al-Mu'tada*, both medieval Arabic cookbooks. In the fifteenth century, the court physician of Sultan Murad II translated the tenth century *Kitab al-Tabìkh*, adding more of his own recipes, and the first Turkish cookbook was born. From there, the Ottoman Turks went on to learn and borrow culinary arts from all over the empire, evolving their cuisine into the one of stuffed vegetables, shish kebabs, and baklavas we recognize in the eastern Mediterranean.

Today, our interaction with other cultures happens on an entirely different level. As information exchange accelerates, global travel rises, and social and technological advancements occur, the way people think, interact, cook, and eat rapidly changes. We can explore new cultures and countries from the comfort of our homes, the Internet gives us access to more information about history than ever before, and an increase in migration means we can experience foreign cultures right in our backyards.

The spirit of Arab cuisine lies in these kinds of journeys that our dishes and customs have taken, and in the experiences and history they have endured, to tell a tale of unique culinary transformation and transmission. *The Arabesque Table* is the tale that celebrates this rich past while showcasing what it has evolved into today. It is a journey from the earliest Arabic cookbooks on record to the dishes being cooked by cutting-edge Arab chefs and home cooks across the region and abroad. It is meals steeped in history but reimagined for our lifestyles today.

A Word on Terminology

One of the issues we face in history and politics, and the social sciences in general, is a lack of agreed-upon terminology. Where does one region start and end? Where exactly did the Spice Routes pass and what do they refer to? And for our purpose, what exactly is the Middle East and how is it different from the Arab world?

The term "Middle East" only really came into use in the early twentieth century as a European perception of a region between Western Europe and the British colony of India in the East. Today, there are different definitions for the Middle East, which often overlap and change according to shifting perspectives. Some include Iran and Turkey, others add in some countries of the Mediterranean, and others yet will include North Africa and different parts of the Islamic world. But we continue to use the term Middle East in the culinary world, usually without specificity, because it's sensually evocative and easy to grasp.

The Middle East is a vast and fluid area, but its collective culture has been shaped by a common history reflecting a long acculturation process under Arab and Islamic rule. When I think of the Middle East, I think of the Arab world, of the twenty-two countries stretching from the Atlantic Ocean to the Arabian Sea. When we go as far back in culinary history as I have in this book, we also see it is Arab culture that defines the historic cuisine of the region, not artificial geographic terms like "Middle East." That is why I have chosen to use the terms "Arab/Arabic" to more accurately portray the dishes and history of this region. The recipes within are inspired by the cuisines and ingredients of the entire region, from Morocco and Sudan to Lebanon, Palestine, and the Arabian Gulf. Given my background and the personal nature of this book, the bulk of inspiration is naturally from the Levant—or present-day Palestine, Lebanon, Syria, and Jordan. I say inspiration because many of these recipes have been influenced by different culinary traditions, by my travels, or by access I had to ingredients, while others either have been adapted to suit our modern lifestyle or have their roots in history, in ancient Arab recipes, reimagined for today's cook.

The Arabesque Table

Having spent the better part of the last three years researching Arabic food, I see just how intertwined the roots of cuisine across the world are and how heavily we influence each other over the course of history. The truth is, the past of the Arab world has not always been peaceful. The rise and fall of empires has left no one in the region unscathed, but our cuisine has emerged stronger and richer as a result. It is a cuisine predicated on hospitality, and whose ingredients and dishes chart the changing face of a region that has existed since the dawn of civilization, and whose sphere of influence has reached every corner of the world.

Choosing a name to convey the spirit of this book took longer than writing it. In fact, I submitted my second draft of the manuscript and completed the photo shoot without a title in mind. In hindsight, this turned out to be a blessing, because rather than forcing the book to fit into a title, the title ultimately emerged from the journey of writing this book and the many lessons I learned along the way.

I was sitting in my childhood garden, sipping on lemonade sweetened with homemade rose syrup, when my mother asked what was on my mind. My head was bent down, my fingers mindlessly tracing a pattern on the tiled table in front of me. "I can't think of an appropriate title for the book," I said. We chatted for a long time, but still, no title felt right. For weeks I sat at this table in the afternoons, writing, thinking, and chatting, mindlessly observing the patterns, before I realized what I was looking for had been in front of me all along. I had been putting the finishing touches on this book at an arabesque table.

Arabesque is an ornamental design of intertwined flowing lines originally found in Arab and Islamic art. The intricate patterns draw inspiration from the natural world to create intersecting and everchanging patterns.

Just like its namesake, this book weaves recipes and stories of past and present to tell a tale of culinary evolution as old as cuisine itself. No cuisine is a straight line stretching infinitely back in time. Rather, it is just like an arabesque pattern, flowing and intertwined, its beauty not intrinsic but enriched by the kaleidoscope of interlaced and potentially infinite designs that inspired this title.

If there is one thing I want this book to convey, it is that we are always moving forward, learning from others, adapting and evolving; but without understanding our history and where we've come from, we cannot sustain our journey forward with integrity. That's why the recipes within have built on a solid past even as they extend into the future. They may take inspiration from various culinary traditions, they may push beyond what we recognize and show us new possibilities, but they remain firmly rooted in a deep awareness of, and appreciation for, the past from which they have risen. So I urge you to approach this book in that same spirit, keeping in mind the porous nature of cuisine and the wealth that comes from culinary diffusion, but only so long as we respect the historic origins of our food and their contribution to our cuisines today.

Ingredients

One of the things I have tried to convey with this book is the fluid nature of cuisine: how vastly recipes change over time, how recipes attributed to one culture have their origins in another, and how historic trade routes have shaped not only the course of history but the very face of our cuisine as we know it.

My fascination with this topic started a few years ago when I realized how many national dishes were made of ingredients not native to those nations. When I started researching where crops come from, I was surprised to see just how much of what is consumed around the world is native to our region. Artichokes, asparagus, beets, cabbage, carrots, cauliflower, dates, grapes, okra, olives, peas, pulses of varying kinds, and turnips are all native to Western Asia (a pragmatic rather than exact term, translating roughly to present-day Middle East and parts of the Mediterranean and North Africa). But the advent of trade allowed the domestication of other vegetables in the region that thrive there today—thanks to complex irrigation systems developed in ancient times—like summer squash, eggplants (aubergines), cucumbers, tomatoes, and potatoes.

The history of these various crops is touched on in the headnotes of relevant recipes. This ingredient section, however, delves into Arab pantry staples—the way a pantry section in any cookbook would—but offers more information on the origins of each and how it made its way into Arab cuisine.

Aleppo Pepper
Chilies are native to South and Central America but made their way to the Middle East along the Silk Road sometime during the fifteenth and sixteenth century Columbian Exchange. Because environmental factors (terroir) affect a crop's phenotype, chilies grown in Aleppo have a distinct flavor, even compared to those grown in neighboring Turkey. Usually sold dried and coarsely ground, they have a marked bright red color and a complex flavor that goes well with the strong, earthy ingredients of Arab cooking. If Aleppo pepper is called for in a recipe, you can substitute with other peppers such as Urfa, Marash, and Antep, named after the respective Turkish towns in which they grow (Sanliurfa, Kahramanmaras, and Gaziantep).

Almond
Native to West and Central Asia (roughly present-day Iran and the Middle East), the almond was of great importance in early Arab cookery, not only for garnish and flavor, but also as a thickening agent. In fact, it was initially used as the thickening agent in sweet milk puddings in medieval Arab cookery, from which Europeans adopted the idea for blancmange (a panna cotta–like dessert). The Arab influence on Europe made the almond ubiquitous in European cuisine, particularly Spanish cuisine. In the Middle East, almond is eaten at all phases of maturity, from green picked right off trees and dipped in salt, to dried, cracked, and toasted, and every option in between.

Aniseed
Not to be confused with star anise, aniseed is a plant native to the Levant. The seeds of this flowering plant have an unmistakable sweet flavor, reminiscent of licorice and fennel. The primary ingredient in flavoring arak, the Arab alcoholic drink of choice, aniseed is also used widely in baked desserts and breads, or simply boiled and the water sipped to aid with digestion. It can be sourced online or in specialty grocery stores.

Bulgur
Usually made out of durum wheat, a species of wheat native to the Middle East, bulgur is made by parboiling the wheat until plump, then drying it and cracking it into different sizes. The fine grain is used mostly for making kubbeh, the medium for making tabbouleh, and the coarse one for cooking. In grocery stores they are often marked as #1, #2, and #3, with #1 being the finest.

Dill
Although Eastern European is the cuisine most likely to spring to mind when you think of dill, the plant itself is native to the Levant and from the same family as the aniseed plant. It is the dill seed that is most prevalent in Arab cooking—Gazan and Egyptian in particular—more so than the fronds. Since it is widely available, I love to incorporate the fronds in large quantities into salads (see Dill, Mint, and Cranberry Almond Salad, page 104).

Lemon
Ubiquitous in Arab cooking, lemons are actually native to Southeast Asia. But the lemon's spread throughout the Mediterranean and Europe was the result of Arab conquest in the region. It was the Arabs who also spread the lemon eastward to China where its name *li mung* is a derivative of the Arabic word *leymun*. But it is the Arab kitchen that probably makes the most use of this fragrant fruit, not only in its fresh form, but also preserved and dried.

Lentil
Lentils originated in the Near East and have been cultivated since antiquity. The seeds come in various sizes and colors, with the brown and red (essentially a split brown lentil) ones being the most commonly used in Arab cooking. I have found, however, that I like using other varieties like beluga and French green (Puy) lentils for recipes where I want the lentils to retain their shape and texture.

Nigella Seed
"It cures everything, except death," or so many Muslims believe the prophet Mohammed to have said about the nigella seed. Native to the region, there are records of it being used as far back as four thousand years. Not to be confused with black sesame, onion seeds, or black cumin, nigella seed has a strong herby, albeit bitter, flavor. It is mostly used in small quantities to flavor baked goods, although some people grind it finely and mix it with honey, then use it as you would peanut butter. Palestinians also make a black cake flavored entirely with nigella. I love its distinct taste, but for many it can be a love-it-or-hate-it flavor.

Olive Oil
If there is one ingredient more meaningful than any other to the Arab world, to the Levant (Syria, Lebanon, Jordan, and Palestine) in particular, it is the olive and its ensuing oil. Rife with symbolism and holding history as ancient as humanity itself, the olive tree's origin can actually be traced to the Levant. Historic documents show its value to have been five times that of wine and two and a half times that of other oils. Its rising popularity today has, unfortunately, left plenty of room for adulteration, making it one of the most tainted industries in the world. Just because a bottle in the grocery store says "extra-virgin" does not mean it is, nor does it guarantee that it is exclusively olive oil. But price is usually a good indicator, as is Protected Designation of Origin (PDO). Since good olive oil is worth seeking out, here are a few things to look for when buying: oil is packaged in darker bottles or tins, it has a date of harvest or pressing, it is not mass marketed, and it is single-source origin or has a PDO.

Orange Blossom and Rose Water
Floral waters go back centuries, with medieval banquets probably smelling more of perfume than food. People used these distilled waters to perfume themselves before and after eating, but also to finish off and flavor countless dishes, both savory and sweet. They are as they sound, waters distilled with the essence of different flowers. They do not have deep flavors, the way vanilla might, but rather very strong aromas that are transportive. They are the first flavor to hit your taste buds and the last one to linger. If overused, they can lend an overpowering and bitter taste, so use sparingly until you know how strong the particular brand you have is. My preferred one is Mymouné, because it is naturally distilled in Lebanon the way it has been for centuries.

Pine Nut
There are many different species of pine nuts, but the ones used in the Middle East come from the stone pine, which is native to the Mediterranean region. They are distinguished

by their more slender shape and uniform texture and color, and their flavor is more buttery and sweet. Evidence of their use goes back to biblical times, and to this day, they are used as garnish or to flavor rice, stuffings, and desserts. Their use in desserts across Europe can in fact be traced to the Arab influence on medieval European cookery. Today, they are one of the most expensive nuts on the market, second only to macadamias; but since they are used in small quantities, it is worth it to buy the best you can find.

Rice
The world's earliest known evidence of rice cultivation goes back thousands of years to either China or Korea, but its journey to becoming the staple food for half of humanity was relatively slow. Most likely brought from Asia to the Near East by the Persians, it was not a staple and only started to be grown in Egypt after the sixth or seventh century. During the Golden Age of Islam (eight to fourteenth century AD), Arabs spread rice to Europe and North Africa, and the Columbian Exchange brought rice to the New World. Although rice became an important part of the Arabic culinary repertoire, it was generally reserved for the wealthy. Only in the last few decades has it replaced wheat and its ensuing products as a staple grain.

Semolina
Like bulgur, semolina is also made out of durum wheat, a species of wheat native to the Middle East. The difference is that it is not parboiled, and the brittle grains are coarsely milled into sharp chips. This process makes it a tough grain that does not become a starchy paste when cooked. Instead, it lends dishes a light, granular texture. It is used mostly in desserts in the Arab world and comes in varying degrees of coarseness from fine to medium to coarse. Do not confuse it with Italian semolina flour or farina, which cannot be substituted for it in dishes.

Sesame Seed
One of the first oilseed plants to be domesticated, it is native to Egypt or the Near East, but has been cultivated in other parts of Africa and India since ancient times. In the Middle Ages, untoasted sesame oil was the oil of choice for cooking in the Arab world. Today, this oil is still used but less predominantly, and the seeds are used in baked goods and desserts. But the largest use of sesame seeds in the Middle East is in the form of tahini, the paste made by grinding the seeds.

Sumac
Sumac is a flowering shrub that grows wild in the Middle East and in parts of North America. The hairy berries of the shrub are dried and their skins (not the inner seeds, which are bitter) are ground and used to add a sour, citrusy flavor to food. Its use is recorded in medieval Arabic cookbooks and it continues to be widely used across the region today. Unfortunately, it is one of the spices that is frequently adulterated, with beet powder used to bulk it up, or salt added to increase weight and control humidity, or citric acid incorporated to make up for loss of sourness. That's why it is important to source from a trusted vendor, or if it grows wild in your region, then simply forage, dry, and grind your own.

Tahini
Sesame seeds were traditionally grown for their oil, but by the tenth century there are references in Arabic cookbooks to tahini, the paste made from grinding sesame seeds. It can be made from hulled or unhulled seeds and from toasted or untoasted seeds, all of which impact its flavor. It does have a strong, earthy taste with bitter undertones, but it should be a very pleasant bitterness with a hint of sweetness when it first hits the palate. Your best bet is to try several brands and gauge which you like best, because when used in large quantities the quality definitely makes a difference to the final flavor of your dish. Tip: Rotate between storing the jar upside down and upright every week or so to prevent the oil from separating.

Za'atar
One of the most misunderstood ingredients of the Middle East, *za'atar* is actually the name of a plant native to the Levant. It is much more closely related to oregano than it is to thyme, with the scientific name *Origanum syriacum* (or Syrian oregano). The leaves of this herb are dried and ground, then mixed with sesame seeds, salt, and sumac to form the condiment widely recognized in the West as za'atar. In the Arab world, there are different names like za'atar halabi, or za'atar lebnani, or duqqa to refer to the different blends that include ingredients and flavoring such as cumin, other spices, and even nuts. But at its most basic, the traditional za'atar blend is dried za'atar leaves, sesame seeds, sumac, and salt.

Basics

My grandfather always told us a story when we were growing up about a salt merchant's son who set sail to a faraway land to sell salt, which had become too commonplace in their part of the world. Upon arriving at the king's palace in the new city, he was scolded and turned away by the ruler for trying to sell him "white dirt." The boy had one simple request before leaving: join the servants for a meal in the kitchen. While there, he secretly sprinkled salt into the food. In the evening, the king ate with much gusto and asked the cook what he had done to transform those dishes into the best meal he'd ever enjoyed. Upon discovering the boy's role in this transformative meal, the king rewarded him by marrying him to his daughter and sending them back to the boy's land with sacks of gold coins and jewels.

This fable, I now know, exists in many cultures. When my grandfather told it to us, his message was that if you can't accomplish something one way, don't give up, just try another way. The moral I take from it today is vastly different, however. It's no longer just about persistence. It is about embracing what we don't know, about evolving and improving by learning from others. Nowhere is this more relevant today than in the world of food.

If we look at the origin of much of what we cook, we will notice it was often based in necessity. Before refrigeration, salting and curing were ways to preserve meats. Pickling and brining were ways to preserve vegetables, while drying was a way to preserve herbs and spices. The results of many of these processes, however, are so delicious that we continue to use the same methods today, even if mostly for flavor.

To celebrate the evolution of cuisine throughout time, it is important to understand where it has come from and what forces of change have shaped its current face. That is why, as always, I chose to start this book with a chapter of basic recipes—perhaps not the most exciting dishes in the book, but ones that can complement many a meal or take a dish from basic to brilliant—dishes that in some shape or form have existed almost as long as Arab cuisine has. Among the recipes in this chapter are quick pickles (page 25) to brighten up a meal, a spice mix (page 27) to add depth of flavor to basic ingredients, and an easy flatbread recipe (page 30) to complement numerous recipes in this book. I hope you will think of the following recipes as the "salt" of this book—they might look basic on first glance, but they make a world of difference and add ample flavor when used in tandem with the other dishes throughout.

Shattah Chili Paste

My parents' kitchen often felt like a factory: pickling vegetables, pressing pomegranates, butchering meat, making molasses, and preserving juices. The list goes on, but there was always something happening. In the summer, when red chili peppers were in season and the sun was hot, it was time to make *shattah*, or fermented red chili paste. My father would buy bags and bags of red chilies, leave them out for a couple of days on cloth sheets to dry in the sun, and then he would pass them through a meat grinder before setting them back out in the sun to continue fermenting. Although delicious, it was quite the project! So this is a much easier and faster way to get the same flavor. Choose a variety of red chili pepper whose heat you can handle, and if you prefer it milder, you can always substitute bell peppers for some of the hot chili peppers.

Makes about 1¼ cups (10 oz/280 g)

- 1 lb 2 oz (500 g) fresh red chili peppers, such as long hots, jalapeños, or Anaheim
- 1 tablespoon salt
- 2 tablespoons olive oil, plus more for sealing

Preheat the oven to 250°F (120°C/Gas Mark ½).

Remove the stems from the chilies and halve each lengthwise. Seed about half of the chilies.

Arrange the chilies cut-side up on a baking sheet and dry out in the oven until the chilies have started to dry and shrivel around the edges, 1 hour to 1 hour 30 minutes. The exact amount of time will depend on the size and variety of chili you are using, so keep an eye out and adjust accordingly.

Allow to cool completely, uncovered, at least 1 hour and up to 1 day.

In a food processor, combine the chilies and salt and process until coarsely ground. You don't want it to become a liquid paste, but you also don't want to see big pieces of pepper skin; it should be somewhere in between. (Alternatively, put the chilies through a meat grinder.) Transfer the chili paste to a bowl, add the olive oil, and mix until evenly combined.

Pour the chili mixture into a 16 oz/450 g glass jar or airtight glass container. Gently tap the jar on a soft flat surface to even out the top. Wipe any chili paste from the edges and drizzle olive oil on top until the surface is fully covered. Seal and store in the refrigerator. Chili paste will keep for at least 1 month, as long as the surface remains covered in olive oil and you use a clean spoon each time you take some out.

Note: An alternative to oven-drying is to grind the chilies fresh, mix with the salt, and cook on the stovetop over low heat, maintaining a very gentle simmer and stirring periodically, until much of the water has evaporated. Exact time will vary, but somewhere between 20 minutes and 1 hour, depending on the chili variety and its liquid content. It should have the consistency of runny jam or thick tomato sauce when warm, and it will thicken more when cooled. Cool completely before storing in a sterilized jar.

Shattah Chili Paste (1); Amba Tahini (2) p. 24; Beet, Cauliflower, and Turnip Pink Pickles (3) p. 25; Turmeric and Fenugreek Quick Pickles (4) p. 25; Split Pea Falafel (5) p. 185

Amba Tahini

Amba, which "means" mango in the Indian language of Marathi, is a fermented condiment of mangoes and fenugreek and is very popular in Iraqi and Indian cuisines. Legend has it that the Baghdadi-born Sassoon family of Bombay invented it in the late nineteenth century. Its varieties and methods of preparation are countless, depending on who is making it. *Amba*—which penetrated Palestinian cuisine through Iraqi Jewish immigrants to the country—was part and parcel of eating falafel for anyone growing up in Jerusalem. I couldn't envision a sandwich without it. To me, this condiment encapsulates the ethnic, cultural, and physical boundaries that only food can cross. Traditionally made with mangoes, the process of pickling and fermenting is time-consuming and not always straightforward. Since it is often eaten alongside tahini, here I make a sauce out of tahini and traditional *amba* spices, giving you the best of both worlds in a fraction of the time.

---

p. 23

Makes about 1¼ cups (300 ml)

½ cup (4 oz/120 g) tahini
4 tablespoons fresh lemon juice
¼ cup (2 oz/60 g) yogurt
½ teaspoon salt
¼ teaspoon ground cumin
¼ teaspoon ground fenugreek
¼ teaspoon ground turmeric

In a bowl, combine the tahini, lemon juice, yogurt, salt, cumin, fenugreek, and turmeric with 4 tablespoons water. Mix until smooth and evenly incorporated. If you prefer it less thick, add more water, 1 tablespoon at a time, and mix until it reaches your desired consistency. The sauce will keep in the refrigerator, covered, for up to 3 days.

Beet, Cauliflower, and Turnip Pink Pickles

Every barbecue, every wedding, and every summer evening gathering across the Middle East will have plates of pickles on the table, from cucumbers and olives to small bowls of bright yellow cauliflower and carrots or vivid pink turnips and beets. Many of those pickles are actually ferments, usually requiring a couple of weeks to interact with salt before being ready to eat. But one kind, referred to as "quick pickles" across the Levant or *torshi* in Iraq and the Gulf, is ready to eat almost immediately. It is made by boiling water, vinegar, and spices, then pouring them over cut vegetables in a jar and refrigerating. The one here, recognized for its distinct bright pink color, is traditionally made with turnips. I use a mixture of cauliflower and turnips, but you could opt for just one or the other. The only non-negotiable item is the beet because that's what gives these pickles their distinct color.

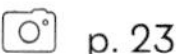 p. 23

Makes one 1½-quart (1.5-liter) jar or three 1-pint (475 ml) jars

- 1 small head cauliflower (about 1 lb/450 g), washed and cut into small florets
- 1 small turnip (about 6 oz/175 g), washed and cut into bite-size pieces
- 1 small beet (about 6 oz/175 g), peeled and cut into bite-size pieces
- 1 cup (8 fl oz/250 ml) apple cider vinegar or distilled white vinegar
- 3 tablespoons coarse sea salt

Tightly pack the cauliflower, turnip, and beet into a 1½-quart (1.5-liter) screw-top glass jar or three 1-pint (475 ml) glass jars.

In a large saucepan, combine 3 cups (24 fl oz/700 ml) water, the vinegar, and salt and bring to a boil over medium-high heat, stirring until the salt dissolves. Remove from the heat and pour over the vegetables until covered completely. Allow to cool, then screw on the lids and refrigerate.

The pickles are ready to eat within a few hours, but will taste better after a couple of days. Refrigerated, pickles will keep for 2–3 months.

Turmeric and Fenugreek Quick Pickles

What vegetables you use in quick pickles is discretionary, but cauliflower and carrots are the standard ones, with people sometimes adding cabbage, bell peppers, chili peppers, even cucumber, celery, turnip, or green beans into the mix. As for spices, there is a blend sold across the Middle East specifically for pickles, which I replicate here by mixing curry powder, turmeric, and fenugreek.

---

p. 23

Makes one 1½-quart (1.5-liter) jar or three 1-pint (475 ml) jars

- 1 lb (450 g) cauliflower (about 1 small head), washed and cut into small florets
- ½ lb (225 g) carrots (3 or 4 medium), peeled and sliced into rounds
- 1 cup (8 fl oz/250 ml) apple cider vinegar or distilled white vinegar
- 3 tablespoons coarse sea salt
- ½ teaspoon curry powder
- ¼ teaspoon ground turmeric
- ⅛ teaspoon ground fenugreek (optional; not necessary if the curry powder has fenugreek in it)

Tightly pack the cauliflower and carrots into a 1½-quart (1.5-liter) glass jar or three 1-pint (475 ml) jars and set aside.

In a large saucepan, combine 3 cups (24 fl oz/700 ml) water, the vinegar, salt, curry powder, turmeric, and fenugreek (if using) and bring to a boil over medium-high heat, stirring until the salt dissolves. Remove from the heat and pour over the vegetables until covered completely. Allow to cool, then cover and refrigerate.

The pickles are ready to eat within a few hours, but will taste better after a couple of days. Refrigerated, pickles will keep for 2–3 months.

Nine-Spice Mix

Ask an Arab person for any recipe, and the ingredients list will almost surely include *baharat*. *Baharat* simply means "spices," and each region has its own mix. While generic blends are easily purchased from spice vendors, families often have their own unique iterations. The one here, which I not very creatively named according to its ingredients, is the spice mix I grew up on. My mother made it at home and used it with most of our dishes, sometimes supplementing with whatever flavor needed to shine. It's such a handy mix if you cook Arabic food at home, even if just once a week, that I urge you to make it. But if you are not so inclined, you can substitute with store-bought Lebanese 7-spice blend or *baharat*.

Makes about 1 cup

6 tablespoons allspice berries
6 small cassia bark or cinnamon sticks
3 tablespoons coriander seeds
1 tablespoon black peppercorns
1 teaspoon cardamom seeds or 10 whole cardamom pods
½ teaspoon cumin seeds
10 whole cloves
2 blades of mace
1 nutmeg

In a large dry frying pan, toast all the spices over medium-low heat until you begin to smell the aroma of the spices, about 10 minutes. Stir with a wooden spoon periodically to ensure the spices do not burn.

Remove the pan from the heat and set aside to cool completely, about 1 hour. This step is crucial because if the spices are not cooled properly, they will form a paste when ground rather than a powder.

Transfer all the roasted spices to a heavy-duty spice grinder and grind until you achieve a fine powder. Store the spice mix in an airtight container. It will keep for several months although the aroma will fade with time.

Note: In most recipes that call for separate spices like allspice, cinnamon, nutmeg, and black pepper, you can always add up the total number of teaspoons and substitute with an equal amount of this mixture. It will give you a slightly different flavor profile, but will still be quite delicious.

Fermented Green Chilies, Walnuts, and Garlic in Olive Oil

Fermentation is probably as old as humanity itself, with cultures using it for foods and beverages throughout history. Although it is making a comeback now both in modern gastronomy and health cuisines, it has long been a big part of the Arab kitchen. One of the most popular and widely recognized ferments in the Levant is *makdoos*, baby eggplants filled with red peppers, garlic, and walnuts, then salted and preserved in oil. My favorite part is usually the walnut mixture, so in this version I skip the eggplants altogether and use a mixture of chilies instead, which is all crunch and delicious flavor. Although you can leave it out on the counter—the oil is a great preservative—and consume within a few weeks, I still recommend you refrigerate it after it has fermented for about 1 week. We most often serve this *makdoos* alone with bread as part of breakfast or a mezze spread, but you can use it to top hummus or labaneh, in sandwiches, with pastas, or any other way you choose because it truly adds a distinctive pop of flavor.

Makes about 2½ cups

- 12 oz (350 g) fresh green or red chilies or a combination (roughly 10 jalapeño-size chilies)
- 1 very small red or green bell pepper
- 1 tablespoon coarse sea salt, plus more for sprinkling
- 4–5 cloves garlic, finely chopped
- ¾ cup (2¾ oz/75 g) walnuts, chopped into small pieces
- Extra-virgin olive oil

Finely dice the chilies and bell pepper and place in a mesh sieve set over a bowl. Sprinkle with some salt and set aside for 15–30 minutes, until some of the water has been released.

Give a final stir in the sieve to release any water, then transfer the chilies and pepper to an approximately 3-cup (710 ml) screw-top jar or airtight container. Add the garlic, walnuts, and 1 tablespoon salt and toss to combine. Pour enough olive oil to cover, making sure no pieces of chili or garlic are exposed, and tightly seal the jar.

Keep at room temperature for about 1 week to ferment, then store in the refrigerator where it will keep for several months as long as it is always covered in olive oil and a clean spoon is used to scoop some out. If using directly from the refrigerator, scoop out what you need (the oil will have solidified) and give it a few minutes to come back to a liquid state.

Variation: I also make a version of this without the walnuts and keep a jar in the refrigerator, where I spoon it out and use it as a base when cooking. You can fry tomatoes, eggs, potatoes, seafood, or anything else you desire in it. I struggle to think of anything whose flavor is not amplified by being cooked in chili and garlic oil.

Fermented Green Chilies, Walnuts, and Garlic in Olive Oil

Unleavened Flatbread

The "staff of life" as it is often called, bread has historically been the staple without peer. Cultures across the globe have cultivated their native grains—from corn and sorghum to wheat and barley—to make a variety of leavened and unleavened breads. If availability was the mother of those inventions, then necessity was the mother of mine. You see, leavened pita bread requires some advance planning, time, and patience. So when I woke up one morning and started to prepare breakfast, only to realize I was out of bread and needed to have school lunches packed and out the door in a couple of hours, I had to get creative. I resorted to making this quick unleavened bread, very similar to a Mexican flour tortilla, but using olive oil in place of the traditional shortening and a bit of yogurt to soften the dough. Making them was a revelation—not only were they easier than pita bread to prepare, but they were also versatile—just as perfect for dipping as they are for rolling (think the shawarma wraps on pages 137 and 156). They also freeze very well and thaw in a few minutes.

Makes 8–10 flatbreads

- 3 cups (14 oz/400 g) all-purpose (plain) flour, plus more for dusting
- ⅔ cup (3½ oz/100 g) whole wheat (wholemeal) flour
- 1 teaspoon salt
- 1 teaspoon baking powder
- ¼ cup (2 oz/60 g) regular or Greek yogurt
- 2 tablespoons olive oil

In a large bowl, combine the flours, salt, and baking powder and whisk briefly to combine.

Add the yogurt, olive oil, and most of 1 cup (8 fl oz/250 ml) water. Mix through with your fingers, gradually adding more water and kneading until the dough comes together. If the mixture feels a little sticky, leave it for 5–10 minutes, then come back and knead again for a few more minutes until you have a soft but robust ball of dough.

Divide the dough into 8–10 balls and place on a well-floured baking sheet. Cover the balls of dough with plastic wrap (clingfilm) or a clean tea towel and allow to rest for at least 20 minutes.

Heat a dry cast-iron or heavy-bottomed skillet over medium heat. Take a ball of dough and on a floured surface with a well-floured rolling pin, roll it out to a round about 8 inches (20 cm) in diameter. This is a very soft dough and you will need to rotate it around and flip it over a few times, so don't hesitate to use as much flour as necessary.

Place the bread in the preheated skillet and cook until there are brown specks on the bottom side and some parts of it are starting to puff up, 35–45 seconds. Flip over and cook until the other side is freckled, another 30–40 seconds. Avoid overcooking the bread as it will become too crisp and lose its softness.

Transfer the cooked bread to a tea towel and cover with another towel. Repeat with the remaining portions of dough (if necessary, use paper towels to clean out any accumulating flour in the pan after every two or three breads). Stack the cooked breads on top of each other between the two tea towels, as this helps the bread retain its moisture and softness.

If not eating the flatbreads within the hour, transfer the towel-wrapped breads to a zipseal plastic food bag where they can keep for several hours. This bread will keep in the freezer for about 3 weeks. Simply reheat in a frying pan for a few seconds on each side when ready to eat.

Toum Sauce

This versatile garlic sauce—*toum* is the word for "garlic" in Arabic—is a staple Lebanese condiment usually served with grilled meats, particularly chicken. But I also remember frequenting restaurants when I lived in Amman, where as soon as you sat down, before you even looked at the menu, the waiters would place a couple slices of tomato on each person's plate and top them with *toum* sauce and a sprinkling of sumac. So simple yet so flavorful. There are different ways to make this sauce thick, with some people relying on egg whites, others on potatoes, and some exclusively on an extreme amount of oil—I'm talking cups. The recipe below does none of the above, using cornstarch (cornflour) as a thickener to give you this beloved sauce that is healthier (less fat), lasts longer (no raw eggs), and tastes purely of garlic (no potatoes). It is the perfect accompaniment to grilled chicken: Try it in place of the *sahawiq* sauce in Aleppo Pepper Roast Chicken, page 81. Or spread it on bread and top with grilled chicken breast, tomato, and Middle Eastern cucumber pickles for a flavorful sandwich. Or, simply lather it on perfect ripe summer tomato slices and sprinkle with sumac. You can also marinate meats in it or mix it with lemon and olive oil for an easy salad dressing. Whatever you do, this is a sauce I am sure you will come back to over and over again.

Makes about 1 cup (250 ml)

- 2 tablespoons cornstarch (cornflour)
- 4 cloves garlic, sliced
- 1 teaspoon fresh lemon juice
- Salt
- 6 tablespoons good-quality vegetable oil

In a small pot, combine the cornstarch (cornflour) and ¾ cup (6 fl oz/180 ml) water and whisk constantly over medium heat until the mixture thickens and starts to bubble. Remove from the heat and add the garlic, lemon juice, and a pinch of salt. Stir to combine, then set aside to cool slightly.

Transfer the mixture to a small food processor or blender and process until no garlic pieces are visible. If you are able to drizzle the oil while the processor is running, gradually pour the oil in and continue to process until the mixture is a bright white color. If you cannot pour the oil in while the processor is running, pour in the oil in three additions, processing after each one until the mixture is white. Taste at this point and add more salt to taste.

Transfer the garlic sauce to a bowl, cover, and refrigerate until cooled completely. The sauce is now ready to use and will keep in the refrigerator for 3–5 days. Stir well before using.

Orzo Rice

Most stew dishes across the Levant are served with broken vermicelli rice. The vermicelli, traditionally made by hand and air-dried, were added to the dish to prevent the rice from clumping up together when cooked. My grandmother often reminisced about those times, especially before weddings where large quantities of rice were being cooked and the women in the village would get together to make the thin noodles by hand. When I first moved abroad, I didn't have any Middle Eastern grocers close by where I could buy broken vermicelli, so I took to using orzo in its place, an idea adopted from a Turkish friend of mine. I brown the orzo with the ancient Arab fats of choice—untoasted sesame oil and ghee—for added flavor, but it would work with other fats as well.

---

p. 91

Serves 4–6

2 cups (14 oz/400 g) rice, such as jasmine or short-grain
2 tablespoons untoasted sesame oil, olive oil, or vegetable oil
1 tablespoon (15 g) unsalted butter or ghee
⅔ cup (3½ oz/100 g) orzo
1 teaspoon salt

Rinse the rice under running water until the water runs clear. Let soak in a bowl of water for at least 15 minutes and up to 30 minutes. Drain and set aside.

In a medium-size pot, heat the oil and butter over medium heat. Add the orzo and stir constantly until it is a golden-brown color, about 5 minutes.

Add the drained rice and toss to fully coat in the oil. Pour 2½ cups (20 fl oz/550 ml) water into the pan, add the salt, and bring to a boil. Boil for about 3 minutes, give it one more stir, then place a tea towel over the pan, close the lid tightly, and remove from the heat. Let it sit for 10–15 minutes. Remove the lid, fluff with a fork, and serve.

Dairy + Eggs

The chicken pen had a corrugated metal roof the color of wine or bricks, bearing the mark of the years. I don't remember much about it other than the hay that lined its floor and the chickens in each corner. The image imprinted on my mind is that of my father sauntering in there on the mornings we slept at my grandmother's house to pick two eggs from under the chicken on the right. The whole family ate, so there must have been more eggs, but it's always those two eggs being gathered from the white chicken on the right that I remember the most.

There used to be goats as well, but by the time I was old enough to remember, they were no longer there. Thirty years later, I recognize how that memory tells a story common to all Arab families—a story about how we used to live in harmony with nature and the bounty it graciously provided. While many now opt for supermarket aisles over pastures, it's not uncommon to find families who still choose to raise their own chickens or at least make their own yogurt, cheese, and labaneh. Once you see the ease with which they can be prepared (pages 36, 38, and 40), you may very well start making your own as well!

In many interviews after my first cookbook, *The Palestinian Table*, came out, I was asked about Middle Eastern food staples. Whenever I said dairy and eggs, I received quizzical glances. Indeed, these are usually not the first ingredients that come to mind when you think of the Middle East. Yet dairy—from sheep and goats—and eggs are prevalent in, and form a substantial part of, our diets. In one medieval cookbook (*Kitab al-Wusla ila al-Habib*), there are thirty-eight recipes for eggs, not counting the chicken, lamb, vegetable, and sweet dishes that happen to include eggs. Another tenth-century cookbook (*Kitab al-Tabikh*) dedicates a chapter to the medicinal properties of eggs, describing the nutrition of various kinds of bird eggs and which is suited to each condition.

Dairy also has been a part of the diet since antiquity. In the Levant, there are ceramic vessels thought to be churns dating back to 4000 BCE. By 3000 BCE, there are mentions in archaic Mesopotamian texts of storable dairy products produced at a scale that only items that play a big part in a cuisine would be. In the pre-Islamic era, dairy—mostly camel, but also from sheep and goats—was the most important part of the diet. In the Qur'an, dates and dairy are the main staples.

The recipes in this chapter have come a long way since those times. Some, like Narjissiyeh (page 48)—fava (broad) beans and fried eggs—draw inspiration from ancient texts. Others, like the Herb and Sujuk Quiche (page 52), take a classic Western dish but flavor it with Arabic ingredients. Others still, like the "Secret" Shankleesh Salad (page 45), simplify traditionally elaborate recipes. But at their heart, these egg and dairy recipes are all relatively simple and as well suited for a breakfast or brunch table as they are for a quick lunch or weeknight supper.

Plain Cultured Yogurt

Gone are the days when most Arab families milked their sheep and used that milk to make yogurt and labaneh. Lifestyles have changed and these products are so readily accessible in supermarkets that people just don't trouble themselves anymore. But when you find the fresh-made varieties in farmers' markets, or sold by local artisans, the flavor is definitely superior. So in a return to our old ways, I started to make my own yogurt a few years back. I find something inherently satisfying about it—seeing the transformation, controlling what goes in as well as the outcome, and ultimately eating my handiwork.

Makes about 8 cups (2 kg)

2 quarts (2 liters) whole milk
½ cup (4 oz/120 g) yogurt with active live cultures

In a large (3-quart/liter or larger) heavy saucepan, bring the milk to just below a boil (210°F/98°C) over medium-low heat. If you do not have a thermometer, you will know it is ready when you see a layer of foam on the top and steam begins to rise. Remove from the heat immediately.

Allow the milk cool to about 115°F (45°C), stirring occasionally to incorporate any skin that forms on top. If you are not using a thermometer, you will know it is at the right temperature when your pinkie can withstand being in the milk for 10 seconds before it feels too hot. This can take about 1 hour, but you can speed up the process by putting the pot in the refrigerator. If the temperature of the milk drops below 110°F (43°C), you will need to reheat it slightly to get it back to the 110°–115°F (43°–45°C) range.

Place the yogurt in a small bowl and pour in about ¼ cup (2 oz/60 g) of the warm milk and whisk until smooth. Pour the yogurt mixture back into the pan and stir to combine.

Cover the pan and wrap in a blanket or some tea towels. This is how people traditionally preserved the warm temperature, but you can also set the pan in a turned-off oven. Leave for anywhere from 8–24 hours, depending on how sour and thick you like your yogurt. The longer you leave it, the thicker and more sour it will become.

After this period, the milk will have thickened into yogurt. You can use it right away, but I recommend placing it in the refrigerator for another 1–2 days to further set the yogurt before consuming or draining it (see Labaneh, page 40). Yogurt will keep in the refrigerator for about 2 weeks.

If you plan to make more yogurt at home, set aside about ½ cup (4 oz/120 g) of your first batch to use as the culture starter for your following one, and repeat.

White Cheese with Nigella Seeds

I still remember the large, golden tins of brined cheese arriving at our house every spring from my grandmother's neighbor Aysha. In it were large squares of white cheese—flavored with mastic, mahlab, and nigella seeds—a staple in Arab households, usually made in spring after the sheep have given birth, then preserved in a salt brine until the following year. This recipe is a quick fix for when you want that white cheese flavor but do not have the traditionally made kind on hand. The cream is optional, but it does add richness and produces more curds. The cheese can be served plain with bread, enjoyed with jams, or snacked on straight from the refrigerator.

Makes about 10 ounces (300 g)

- 2 quarts/liters whole milk
- ½ cup (4 fl oz/120 ml) heavy (double) cream (optional)
- 4 tablespoons distilled white vinegar or apple cider vinegar
- 2 teaspoons nigella seeds
- ½ teaspoon ground mahlab (optional; see Note)
- ½ teaspoon ground mastic (optional: see Note)
- 1 teaspoon salt

Line a large sieve with a muslin cloth or several layers of cheesecloth (muslin) and set aside in a sink.

Pour the milk and cream (if using) into a large pot and set over medium heat. Bring to a bare simmer, stirring periodically to make sure the bottom doesn't catch or burn. You will know it's ready once it looks foamy on top. This step should take about 15 minutes.

Add the vinegar, stirring occasionally, until you see the milk curdle and the clear yellowish whey separate from the curds. If after a few minutes it is not separating, add another tablespoon of vinegar and stir until it does.

Carefully pour the mixture into the lined sieve, letting the whey drain into the sink. Once most of the liquid has drained, sprinkle the curds with the nigella, mahlab (if using), mastic (if using) and salt, and mix to combine.

Shape into a round and cover tightly with the cheesecloth. Set the sieve over a bowl to catch any draining whey. Place a plate that fits snugly into the sieve above the wrapped curds, pressing down firmly. Allow to drain at room temperature until cool, then transfer to the refrigerator and continue to drain for another 4–6 hours until solid and holding its shape.

When ready, remove the cheese from the cloth and transfer to an airtight container. It will last for 3–5 days in the refrigerator.

Notes: This is one of the most basic methods of cheese making. It is used across countless cultures and forms the base step for many white cheeses (paneer, ricotta, queso blanco, feta, cottage cheese, etc.) Varying techniques, flavorings, and salting are responsible for the differences among the cheese varieties. The flavors of mahlab and mastic are the first indicators that you are eating an Arabic white cheese. While not vital, they definitely add a unique dimension to this cheese. If you prefer to skip them, you will still come out with a delicious cheese—especially since it is flavored with nigella seeds—but the flavor profile will be slightly plainer.

White Cheese with Nigella Seeds

Labaneh

While labaneh has become a well-recognized spread easily found in most supermarkets, it is not an easy spread to include in recipes because the products vary drastically from brand to brand. From fat and salt content to acidity and texture, it's hard to find a uniform product. The hallmark of good labaneh is a tart, salty, and creamy spread, and it is easiest to control these aspects by making it at home. Incredibly easy to make, the recipes in this book that call for labaneh assume you are using the following homemade version. You can of course substitute with store-bought, but the flavor profile will be slightly different, and you may have to adjust the salt and acid in the recipes.

–

Makes 1–1½ pounds (450–700 g)

4 generous cups (36 oz/1 kg) yogurt, homemade (page 36) or store-bought
1 teaspoon salt
Olive oil, to cover (optional)

In a bowl, stir together the yogurt and salt, mixing until fully combined. Line a colander with cheesecloth (muslin) or white paper towels and scrape in the yogurt. Fold the sides over to cover the yogurt.

Place a plate over the yogurt and set the colander over a bowl to drain. (Alternatively, you can pour the yogurt into a square of cheesecloth, tie together the opposite corners, then tie this to a wooden spoon suspended over a large bowl or pot—similar to a bindle.)

Drain at room temperature overnight (see Note). Once thickened, scrape the labaneh from the cloth and put it into a bowl. Taste and adjust salt if you prefer it saltier, then whisk to incorporate and smooth out.

Store in an airtight container in the refrigerator for up to 2 weeks, or 4 weeks if covered in a thin layer of olive oil.

Note: The consistency of labaneh will depend on how long you drain it; the longer you drain it, the firmer and drier it will become. If using it as a spread, 8–12 hours is enough, but if you are pickling it or rolling it into balls, then you want to remove as much moisture as possible and you want to let it drain for at least 24 hours.

Labaneh, Red Chili, and Egg Salad

Eggs have been a common food, and part of religious rituals even, for as long as history has been recorded, and probably well before. Versatile and with countless uses—from preserving and pickling to scrambling, frying, boiling, and creaming—the humble egg is used by every culture across the globe. I first came across this recipe during a sleepover at a cousin's house in Jordan. We got up to make breakfast and realized halfway through that we only had one egg. "Don't worry," one of my cousins said, "I'll make my grandfather's egg salad!" So she did, and three of us were able to enjoy a single egg. Perhaps the root of this dish then was to stretch out eggs to feed more people, but whatever the origins, it's still a delicious way to enjoy boiled eggs.

–

pp. 42–43

Serves 2–4

4 tablespoons labaneh, preferably homemade (opposite)
1 tablespoon Shattah Chili Paste (page 22), or 2 finely chopped fresh red chilies
1 teaspoon za'atar blend
½ teaspoon salt
4 hard-boiled eggs, chopped (see Note)
2 tablespoons extra-virgin olive oil
Bread, for serving

In a medium bowl, mix together the labaneh, chili paste, za'atar, and salt. Add the chopped eggs and drizzle with the olive oil. Mix everything well to combine. Serve with bread.

Note: The easiest way to chop the egg is to use an egg slicer. First place the egg horizontally and slice. Then, holding all the egg slices together with your hand, rotate it vertically and slice again. You will end up with uniform pieces of chopped egg. If pressed for time, just put the whole eggs in with the labaneh and mash everything with a fork.

Fried Arabic White Cheese

Although the earliest recorded descriptions of halloumi cheese date back to the sixteenth century, the method of preparing it probably dates back to the Byzantine Empire. Common across the Levant and the entire Mediterranean region, this cheese varies in texture and flavor from one locale to the next. I grew up with Akkawi or Nabulsi cheese, the Palestinian varieties named for the cities in which they originated (Akka or Nablus), and they are the kinds I prefer to work with, especially when frying. A very quick and easy dish to make, the cheese can be cut into cubes and deep-fried in vegetable oil for a nice mezze platter; for breakfast, it's divine when shallow-fried in olive oil.

–

pp. 42–43

Serves 2–4

9 oz (250 g) Akkawi, Nabulsi, or halloumi cheese (see Note), cut into thick slices or cubes
Olive oil, for shallow-frying
Pita bread, labaneh, and tomatoes, for serving

If the cheese is too salty, cover with boiling water for 15 minutes, rinse, and pat dry. Set on a plate lined with paper towels in the refrigerator, uncovered, overnight. If using Cypriot/Greek/Turkish halloumi, you can skip this step.

Pour enough olive oil to shallow-fry the cheese into a nonstick medium frying pan. Heat over medium-high heat until hot but not smoking. Place the cheese in the oil, leaving enough space between the pieces so they do not stick together. Cover loosely with a lid to prevent spattering but still allow steam to escape. Once the cheese has reached a golden-brown color on one side, 2–3 minutes, flip over with a fork and fry until the other side is browned, another 2 minutes.

Remove cheese to a plate and serve with pita bread, labaneh, and tomatoes.

Note: How the cheese turns out ultimately depends on the kind of cheese you use and you will probably have to try several different varieties before you find the one you like best. The drier the cheese is, the better the result, so I leave it uncovered in the refrigerator for a few hours and up to one day before frying. This is especially important if you have soaked the cheese in boiling water to remove extra saltiness. If using Halloumi, this is less of an issue as it tends to be a drier variety in general.

1
3

Sujuk Fried Eggs (1) p. 44; "Secret" Shankleesh Salad (2) p. 45; Fried Arabic White Cheese (3) p. 41; Labaneh, Red Chili, and Egg Salad (4) p. 40

Sujuk Fried Eggs

Eggs and meat are a common breakfast combination across the Middle East. Sometimes it is tender cuts of lamb scrambled into eggs, other times it is *basturma* or *sujuk* eaten alongside fried eggs, and in other cases, especially in Egypt, it is ground meat folded into a frittata known as *ijjeh iskandaraniyeh* or "Alexandrian omelet." This recipe, which draws inspiration from those dishes, is reminiscent of the eggs my father made on the weekends when he purchased *sujuk* from the neighborhood butcher. It almost doesn't feel like a recipe because it is so easy and forgiving. I usually crack the eggs over the frying *sujuk* and let it cook until the yolks are done to my liking, but you could just as well scramble the eggs over the *sujuk*. I love to eat it with flatbread, cucumber, and slices of white cheese with a side of sweetened mint black tea.

---

pp. 42–43

Serves 2–4

- 1–2 tablespoons olive oil (optional; see Note)
- 4 oz (120 g) sujuk, preferably homemade (page 124), cut into bite-size pieces
- 4 eggs
- Salt and freshly ground black pepper

For serving:

- Flatbreads, store-bought or homemade (page 30)
- Cucumbers, sliced
- White cheese, such as Akkawi, Nabulsi, or feta, sliced

In a large nonstick frying pan, heat the oil (if using) over medium-high heat until shimmering. Add the *sujuk* and cook, stirring often to brown evenly, until warmed through and starting to brown, about 2 minutes.

Spread the *sujuk* around the pan so you have 4 open areas in which to crack the eggs. Crack an egg into each area (it's perfectly fine to crack the eggs over the *sujuk* if you prefer, or to move all the *sujuk* to the outside perimeter and crack the eggs in the center). With a small spatula, spread the whites around slightly, especially the thicker part surrounding the yolk, to ensure that the eggs cook evenly. Sprinkle with salt and pepper to your liking. Cover and cook until the yolks are at your desired level of doneness, about 3 minutes for runny and 5 minutes for fully cooked. Remove from the heat.

To serve:

Serve hot with flatbreads, cucumbers, and white cheese.

Note: If you use store-bought *sujuk*, you may not need the olive oil. Some store-bought varieties release plenty of fat when heated, so just put it in your hot pan without any oil and fry the eggs in the oil it releases. Homemade *sujuk* is usually a bit leaner, so you will need to use the olive oil for frying.

“Secret” Shankleesh Salad

Shankleesh is a type of cheese in the Levantine kitchen usually made from sheep buttermilk and formed into balls that are aged and dried, then washed and covered with Aleppo pepper and dried za’atar leaves. This is a somewhat complex process, but Arabs have come up with countless easier ways to make these balls at home from curdling yogurt to using labaneh with a mixture of other cheeses. But even those simple processes still involve drying and storing the balls before using them in salads or mezze spreads.
A nifty little secret I learned from my mother, who learned it from the sister of a grocery shop owner in our neighborhood, is to forgo that whole process and use good-quality sheep or goat feta cheese instead. Once crumbled finely and mixed with all the aromatics, you’d be hard-pressed to tell the difference between this version and the original. This is a generous portion, but it can easily be halved.

---

pp. 42–43

Serves 6–8 as part of a spread

- 1 block (8 oz/225 g) feta cheese
- 1 tablespoon Aleppo pepper
- 1 tablespoon dried crushed za’atar leaves (in a pinch use dried oregano or marjoram or even za’atar blend)
- 2 teaspoons nigella seeds
- ½ teaspoon crushed dried mint (optional)
- 1 tablespoon extra-virgin olive oil, plus more for drizzling
- 1 tablespoon fresh lemon juice
- 1½ lb (700 g) tomatoes (4–5 medium), finely diced
- 5 scallions (spring onions), thinly sliced
- 12–15 pitted Kalamata or Nicoise olives, halved
- 4 tablespoons walnut pieces, lightly toasted

Crumble the feta finely with your hands. Set on paper towels for 10–15 minutes to absorb any excess moisture from the brine. Transfer the feta to a bowl and add the Aleppo pepper, za’atar, nigella seeds, and mint (if using) and mix until evenly incorporated.

In a small bowl, mix the olive oil and lemon juice together. Set the dressing aside until ready to use.

To serve, spread the diced tomatoes in a single layer on a serving platter and top with the sliced scallions (spring onions). Drizzle with the olive oil dressing. Spread the crumbled feta mixture on top and drizzle with some olive oil. Top the cheese with the olives and walnuts and serve.

Potato, Onion, and Chili Shakshuka with Za'atar

I'm not sure shakshuka is the most accurate name for this dish, but I figured it would convey the idea best. After all, the word *shakshuka*, which refers to the North African dish of eggs poached in tomatoes, is literally derived from an Arabic word meaning "to pair or mix together." Here we are mixing two classic breakfast foods: eggs and potatoes. This combo is a staple breakfast across the Arab world. Some people scramble the eggs with potato cubes, others make it a frittata and add more vegetables, but here I leave the eggs whole and allow them to fry with the potatoes and other aromatics for a dish that's crispy on the edges, but soft and comforting in the middle. While it's wonderful on its own, if you're like me (or like most Arabs!), you never pass up a chance to eat carbs with carbs, and so we scoop this whole thing up with bread.

Serves 2–4

- 3 tablespoons olive oil, plus more for drizzling
- 1¼ lb (550–600 g) russet (baking) or red potatoes (about 3 medium), cut into ¾-inch (2 cm) cubes
- 1 small red or green bell pepper, cut into ¾-inch (2 cm) pieces
- 2 fresh red or green chili peppers, such as jalapeño or Anaheim, thinly sliced (omit if you don't like spice)
- 1 small onion, diced
- 1 teaspoon salt
- ¼ teaspoon ground cumin
- A few twists of black pepper
- 4 eggs
- 2 teaspoons za'atar blend
- Fresh za'atar or oregano leaves, for garnish

In a large lidded nonstick or cast-iron skillet, heat the olive oil over medium-high heat. Add the potatoes and cook, tossing frequently, until just starting to brown around the edges, 10–15 minutes.

Add the bell pepper, chilies, and onion and continue to cook, tossing periodically, until the potatoes are golden brown and crisp all over, another 15 minutes.

Add the salt, cumin, and black pepper and give everything one more toss. Make 4 wells in the potato mixture with the back of a large spoon and crack an egg into each well. Drizzle some olive oil on top of the eggs and sprinkle with the za'atar. Cover the pan and cook until the whites are set. If you prefer a runnier yolk, you can spoon the whites gently away from the yolk so you have thinner whites that will cook faster.

Remove from the heat, garnish with fresh za'atar leaves, and serve immediately.

Potato, Onion, and Chili Shakshuka with Za'atar

Narjissiyeh

Narjissiyeh literally means "like narcissus" and refers to a class of dishes made with sunny-side up eggs and fava (broad) beans described in the tenth-century cookbook *Kitab al-Tabikh*. It is believed the name was given to the dish because of its vibrant green, white, and yellow colors, just like the narcissus (daffodil) flower. In addition to being beautiful, however, the dish is also delicious. I've adapted the recipe to make it suitable to the way we cook and the ingredients we have available today. It can be made in both vegetarian and nonvegetarian variations. See below for both options.

p. 50

Serves 4–6

For meat version:
4 tablespoons olive oil
1 large onion, finely diced
1 lb (450 g) ground (minced) beef, lamb, or a combination
1 teaspoon salt
½ teaspoon ground coriander
¼ teaspoon freshly ground black pepper
1 cup (125 g) shelled fava (broad) beans, blanched and peeled (see Note)
6 eggs
Bread, for serving

For vegetarian version:
3 tablespoons olive oil
9 oz (250 g) white cheese (such as halloumi, Akkawi, or Nabulsi), cut into bite-size pieces
1 cup (125 g) shelled fava (broad) beans, blanched and peeled (see Note)
6 eggs
Salt and freshly ground black pepper
Bread, for serving

To make the meat version:
In a medium frying pan, heat the olive oil over medium-high heat. Add the onion and cook, stirring, until translucent and starting to brown, 3–5 minutes. Add the meat, salt, coriander, and pepper and cook, breaking up any lumps with a wooden spoon, until the liquid has evaporated and the meat is nicely browned, 6–8 minutes.

Add the fava (broad) beans, tossing to combine, then cook for about 30 seconds.

With the back of a spoon, make 6 wells in the meat mixture and crack an egg into each one. Using the tip of the spoon, spread the whites around slightly, especially the thicker part surrounding the yolk, to ensure they cook evenly. Cover and cook until the yolks are at your desired level of doneness, about 3 minutes for runny or 5 minutes for fully cooked. Remove from the heat and serve immediately with bread.

To make the vegetarian version:
In a medium frying pan, heat the olive oil over medium heat. Add the cheese in a single layer and cook for a couple of minutes on one side until starting to brown (time can vary considerably between brands depending on moisture content, so keep an eye on it), then flip over.

Reduce the heat, to avoid burning the cheese, and add the fava (broad) beans. Crack the eggs evenly over the cheese and fava beans. Sprinkle with salt and pepper. Depending on how salty the cheese you are using is, you may not need to add any salt. Increase the heat to medium and with the tip of the spoon, spread the whites around slightly to ensure they cook evenly. You can also pierce the yolks and allow them to spread over the whites to give a nice marbled look and even flavor. Cook until at your desired level of doneness.

Remove from the heat and serve immediately with bread.

Note: Fava (broad) beans are usually in season in late spring, and the tender early crops are ready to eat as is after shelling. However, if you want to reveal the bright green beans inside, you can peel the skin off the beans. Older beans should be blanched briefly in boiling water, about 1 minute, and then peeled. An easy alternative is to use frozen fava or baby lima beans (butter beans). If you do, simply cover with boiling water for a minute or two, drain, and use as above.

Garlic Yogurt Spaghetti with Pine Nuts

Cooked yogurt is a staple in Arab cooking. It is used as a stew-like sauce for countless items, from cauliflower and meats to kubbeh, *shushbarak*, and rice. Some people serve it as a soup as well. Traditionally made from sheep or goat milk, the yogurt has a sharp, acidic flavor and is generously salted. Cooking it, however, requires constantly stirring to avoid curdling, and if using cow milk yogurt sometimes necessitates using a starch as well. This recipe, though inspired by some of those traditional dishes, uses raw yogurt flavored with fried garlic for a taste reminiscent of the cooked variety, but it is more delicate and lighter to digest. Across the Middle East, people cook some variation of this pasta dish as a "lazy person's" version of the more elaborate ones mentioned above.

p. 51

Serves 4

- Coarse sea salt, for the pasta water
- 1 lb (450 g) spaghetti, linguine, or fettuccine
- 1 lb (450 g) yogurt (not Greek)
- ½ teaspoon salt
- 3 tablespoons olive oil
- ¼ cup (1¼ oz/35 g) pine nuts
- 3 cloves garlic, crushed in a garlic press
- Crushed dried mint, for garnish

Fill a large pot with 4 quarts (4 liters) water and add 2 tablespoons salt and bring to a boil. Add the pasta and cook according to the package directions.

Meanwhile, in a bowl large enough to hold the cooked pasta, whisk together the yogurt and ½ teaspoon salt until smooth and combined.

In a very small frying pan, heat the olive oil over medium heat. Add the pine nuts and cook, stirring constantly until the nuts are a very light golden color. Remove with a slotted spoon onto a plate lined with paper towels and set aside.

To the same pan, add the garlic and fry just until fragrant, but not browned. Garlic can quickly burn, so the minute it becomes fragrant, remove from the heat and pour on top of the yogurt. Stir to combine. The sauce should be salty and tangy, so taste at this point and adjust seasoning as necessary

When the pasta is done, drain, reserving some of the pasta water. Add ¼ cup (60 ml) of the pasta water to the yogurt, whisking to combine, then add the pasta and toss to coat evenly. If the sauce is still too thick, add a little more pasta water and toss lightly.

Transfer to serving bowls and garnish each with the fried pine nuts and dried mint. Serve immediately.

Narjissiyeh

Garlic Yogurt Spaghetti with Pine Nuts

Herb and Sujuk Quiche

Although using eggs and cream in pastry was documented in English and Italian cuisine long before it entered the French, and even though the word "quiche" is borrowed from the German word *kuchen*, which means "cake," quiche as we know it today is an undeniably French dish. It also holds a special place in my heart because the first time I encountered it I was an exchange student in France. It was the first meal my host family gave me and it was the pastry I picked up from the neighborhood boulangerie on my way to university. From tuna-tomato and spinach-salmon to the classic quiche Lorraine, there was no shortage of varieties. So when I started making the spicy sausage sujuk at home (see page 124), my first instinct was to put it in a quiche, in an Arab riff on the classic quiche Lorraine—what a winning combination it was. For ease, you can use store-bought pie dough.

Makes one 9-inch (23 cm) quiche

For the pastry:
- Generous 1 cup (5⅓ oz/150 g) all-purpose (plain) flour
- Generous ¼ cup (1¾ oz/50 g) white whole wheat (wholemeal) flour, or more all-purpose flour
- 1 teaspoon sugar
- 1 teaspoon salt
- 7 tablespoons (3½ oz/100 g) very cold unsalted butter, cut into small cubes
- 1 egg
- 2 tablespoons cold water

For the filling:
- 3 eggs
- 1½ cups (12½ fl oz/370 ml) half-and-half (single cream) or a mixture of ¾ cup (6¼ fl oz/185 ml) whole milk and ¾ cup (6¼ fl oz/185 ml) heavy (double) cream
- ¼ teaspoon salt
- 5 oz (150 g) sujuk, diced into ⅓-inch/1 cm cubes (about 1 heaping cup)
- 3½ oz (100 g) feta cheese, crumbled or grated
- 5 oz (150 g) low-moisture mozzarella cheese, grated
- Small handful of roughly torn fresh oregano leaves, plus more for garnish

Make the pastry:
In a food processor, combine the flours, sugar, and salt and pulse to combine. Scatter the butter cubes evenly over the flour and give 18–20 more pulses to cut it into the dough. In a small bowl, whisk the egg with the 2 tablespoons cold water. Add half the mixture to the flour and give it around 5 pulses. Add the remaining egg mixture and pulse another 5–7 times. The dough should look crumbly but hold together when squeezed. Tip onto a work surface and use your hands to shape it into a disc, without overworking the dough. You can roll the dough out or press it into the pan straight away, but if in a warm environment, it is better to refrigerate it for 30 minutes.

Place the dough between two sheets of parchment paper and roll into a round roughly 12 inches (30 cm) in diameter. Remove the top paper and using the bottom one, invert the dough into a 9-inch/23-cm springform pan or pie dish, then peel off the paper. With your fingers, press the dough about 2 inches (5 cm) up the sides, using a knife to trim uneven edges. Use excess dough to seal cracks. Refrigerate for at least 1 hour or freeze for at least 30 minutes.

Preheat the oven to 425°F (220°C/Gas Mark 7).

Fit a piece of parchment against the dough and top with pie weights (baking beans). Bake for 12–15 minutes. Remove the weights and parchment and bake until the edges just start to brown, another 5 minutes. Remove the pie shell and reduce the temperature to 350°F (180°C/Gas Mark 4).

Make the filling:
In a bowl or large measuring cup (jug), combine the eggs, half-and-half (single cream), and salt and whisk until combined. Scatter the sujuk, feta, mozzarella, and oregano onto the pastry shell. Carefully pour the egg mixture on top. The mixture should fill it exactly, but if your pastry shrank or the sides are not as high as necessary and you find you have extra filling, stop pouring before it spills out of the crust.

Transfer to the oven and bake until set around the edges and the center jiggles very lightly if shaken, 40–45 minutes. Remove from the oven and allow to cool for at least 15 minutes. The quiche can also be made a day in advance and reheated. Serve warm, sprinkling fresh oregano on top, if desired.

Fresh Mint Muhallabiyeh with Chocolate "Soil" Crumbs

Muhallabiyeh is the Arabic version of a simple milk pudding, the first reference to which dates back to the tenth-century Arabic cookbook *Kitab al-Tabikh*. In fact, the origins of French blancmange and Italian panna cotta are thought to date back to the Arab influence on early medieval Europe. Like many dishes during Arab medieval times, the dish was named for a king or leader who favored it most, in this case, for Al-Muhallab ibn Abi Sufra, a leader during the Rashidun and Umayyad Caliphates. The original form of this dish is drastically different from the one recognized today, having included meat and sheep's tail fat and bread topped with a milk custard, then baked. Today, *muhallabiyeh* across the Arab world refers simply to starch-thickened milk pudding flavored with mastic or rose water. Here I take traditional *muhallabiyeh* but pair it with a different flavor combination—mint and chocolate—for a dessert that's both refreshing in flavor and satisfying in texture.

Serves 10–12

For the pudding:
- 4 cups (1 quart/liter) whole milk
- 1 cup (8 fl oz/250 ml) heavy (double) cream
- ¾ cup (4 oz/120 g) sugar
- 4–6 sprigs fresh mint, plus a few leaves for garnish
- ¾ cup (3 oz/80 g) cornstarch (cornflour)

For the chocolate crumbs:
- 1 cup (7 oz/200 g) sugar
- ½ cup (1¾ oz/50 g) unsweetened cocoa powder
- ¼ teaspoon salt
- 4 tablespoons (2 oz/60 g) unsalted butter, melted

Make the pudding:
In a large heavy-bottomed saucepan, combine 3 cups (24 fl oz/750 ml) of the milk, the cream, sugar, and mint sprigs. Bring just to a simmer over medium-low heat, then reduce the heat and cook for an additional 5 minutes to allow the mint to infuse.

Meanwhile, in a small bowl, stir the remaining 1 cup (8 fl oz/250 ml) milk into the cornstarch (cornflour) until fully dissolved.

Discard the mint sprigs then pour the cornstarch mixture into the pan, whisking constantly, until the mixture thickens, 1–2 minutes.

Remove from the heat and pour the pudding into very small dessert bowls or glass tumblers. Refrigerate for at least 4 hours and preferably overnight.

Make the chocolate crumbs:
Line a platter with parchment paper. In a large bowl, whisk together the sugar, cocoa powder, and salt until thoroughly combined. Gradually add the melted butter and continue to mix until evenly incorporated. Transfer the mixture to the lined platter and use a fork to mix until you have coarse crumbs that resemble wet soil. Refrigerate until the mixture hardens and cools completely, about 30 minutes. Break up any big lumps with a fork. Store in an airtight container until ready to serve. The mixture will keep in the refrigerator for several days.

Right before serving, top each bowl of milk pudding with some of the chocolate "soil" and a couple leaves of fresh mint.

Variations: If you're short on time, you can forgo the chocolate soil topping and top the puddings with chocolate cookie crumbs (your favorite dark chocolate cookie), grated dark chocolate (70% cacao), or a drizzle of dark chocolate ganache.

Eggplants + Tomatoes

My grandmother, Teta Asma, must have been around the age I am now when she was raising five children in her tiny Galilean village and working as a schoolteacher. She did all this while embroidering the most delicate needlework (some of which features as backgrounds in this book); while raising goats, chickens, and keeping a garden; and while also daily preparing food for her family that got her recognized as the best cook in the town. But out of all the stories I have heard about those times, one that always comes back to me when I cook with vegetables is how she woke up at the crack of dawn each morning to tend to her garden before heading out to school, picking the perfectly ripe eggplants (aubergines) or tomatoes or peppers to prepare for lunch that day.

Our cuisine is heavily reliant on vegetables. Picking out, even buying, vegetables is seen as an art in the Arab world, from knowing which tomatoes are the perfect ripeness and which eggplants would absorb the least oil when fried, to which peppers would make the perfect chili paste and which size okra won't be slimy when stewed. My grandmother took pride in knowing her vegetables as intimately as she knew her kids and knowing how to coax the most flavor out of them.

The stories of her time tell of a life simpler and more enjoyable than many of ours today, in spite of fewer conveniences than we currently have. Looking at how the village has changed since the days I speak of, I think the real secret was community. It is the sense of community and belonging that gives our lives meaning and makes it possible to manage all we have to do. Today, I find no better way to build community than over food. I chose eggplants and tomatoes for this chapter because, even though not native to our region, they are some of the most widely used in Arab cuisine and are two vegetables that feature in almost every food gathering I have.

Like star-crossed lovers, eggplants and tomatoes came from disparate parts of the world to create such harmonious combinations in Arab cuisine that it's impossible to imagine a time when it wasn't so. But that time indeed existed. A time when, around the ninth century, eggplants were described as having "the colors of a scorpion's abdomen, and a taste like its sting." But by the tenth century, after people discovered how salting could remove the bitter taste, the eggplant had become a pervasive ingredient across the Arab world, evidenced by the numerous recipes for it in *Kitab al-Tabìkh*, the oldest Arabic cookbook on record. Believed to have originated in southern and eastern Asia, the eggplant is now a favorite food on Arab tables with countless ways of preparing it, from smoked, roasted, and fried, to stewed or mashed for a "poor man's caviar."

Tomatoes, another non-native plant originating in Mexico and South America, made their way to the Middle East sometime between the sixteenth and nineteenth centuries. The Arabic word *banadura*, similar to the Italian word *pomodoro*, hints at one possible route—from Italy to Egypt—by which tomatoes came to the Middle East. Their arrival brought a fundamental change to Arab cooking. Stews, the staple Arab dish, started to use tomato as a key ingredient for thickening, souring, and coloring in place of nuts, juices, and saffron as they had done previously. If you look at the cuisine of the Middle East only a few centuries ago, it was very different from the one we recognize today in which tomatoes play such a dominant role.

The recipes here veer from the standards we have come to recognize in Arab cuisines. Instead, they are a combination of classics reimagined (Fried Eggplant, Tomato, and Chili Salad with Toasted Pita, page 62), of meals inspired by other cultures (Grilled Eggplant Salad with Sumac Chicken and Pine Nuts, page 68), or dishes I grew up eating from my Teta Asma (Lamb and Halloumi Pasta Bake, page 72), which I find symbolic of the way ingredients and dishes travel across time and geography to find unique homes in various parts of the world.

Tomato Salad with Labaneh and Za'atar

The perfectly ripe tomatoes of summer are cherished across the Mediterranean where eating them with various white cheeses is common, from Italian caprese to Greek *horiatiki*. In the Middle East, the Levant in particular, this is also the case, but it is less structured. Tomatoes and labaneh, or white cheese, are staples on breakfast and supper tables. The cheese is usually eaten with bread, sometimes with za'atar, and the tomatoes are enjoyed plainly on the side. This salad takes that humble breakfast and assembles it into a more structured dish that's as tasty as it is pretty. If you do not have or want to make labaneh, you could substitute thin slices or small cubes of feta. You could also use soft goat cheese and either crumble it or form it into balls as you would the labaneh.

Serves 4–6

- ¾ cup (3 oz/85 g) labaneh, preferably homemade (page 40)
- Scant 1 tablespoon za'atar blend (optional)
- 1 lb 10 oz (750 g) heirloom or good-quality slicing tomatoes or cherry tomatoes (a mixture of colors looks pretty here)
- 2 tablespoons extra-virgin olive oil
- 1 clove garlic, very finely chopped
- 1 tablespoon fresh lemon juice
- 1 teaspoon sumac
- Maldon sea salt
- 2–3 sprigs fresh za'atar, leaves picked (or use fresh oregano or marjoram, or in a pinch, thyme)
- Bread, for serving

Line a sieve with paper towels and set over a bowl. Spoon the labaneh into the sieve and allow to sit for about 1 hour at room temperature, until some of the liquid has drained and it is drier and easier to roll. Transfer to a bowl, add the za'atar blend (if using), and mix to combine.

Line a flat plate with parchment paper. With lightly oiled hands, roll the labaneh into balls the size of marbles and set on the plate. Cover with plastic wrap (clingfilm) and refrigerate until ready to use.

Slice the tomatoes into rounds ⅓ inch (1 cm) thick and arrange on a serving platter.

In a small bowl, whisk together the olive oil, garlic, and lemon juice. Spoon the mixture over the sliced tomatoes. Sprinkle with the sumac and salt flakes. Top with the labaneh balls and scatter with the fresh za'atar leaves. Serve with bread.

Tomato Salad with Labaneh and Za'atar

Tomato, Cucumber, and Peanut Butter Salad

The more I research food, the more I see the striking similarities across cultures and the nuanced differences at play because of environmental factors and ingredient availability. Take chopped cucumber tomato salad: Indians call it *cachumber* and East Africans *kachumbarì*; Iranians call it *shìrazì* and Turks *choban salatasì*; Balkans and Central Europeans call it *shopska salad*; and Israelis call it Arab salad, while Palestinians call it *saltet falaheen* or "farmers' salad." The differences are minor with varying herbs and dressing ingredients. One Arab variation is to mix the salad with tahini. In Sudan, it is mixed with the more widely available peanut butter instead. Taking inspiration from the Sudanese version, this mixed chopped salad with peanut butter is one of my favorite sides to grilled meats and rice dishes, but is also perfect on its own with fresh bread.

Serves 4

4 tablespoons unsalted peanut butter (see Note)
2 tablespoons fresh lime juice
½ teaspoon salt
1 large tomato (8½ oz/240 g), cut into ⅓-inch (1 cm) dice
1 mini cucumber, cut into ⅓-inch (1 cm) dice
2 scallions (spring onions), thinly sliced
2 tablespoons finely chopped fresh cilantro (coriander)
1 green chili, finely chopped

In a medium bowl, combine the peanut butter, lime juice, and salt and stir to combine. It might appear pasty, but that is fine because the juices from the vegetables will thin it out.

Add all the vegetables and mix with a spoon to incorporate.

Note: You can use creamy or crunchy peanut butter, but the recipe assumes it is unsalted either way. If your peanut butter has salt in the ingredients list, then start out with ¼ teaspoon salt, taste when combined, and adjust accordingly.

Sudanese Peanut Butter Eggplant Mutabal

Eggplant (aubergine) *mutabal*, or baba ghanouj as many refer to it, is usually made with fire-roasted eggplants for a smoky flavor. In *The Palestinian Table*, I confessed to not liking it much and shared my grandmother's version, which uses fried eggplants instead. Countless people told me they were converted after trying the fried version. When I mentioned this to one of my cousins, whose husband is Sudanese, she told me of a similar dish her husband makes that is flavored with peanut butter instead of tahini—not surprising since Sudan is one of the largest exporters of peanuts. In fact, in Arabic, peanuts are called fool Sudani or "Sudanese beans," similar to the way we refer to pistachios as *fistuk Halabi*, which means nut of Aleppo. This recipe is my version, adapted from the Sudanese dish known locally as *salata aswad*. Very forward on the peanut flavor, this dish is delicious served as a side or part of a mezze spread with bread or even crackers.

---

p. 61

Serves 4

- ½ lb (450 g) eggplants (aubergines), 4 small or 2 medium or 1 large
- 2 tablespoons olive oil, plus more for drizzling
- 1 small onion, chopped (about ½ cup)
- 1 jalapeño or other green chili, finely chopped (optional)
- ½ teaspoon salt, plus more for sprinkling
- 1 clove garlic, crushed or finely chopped
- ½ teaspoon tomato paste (purée)
- ½ lb (450 g) tomatoes (2 medium to large), cut into small dice
- 2 tablespoons creamy unsalted peanut butter
- 2 teaspoons fresh lime juice, plus more to taste
- Bread, for serving

Preheat the oven to 500°F (260°C/Gas Mark 10) or as high as it will go.

Make 2 or 3 deep incisions in the eggplants (aubergines) and place on the baking sheet. Roast until cooked through and the skin is crisp and cracks when pierced with a knife, about 1 hour. Remove and set aside to cool.

When cool enough to handle, peel the eggplants, roughly mash with a fork, and place in a mesh sieve set over a bowl to drain excess liquid.

In a medium pot, heat the olive oil over medium-high heat. Add the onion, jalapeño, and salt and cook, stirring occasionally, until browned and starting to crisp around the edges, 10–20 minutes. Time will depend on the variety of the onion and strength of heat.

Add the garlic and cook for about 1 minute, until fragrant, then add the tomato paste (purée) and cook for another minute until evenly incorporated.

Add the diced tomatoes to the pot and cook until they have softened and broken up, 5–8 minutes. Add the peanut butter and continue to stir until well combined.

Reduce the heat, add the roasted eggplants, and continue to cook, stirring regularly and mashing lightly, until the mix comes together in a chunky paste, another 3–5 minutes. Stir in the lime juice to incorporate. Taste and add more lime and salt to your liking. Remove from the heat and allow to cool slightly before serving.

Spoon into a bowl, drizzle with more olive oil, if desired, and serve with bread. Can be served warm, cool, or at room temperature. Leftovers can keep in the refrigerator, tightly covered, up to 4 days.

Fire-Roasted Eggplant and Tomato Mutabal

When my grandmother used to bake her bread on a wooden fire out in a communal courtyard with other neighborhood women, she would often take some eggplants (aubergines), tomatoes and green chilies and roast them on the remaining embers. She would mash the roasted pulps together and then mix with fresh parsley, garlic, and olive oil. Most similar methods of vegetable preparation in Arab cooking are referred to as *mutabal*, which literally means "seasoned" or "flavored." This recipe is a more modern adaptation of my grandmother's basic one, perfect with bread as part of a mezze but is equally good eaten with tortilla chips the way you would scoop up salsa.

Serves 4–6 as part of a spread

- 1 large (about 1¼ lb/550 g) eggplant (aubergine)
- 1 large tomato (about 9 oz/250 g), halved and cored
- 1 small onion, halved
- 1 jalapeño pepper
- 1½ tablespoons fresh lemon juice
- 1 tablespoon extra-virgin olive oil, plus more for drizzling
- 1¼ teaspoons salt
- 1 clove garlic, crushed in a garlic press or finely chopped
- Small handful of cilantro (coriander), finely chopped, plus more for garnish
- Slivered almonds, toasted, for garnish

Preheat the oven to 500°F (260°C/Gas Mark 10) or as high as it will go.

Make 2 or 3 deep incisions in the eggplant (aubergine) and place on a baking sheet along with the cut tomato, onion, and jalapeño pepper.

Transfer to the oven and roast until the vegetables are charred on the outside and tender on the inside, 30–40 minutes. The eggplant may need more time, depending on size, so you can remove the tomato, onion, and jalapeño and set aside while you continue to roast the eggplant. You can tell the eggplant is done when the skin is crisp and cracks when pierced with a knife. Remove and set aside to cool.

When cool enough to handle, peel the vegetables. You can leave the skin on the jalapeño and tomato if you wish. With a fork and knife, finely chop the eggplant and place in a mesh sieve set over a bowl to drain excess liquid.

In a mini food processor, combine the tomato, onion, and jalapeño and pulse until coarsely chopped. Add the mixture to the eggplant in the sieve and mix until combined, then leave in the sieve for another 15 minutes or so to drain.

Transfer the mixture to a bowl, add the lemon juice, olive oil, salt, garlic, and cilantro (coriander) and mix to combine. The *mutabal* can be used immediately or it will keep in the refrigerator, tightly covered, up to 3 days.

To serve, spoon into a serving bowl, drizzle with olive oil, and garnish with chopped cilantro and toasted almonds.

 Fire-Roasted Eggplant and Tomato Mutabal (1); Sudanese Peanut Butter Eggplant Mutabal (2) p. 59

Fried Eggplant, Tomato, and Chili Salad with Toasted Pita

Whenever my mother made *maqlubeh* for us growing up, she would have a platter of fried eggplants (aubergines) off to the side in the kitchen. I would take a few slices, slip them into a pita bread with some tomatoes and green chilies, then drizzle a very sour tahini sauce on top. It was, and remains, one of my favorite sandwiches of all times. As simple as it sounds, the flavors and textures were sublime. This salad is my take on those childhood sandwiches.

Serves 4 as an appetizer or as part of a spread

2 oz (60 g) white pita bread

For the sauce:
4 tablespoons tahini
2 tablespoons yogurt
1 tablespoon fresh lemon juice, plus more to taste
¼ teaspoon salt, or to taste

For the eggplant:
1 medium (about 12 oz/350 g) eggplant (aubergine)
Vegetable oil, for deep-frying
Salt

For serving:
1 small tomato, finely diced
1 small green chili, thinly sliced

Preheat the oven to 350°F (180°C/Gas Mark 4).

Cut the pita bread into ¾-inch (2 cm) squares and arrange on a baking sheet. Bake, moving the bread around from time to time, until the squares are completely dry and crisp and starting to darken in color, about 15 minutes. Remove and set aside. (This step can be done a couple of days in advance and bread stored in a zip seal bag or airtight container at room temperature.)

Make the sauce:
In a bowl, stir together the tahini, yogurt, 3 tablespoons water, the lemon juice, and salt. Taste and adjust the salt and lemon to your liking. Set aside.

Make the eggplant:
Halve the eggplant (aubergine) lengthwise, then in half lengthwise again, then cut each strip crosswise into cubes.

Pour about 3 inches/7 cm vegetable oil into a deep-fryer or heavy Dutch oven (casserole) and heat to 350°F (180°C) or until a morsel of bread immediately rises to the surface when dropped in. Pat the eggplant dry with paper towels. Working in batches, fry the eggplant until golden brown, 5–8 minutes. Remove with a slotted spoon and drain on paper towels. Sprinkle with salt.

To assemble:
Scatter the toasted pita in a serving platter. Spread the fried eggplant evenly on top. Drizzle the tahini sauce over the eggplant. Top with the diced tomato and chili. Serve immediately.

Fried Eggplant, Tomato, and Chili Salad with Toasted Pita

Roasted Eggplant with Vegetables, Olives, and Walnuts over Tahini

Eggplants (aubergines) are one of the most widely used vegetables across the Middle East, probably because they are such a wonderful vessel for flavor with a creamy yet hearty texture. Two of the most popular dishes are eggplant *mutabal* (roasted eggplants mixed with tahini) and *bìtìnjan al rahìb* or "monk's eggplant" (roasted eggplant mixed with fresh vegetables). This salad is the best of both worlds because it allows you to savor the unique elements of each dish through a harmonious layering of flavors. A deconstructed *mutabal* of sorts, it combines the classic tahini sauce with the vegetable variation in a new way, adding uncommon ingredients like olives and walnuts. Perfect with bread, it's so delicious you just might find yourself eating it alone by the spoonful.

Serves 6–8 as part of a spread

For the tahini base:

½ cup (4 oz/120 g) tahini
4 tablespoons fresh lemon juice
4 tablespoons yogurt
½ teaspoon salt

For the eggplant mixture:

2 medium eggplants (aubergines), about 2¼ lb/1 kg total
2–3 green chilies or jalapeño peppers, seeded and finely diced (remove the membranes for less spice or substitute with ½ green bell pepper)
½ red bell pepper, finely diced
1 small tomato, finely diced
20 pitted green olives, thinly sliced
½ cup (2 oz/60 g) walnuts, toasted and finely chopped
2 cloves garlic, crushed in a garlic press or grated on a Microplane
2 tablespoons finely chopped fresh parsley
3 tablespoons extra-virgin olive oil
2 tablespoons pomegranate molasses
2 tablespoons fresh lemon juice
1 teaspoon salt

Preheat the oven to 500°F (260°C/Gas Mark 10). Line a baking sheet with foil for easy cleanup.

Prepare the tahini base:
While the oven preheats, in a bowl, stir together the tahini, lemon juice, 3 tablespoons water, the yogurt, and salt until smooth and evenly incorporated. You want a spreadable consistency slightly thicker than Greek yogurt. If it's too thick, add a tablespoon of water at a time, stirring to incorporate, until you reach the desired consistency. Cover and set aside.

Prepare the eggplant mixture:
Make 2 or 3 deep incisions in the eggplants (aubergines) and place on the baking sheet. Roast until cooked through and the skin is crisp and cracks when pierced with a knife, about 1 hour. Remove and set aside to cool.

When cool enough to handle, peel the eggplants. With a fork and knife, finely chop the eggplants and place in a mesh sieve set over a bowl to drain excess liquid.

Transfer the eggplants to a large bowl and add all the remaining ingredients. Mix until well combined.

To serve, spoon the tahini mixture into a shallow bowl and use the back of a spoon to make a well in the center. Place the eggplant *mutabal* in the center and serve.

Roasted Eggplant with Vegetables, Olives, and Walnuts over Tahini

Fried Garlic Tomatoes

On days when one is tired of cooking traditional food, it is quite common for Arab families to do something called *maqalee*, which simply means "fried foods," or *nawashif*, which means "dry foods" (as compared with the usual sauces and stews). On such days, you'll find the dinner table filled with simple dips, spreads, and bread and, of course, fried vegetables like eggplants (aubergines), potatoes, cauliflower, and tomatoes. Although the tomatoes are usually fried until they break down into a thick, chunky sauce, I prefer to make these delicious garlic ones the way my mother does, retaining their shape and impressive look and allowing you to taste each element fully. Summer tomatoes or good-quality heirlooms that are fleshy and not filled with watery seeds are the best varieties for this dish.

Serves 4 as part of a spread

- 4–6 large fleshy tomatoes (about 2¼ lb/1 kg)
- 4 tablespoons olive oil
- 10 large cloves garlic, finely chopped (not crushed)
- 2–3 fresh green chilies, finely chopped
- ½ teaspoon salt
- Small bunch of fresh mint leaves, finely chopped, or 2 teaspoons crushed dried mint
- Bread, for serving

Using a sharp knife, slice each tomato horizontally in half (through the equator).

Arrange the tomato halves cut-side down in a frying pan large enough to fit the pieces snugly. Pour the olive oil over the tomatoes and set the pan over medium heat for about 5 minutes.

Flip the tomatoes over and scatter half the garlic and chilies on the tomatoes and the other half in the oil. Sprinkle with the salt, cover the pan, reduce the heat, and cook until the tomatoes have started to soften but still retain their shape, about 15 minutes. Check on the tomatoes several times while cooking and, tilting the pan, spoon some of the oil mixture over the tomatoes. When almost done, sprinkle the mint over the tomatoes, cover the pan, and cook for another minute or two.

Remove from the heat and serve immediately with fresh bread to mop up all the delicious juices. Leftovers can be lightly mashed with a fork or blitzed in a blender and used as a tomato sauce base for any recipe calling for it. Frozen leftovers will keep for at least 2 months.

Broiled Eggplant Salad with Sumac Chicken and Pine Nuts

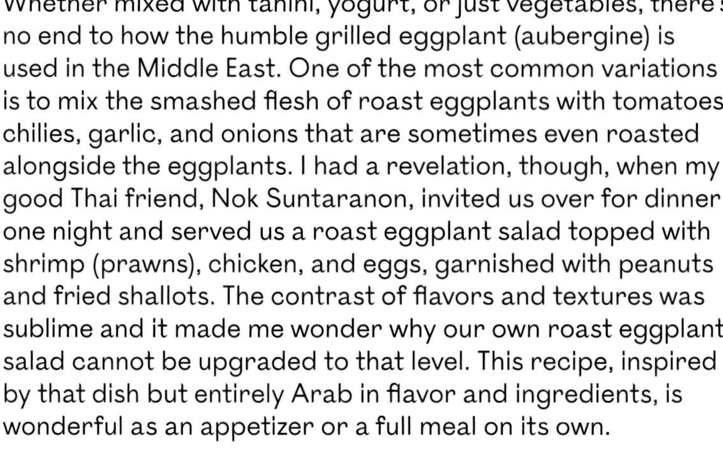

Whether mixed with tahini, yogurt, or just vegetables, there's no end to how the humble grilled eggplant (aubergine) is used in the Middle East. One of the most common variations is to mix the smashed flesh of roast eggplants with tomatoes, chilies, garlic, and onions that are sometimes even roasted alongside the eggplants. I had a revelation, though, when my good Thai friend, Nok Suntaranon, invited us over for dinner one night and served us a roast eggplant salad topped with shrimp (prawns), chicken, and eggs, garnished with peanuts and fried shallots. The contrast of flavors and textures was sublime and it made me wonder why our own roast eggplant salad cannot be upgraded to that level. This recipe, inspired by that dish but entirely Arab in flavor and ingredients, is wonderful as an appetizer or a full meal on its own.

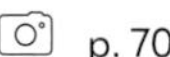 p. 70

Serves 4

2¼ lb (1 kg) eggplants (aubergines), about 4 medium or 2 large

For the dressing:
4 tablespoons fresh lemon juice
4 tablespoons extra-virgin olive oil
2 large cloves garlic, finely chopped
1 teaspoon salt
Pinch of sugar (optional)

For the chicken:
2 tablespoons olive oil
9 oz (250 g) ground (minced) chicken or chicken breasts/thighs cut into very small chunks
1 teaspoon salt
½ teaspoon ground cumin
¼ teaspoon freshly ground black pepper, or more to taste
1 tablespoon sumac

For assembly:
2 medium tomatoes, finely chopped
1 green or red chili, finely chopped (optional; omit for nonspicy version)
1 small bunch of parsley, finely chopped
1 small bunch of cilantro (coriander), finely chopped
1 small shallot, thinly sliced
4 tablespoons pine nuts, lightly toasted

Adjust a rack to 6–8 inches (15–20 cm) below the broiler (grill) element and preheat the broiler to high. Line a baking sheet with aluminum foil.

Pierce the eggplants (aubergines) a few times with a fork all over to avoid them exploding in the oven. Place the eggplants on the lined baking sheet and broil, turning occasionally, until charred on all sides and tender on the inside, 30 minutes to 1 hour, depending on the size. The eggplants are ready when they are collapsing and the outside feels crisp and easily breaks when touched. Remove from the oven and close the foil around the eggplants to hold in the steam. This will make the eggplants easy to peel. Allow the eggplants to rest for 15–30 minutes.

Meanwhile, make the dressing:
In a small bowl, mix together the lemon juice, olive oil, garlic, salt, and sugar (if using). Set aside.

Open the foil package of eggplants and with your fingers, carefully peel away the skin, trying to keep the eggplants intact as much as possible. Transfer to a sieve set in a large bowl and let sit for 10–15 minutes to allow the liquid to drain.

Meanwhile, prepare the chicken:
In a nonstick or heavy-bottomed frying pan, heat the olive oil until shimmering but not smoking. Add the chicken, salt, cumin, and pepper and fry, stirring regularly, until the chicken is cooked through and starting to brown around the edges, 6–8 minutes. Add the sumac, give one final toss, and remove from the heat.

To assemble:
Arrange the eggplants on serving platter and drizzle with half of the dressing. Arrange the chicken mixture over the eggplants. Top with the tomatoes, chili (if using), parsley, cilantro (coriander), and shallot. Drizzle the remaining dressing on top, sprinkle with the pine nuts, and serve.

Note: If you have a gas burner, you could also roast the eggplants directly over the flame, but it will be much messier. You can, however, line under the burners with foil for easier clean up. To roast, use metal tongs to hold the eggplants above the flame and turn until charred on all sides. Then place in a bowl, cover with plastic wrap (clingfilm), and allow to rest for 15–30 minutes. Continue with the recipe as above.

Mussels in Arak, Saffron, and Tomato Broth

Mussels are not common in Arab kitchens. In fact, the first time I ever had them I was a teenager in France and my father had seen them in a market and insisted on cooking them for us with white wine. From that day, I was converted. Today, when I order mussels at restaurants, it's rarely to eat the mussels themselves. It's usually because I want plenty of crusty bread to mop up the delicious sauce with. The broth in this recipe is perfect for that. Reminiscent of various Mediterranean fish stews, the flavors here are pungent and aromatic. I use arak because it's the anise liquor of choice in Arab households, but you can sub with raki or ouzo.

 p. 71

Serves 4–6

1 tablespoon (15 g) unsalted butter
1 tablespoon olive oil
1 small bulb fennel (some fronds reserved), finely chopped
1 medium carrot, finely diced
1 shallot, thinly sliced
2¼ teaspoons salt
4 cloves garlic, finely chopped
3 tablespoons arak, raki, or ouzo
1 can (14 oz/400 g) crushed (finely chopped) tomatoes
Generous pinch of saffron threads
½ teaspoon Aleppo pepper
¼ cup (60 ml) heavy (double) cream
2 lb (900 g) mussels, scrubbed and debearded
Crusty bread, for serving

In a large heavy-bottomed pot, heat the butter and oil over medium heat. Add the fennel, carrot, shallot, and 1 teaspoon of the salt and cook, stirring occasionally, until the vegetables are softened and starting to brown, about 15 minutes. Add the garlic and continue to cook for another 2–3 minutes until fragrant.

Pour in the arak to deglaze the pan and use a wooden spoon to scrape the browned bits from the bottom. Allow to cook for 1 minute, then add the tomatoes, 1 teaspoon of the salt, and 4 cups (32 fl oz/ 950 ml) water and bring to a boil. Continue to cook for a couple of minutes, then reduce the heat, add the saffron heads, and simmer for 30 minutes to meld the flavors.

Add the pepper, then taste and add the remaining ¼ teaspoon salt if needed. Pour in the cream and stir to combine.

Add the mussels, increase the heat to high, cover, and cook until the mussels open, about 5 minutes. Discard any mussels that remain closed at this point.

Divide the mussels among serving bowls and pour more sauce on top. Garnish with the reserved fennel fronds. Serve with crusty bread.

Broiled Eggplant Salad with Sumac Chicken and Pine Nuts

Mussels in Arak, Saffron, and Tomato Broth

Lamb and Halloumi Pasta Bake

Legends abound as to the origins of pasta and the direction of its spread across the world, but academic research often points to the Fertile Crescent as its origin. Evidence includes the cultivation of durum wheat, a grain native to that region; the Arabic and Turkic names of related food items even in countries like China; and the first-ever mention of pasta in the tenth-century Arabic cookbook *Kitab al-Tabikh*. This fascinating and uncertain history aside, processed pasta as we know it today was not historically a staple food in the Levant. In recent decades, however, the varieties and availability of packaged pasta—often imported from Italy—have grown. But when my grandmother was a young woman, they only had access to spaghetti-like varieties. So on occasion, she would mix it with meat and tomatoes and, if feeling decadent, top it with some white cheese and bake it. This recipe is adapted from hers and one that I find deeply symbolic of how our foods travel across geography and time, finding unique homes and methods of preparation wherever they end up in the world.

Serves 4–6

- 1 lb (450 g) lean cut of lamb or beef
- 4 tablespoons olive oil, plus extra for pasta
- 1 large onion, finely chopped
- 1 green chili, deseeded and finely chopped
- 2½ teaspoons salt, divided
- 3 cloves garlic, finely minced
- 2 cans (14 oz/400 g each) crushed tomatoes
- 1 teaspoon finely chopped fresh za'atar or oregano leaves (optional)
- 1 lb (450 g) bucatini pasta (or any pasta of choice suitable for baking, such as penne, fusilli, or ziti)
- 5 oz (150 g) halloumi cheese, grated
- 3½ oz (100 g) low-moisture mozzarella, grated

Use a sharp knife to cut the meat into very thin bite-size pieces. This is easier if the meat has been partially frozen beforehand.

Heat the olive oil in a large pan over medium heat. Add the onion and chili with ½ teaspoon of the salt and cook, stirring periodically, until softened and starting to brown, 5–6 minutes. Add the garlic and continue to cook until fragrant, another minute or two.

Increase the heat to high and add the meat and 1 teaspoon salt. Cook, stirring regularly, until any released water evaporates and the meat starts to brown, 6–8 minutes.

Add the tomatoes and the remaining 1 teaspoon salt, bring to a boil, then reduce the heat to low and simmer until the flavors have melded, the meat is meltingly tender, and the sauce has darkened in color, 40–50 minutes. Check on the sauce a few times as it simmers and if it appears to be thickening too much, add a couple splashes of water. You want the consistency to be slightly runny because the pasta will absorb some of the liquid as it bakes. Remove from the heat and add the za'atar or oregano leaves (if using), and set aside.

As the sauce simmers, preheat the oven to 400°F (200°C/Gas Mark 6) and bring a pot of well-salted water to a boil. Add the pasta to water and cook to al dente, generally 2 minutes less than on package instructions.

Drain the pasta and transfer to a baking dish, adding a tablespoon of oil so it doesn't clump up. Pour the meat and tomato sauce over the pasta and give it a very gentle toss. Top with the grated cheeses, cover, and bake until bubbling and cheese is melted, 30–40 minutes. Uncover the dish and broil until the cheese is crisp and browned to your liking, 5–6 minutes.

Remove from the oven and allow to sit for 10 minutes before serving.

Lamb and Halloumi Pasta Bake

Eggplant-Wrapped Kafta Rolls in Tomato Sauce

Eggplants (aubergines) and meat are one of the most widespread combinations across the Middle East and Mediterranean. From Iraqi *tepsì baytinìjan* and Turkish *permak kebabì*, to Greek moussaka and Levantine *mnazaleh*, there are probably as many variations as there are cooks. Here I draw inspiration from different cuisines and cooking methods to create a unique but easy dish that's impressive to serve company, yet equally perfect for a weeknight dinner, as it can be prepped in advance and then quickly baked in the oven. The ingredients list is deceptively long, but it is actually quite simple and quick to put together. Perfect alongside vermicelli or plain rice.

Serves 4–6

For the eggplant:

3 medium globe eggplants (aubergines), about 3½ lb (1.5 kg) total
Vegetable oil, for frying

For the lamb kaftas:

1 lb 12 oz (800 g) coarsely ground (minced) meat: beef, lamb, veal, or a combination
3 oz (85 g) pita bread or white bread with crusts removed, roughly torn
1 small tomato, quartered
1 small onion, quartered
1 large clove garlic
1 green chili (optional)
2 tablespoons chopped fresh cilantro (coriander)
2 tablespoons chopped fresh flat-leaf parsley
1 tablespoon olive oil
1 tablespoon salt
1 tablespoon Nine-Spice Mix (page 27), baharat, or Lebanese 7-spice blend

For the tomato sauce:

2 cans (14 oz/400 g each) crushed (finely chopped) tomatoes
1 tablespoon olive oil
1 teaspoon salt
2 cloves garlic, minced

For serving:

Orzo Rice (page 33) or bread

Prepare the eggplant:

Cut each eggplant (aubergine) lengthwise into slices ⅔ inch (1.5 cm) thick. You should end up with 15 slices. If you end up with fewer slices (if your eggplants are perhaps narrower but longer), reduce the number of kaftas accordingly.

In a large nonstick frying pan over medium-high heat, pour enough vegetable oil to shallow-fry the eggplants. Heat until hot, but not smoking. Place a few eggplant slices in the oil making sure not to overcrowd. Fry until golden brown, 3–5 minutes per side. Remove and place on a paper-towel-lined plate to drain, continue until all slices are fried.

Prepare the lamb kaftas:

Preheat the oven to 425°F (220°C/Gas Mark 7). Line a sheet pan with parchment paper.

Place the meat in a large bowl.

In a food processor, combine the bread, tomato, onion, garlic, chili (if using), cilantro (coriander), parsley, olive oil, salt, and spice mix and pulse to a coarse paste. Pour the mixture over the meat in the bowl and mix very well with your hands until fully combined.

Shape the meat mixture into 15 kafta sausages. The mixture will be soft, so oil your hands or wear disposable food gloves to shape the kafkas.

Arrange the sausages in a single layer on the lined sheet pan and transfer to the oven. Cook until the kaftas have started to brown, 15–20 minutes. Remove and set the sausages aside. Pour any juices from the pan into a medium bowl and set aside for the tomato sauce.

To assemble the dish, set an eggplant slice vertically in front of you. Place a kafta sausage crosswise at the bottom of the eggplant slice and roll up. Set, seam-side down, in an 9-inch (23-cm) round or 9 × 13-inch (23 × 33 cm) baking pan. Repeat to roll up all of the kaftas.

Make the tomato sauce:

To the bowl of kafta cooking juices, add the crushed tomatoes, ½ cup (4 fl oz/120 ml) water, the olive oil, salt, and garlic. The sauce should be easily pourable because it will thicken in the oven, so add up to ½ cup (4 fl oz/120 ml) additional water if it appears too thick.

Pour the sauce over the eggplant rolls and transfer to the oven. Bake until the sauce is bubbling and slightly thickened, 15–20 minutes.

To serve:

Remove from the oven, let stand for 5 minutes, then serve with orzo rice or bread.

Eggplant-Wrapped Kafta Rolls in Tomato Sauce

Easy Eggplant Maqlubeh

One of my favorite things to eat is the quintessential Palestinian dish *maqlubeh*. Usually reserved for weekends and larger gatherings, it is time-consuming, but is a labor of love also. Since I often crave this dish, and my daughters ask for it, I've streamlined it into an easier version that tastes just as good but is fit for a weeknight dinner. Also, a few small tweaks—roasting the eggplants (aubergines) instead of frying, doctoring store-bought stock, and using chicken breasts—give an equally delicious outcome. It's delicious on its own or with a side of yogurt and mixed chopped salad.

Serves 4

For the chicken:

3 medium-size chicken breasts (1¼–1½ lb/575–680 g total)
1 teaspoon salt
1 teaspoon Nine-Spice Mix (page 27), baharat, or Lebanese 7-spice blend
1 teaspoon olive oil
1 tablespoon ghee

For the eggplants and rice:

2 medium eggplants (aubergines), about 2 lb/900 g total
Olive oil, for brushing
3 cups (19½ oz/550 g) jasmine rice
4 cups (32 fl oz/950 ml) chicken stock (homemade or store-bought)
1 teaspoon Nine-Spice Mix (page 27), baharat, or Lebanese 7-spice blend
1 teaspoon tomato paste (purée)
1 teaspoon salt, plus more as needed
½ teaspoon ground turmeric
Slivered almonds, toasted

Prepare the chicken:
Slice each chicken breast into 3 or 4 pieces and set in a shallow bowl. Add the salt, spice blend, and olive oil and mix to evenly coat. Let marinate in the refrigerator as you prepare the remaining ingredients.

Preheat the broiler (grill) to high. Line a baking sheet with parchment paper.

Prepare the eggplants and rice:
Slice the eggplants (aubergines) crosswise into rounds ¾ inch (2 cm) thick. Brush both sides with olive oil. Place the eggplant slices on the baking sheet and broil (grill) until the exterior is a deep golden-brown, 8–10 minutes on each side. Remove and set aside.

While the eggplants are roasting, wash the rice until the water runs clear, then add to a bowl with water to cover and leave to soak for 15 minutes. Drain and set aside.

Pour the stock into a large spouted measuring cup (jug) or small pot and stir in the spice blend, tomato paste (purée), salt and tumeric to combine.

In a large (9- to 10-inch/23- to 25-cm) nonstick pot (preferably not deeper than 6 inches/15 cm), heat the ghee until shimmering but not smoking. Add the chicken in a single layer and cook until nicely browned on the bottom, 3–5 minutes. Flip and cook for another 3–5 minutes to cook through. Remove the chicken, reserving the fat in the pot. Set the chicken aside.

Spread about one-third of the drained rice evenly in the bottom of the pot. Arrange the eggplant slices over the rice, then top with the chicken. Top with the remaining rice.

Gently pour the stock mixture on top until it comes to about ¾ inch (2 cm) above the rice. Set a plate on top of the rice to help maintain the shape during cooking and bring to a boil over medium-high heat. Taste the broth and add more salt if necessary. You may need to add up to another teaspoon of salt.

Cook for 15 minutes, then reduce the heat, remove the plate but return the cover, and simmer until the rice is fully cooked with no bite, 15–20 minutes. Remove from the heat and set aside, covered, to rest for 10–15 minutes.

To serve, remove the lid and place a large inverted serving platter over the pot of rice. Using both hands, flip the pot over, and slowly lift to reveal a beautiful cake-shaped rice dish. Give a little shake to disperse the rice, then top with the toasted almonds and serve.

Easy Eggplant Maqlubeh

Pomegranates + Lemons

In the middle of my parents' courtyard is a lemon tree, and around the edges, limes and navel oranges. But the lemon tree is the oldest, largest, and most special. Even my daughters always ask, "When will we visit Seedo and Teta to pick lemons?" We use its blossoms to make a jam that turns bright pink on its own; its juice for cooking, cordials, and lemonade; and at the start of the season we slice the whole lemons, skin and all, sprinkle with salt, and eat as a snack. For use throughout the year, in addition to freezing its juice, we also preserve the lemon in salt.

On the edges of my family's garden are two pomegranate trees. Every year in late summer, my father spends his afternoons picking pomegranates, peeling and seeding them so that not a single seed is squashed, and then we eat what we can and the rest we juice to make cordials and molasses. Just as our ancestors did, we do this to keep our bounty alive from one season to the next. For our ancestors, however, much of the food they prepared was born of necessity. We still enjoy some of these foods today, but probably more for their flavor than for their practicality. Preserved lemons are one such example. Lemons only made their way to the Middle East and the Arab world sometime between the eighth and tenth centuries, but have become a staple in the cuisine since. Preserved lemons, often associated with North African cuisine, have been prevalent in the entirety of Arab cooking since ancient times. That's why the thirteenth-century Syrian cookbook *Kìtab al-Wusla ìla al-Habìb*, in a section on variations to salt-preserved lemon recipes, starts out with the sentence, "The first recipe is so well known it need not be described."

Pomegranates were one of the first fruits cultivated by humans in the region, and pomegranate molasses also falls into the category of well-known preparations across the Middle East. One of the first references to the molasses is in the tenth-century Arabic cookbook *Kìtab al-Tabìkh*, where it is listed alongside other condensed juices, each used for a specific medicinal purpose. Today, pomegranate molasses belongs more in the kitchen than in the medicine cabinet. Readily available in stores, it still remains a staple prepared by many in their homes.

Both preserved lemons and pomegranate molasses are used to impart sour flavor to dishes. Preserved lemons tend to be consistent across brands, but pomegranate molasses is a different story. Due to the laborious nature of preparing it, many brands will thicken it with sugar and starch and include additives like citric acid. While the surest way to have the best kind is to peel and juice your own and then reduce it until thickened, the process can be tiresome. So simply make sure you buy a trusted brand, where only pomegranate juice is in the ingredients list.

Historically, dishes hailing from coastal towns where citrus was grown in abundance relied on lemons, whereas landlocked corridors, like the area extending from Aleppo to Damascus, relied on more local ingredients like pomegranate molasses. Both impart sour notes, but the flavors are distinct. Pomegranate verges on the sweet while lemons are more astringent, albeit in a pleasant way. Whether it's a dish based on ancient texts (Flounder with Olives, Pistachios, and Lemon, page 94), a trusted classic elevated with unique flavors (Pomegranate Molasses and Aleppo Pepper Roast Chicken, page 81), or a simple vegetable made sublime with a few sharp ingredients (Okra in Lemon-Cilantro Sauce, page 88), a sour note is the common thread running throughout this chapter.

Olive, Cheese, and Pomegranate Molasses Salad

Having grown up where the world's oldest olive trees are said to exist, it is no surprise that olives were a staple on my family table, as they are on almost every Palestinian and Arab table. My family harvested our groves throughout the season, from the early plump green olives to the later sweet black ones. At its simplest, we had green olives marinated in red chilies. To be a bit more elaborate, we added garlic and cubes of lemon, and on rare occasions, small cubes of white cheese. The olives were so flavorful that you really didn't need to add much to them. The olives you buy in supermarkets today, however, have largely been washed of their original flavor so they require a bit more coaxing to get them to truly shine. This dish really transforms the olives and is perfect as part of a mezze spread, as a topping for hummus or labaneh, or even mixed in with pasta.

Serves 4 as part of a spread

- 1 large clove garlic, crushed in a garlic press
- 1 tablespoon pomegranate molasses
- 1 tablespoon extra-virgin olive oil
- ½ teaspoon Aleppo pepper or paprika
- ½ teaspoon tomato paste (purée)
- ½ teaspoon cumin seeds, lightly toasted, or ¼ teaspoon ground cumin
- 1 cup (5¼ oz/150 g) pitted green olives (preferably Castelvetrano or Frescatrano)
- 1 scallion (spring onion), thinly sliced
- 4 tablespoons finely diced yellow or orange bell pepper (about ¼ large pepper)
- ½ cup (2½ oz/70 g) diced halloumi, Akkawi, or Nabulsi cheese
- 3 tablespoons coarsely chopped lightly toasted walnuts
- 2 sprigs fresh za'atar, oregano, or marjoram, leaves picked and coarsely chopped

In a medium bowl combine the garlic, pomegranate molasses, olive oil, Aleppo pepper, tomato paste (purée), and cumin and stir to combine.

Add in all the remaining ingredients except the fresh za'atar and toss to evenly coat. Transfer the salad to a serving bowl, scatter the fresh za'atar leaves and serve.

The salad will keep in the refrigerator for a couple of days. If you want it to keep longer, up to 1 week, only add the olives to the marinade, then take out the portion you want to serve and mix it with a portion of the cheese, bell pepper, and scallion right before serving.

Note: I like to keep the olives whole and even use ones with the pit because they look nicer when served. If you are going to toss with pasta or use as a topping, however, you can slice the olives thinly to spread the marinade more evenly and make eating easier.

Pomegranate Molasses and Aleppo Pepper Roast Chicken with Spicy Sahawiq Sauce

One of my favorite dishes as a child was the chicken my mother roasted in the oven. It had extremely crispy skin with such deep layers of flavors that I often gave up my chicken in exchange for the skin on someone else's piece. Today, my oldest daughter does the same, fighting us all for the crispy bits. Luckily, this dish has crispy and flavorful bits to spare. The choice of spices is not traditional, but it's the version my mother has always made at home. Most of the chicken dishes found in the earliest known Arabic cookbooks were cooked in plenty of fat—usually untoasted sesame oil—over open flame. They leaned toward the sweet and were usually fragrant with the use of floral waters, saffron, and myrrh. This version strays quite a bit from those flavors with a spicy, pungent profile. For even more kick, I serve it with the Yemenite hot sauce *sahawiq*, but I mix it with labaneh because at home we often ate this sauce with bread and labaneh next to grilled meats, so this harks back to that delicious combo.

Serves 4

For the chicken:

- 1 tablespoon untoasted sesame oil or olive oil
- 1 tablespoon garlic granules
- 1 tablespoon pomegranate molasses
- 1 tablespoon soy sauce
- 1 teaspoon tomato paste (purée)
- 1 tablespoon salt
- 2 teaspoons Aleppo pepper
- 1 teaspoon sumac
- 1 teaspoon Nine-Spice Mix (page 27), baharat, or Lebanese 7-spice blend
- 1 teaspoon crushed dried za'atar leaves, or ½ teaspoon each dried oregano and thyme
- ½ teaspoon ground coriander
- ¼ teaspoon ground cumin
- 1 whole chicken (4–4½ lb/1.5–2 kg), spatchcocked, cut in half, or jointed

For the sauce:

- 1½ cups (1½ oz/45 g) sprigs fresh cilantro (coriander)
- ½ cup (½ oz/15 g) sprigs parsley
- 2 or 3 jalapeño peppers, seeded
- 2 cloves garlic, peeled
- 2 tablespoons labaneh, preferably homemade (page 40)
- ¼ cup (2 fl oz/60 ml) extra-virgin olive oil
- 3 tablespoons fresh lemon juice
- 1 tablespoon pomegranate molasses
- 1 teaspoon salt
- ½ teaspoon ground cumin

Prepare the chicken:

In a bowl large enough to hold the chicken in whatever form it's in, combine the oil, garlic granules, pomegranate molasses, soy sauce, tomato paste (purée), salt, Aleppo pepper, and all the spices and herbs and mix well. Add the chicken and turn to coat with the marinade on both sides and under the skin as well. Refrigerate, uncovered, for at least 2 hours but preferably overnight.

Preheat the oven to 425°F (220°C/Gas Mark 7), convection if available. Line a sheet pan with parchment paper.

Arrange the chicken skin-side up on the prepared pan. Transfer to the oven with the legs toward the back of the oven. Roast until the skin is crispy and dark golden brown and an instant-read thermometer registers 165°F (74°C) in the thickest part, 1 hour to 1 hour 10 minutes. If you prefer the skin much crispier and don't mind slightly drier meat, roast for an additional 10–20 minutes. The exact timing will depend on the weight and variety of chicken, and how you have cut it. Jointed pieces will take less time than spatchcocked, so check throughout for doneness and desired crispiness. Remove from the oven and let sit for 10 minutes before serving.

Meanwhile, prepare the sauce:

In a mini food processor or blender, combine the cilantro (coriander), parsley, jalapeños, garlic, labaneh, olive oil, lemon juice, pomegranate molasses, salt, and cumin and blend until finely chopped and combined. Transfer to a small serving bowl.

Carve the chicken and serve, passing the sauce around for each person to drizzle over their portion.

Shiitake Mushroom Fatteh with Walnuts, Dill, and Pomegranate Molasses

Fatteh, derived from an old Arabic verb meaning "to break bread and steep in liquid," is a common dish across the Middle East. The base is bread, but the toppings vary from eggplants (aubergines) and chickpeas, to rice and a variety of meats. The sauces are just as varied with some yogurt-based, others tahini-based, and others broth- or lemon-based. Moona, a restaurant in Boston serving up creative Middle Eastern dishes based on pantry ingredients (*moona* means "pantry" in Arabic), has a version made with mushrooms. The first time I tried the dish, I was skeptical. "Mushrooms?!" I thought. But I was blown away by the flavors and textures. Mushrooms have an earthy, meaty taste that is superbly complemented by the sweet tartness of pomegranate molasses, the crunchiness of the toasted bread and nuts, and the brightness of the yogurt-tahini dressing. Just another example of how pushing boundaries can lead to delicious surprises.

Serves 4

2 large or 4 small thin pita breads in ¾-inch/2 cm squares (6 oz/165 g or 2½ generous cups)

For the yogurt sauce:
1⅓ cups (10½ oz/300 g) yogurt
3 tablespoons tahini
2–3 tablespoons fresh lemon juice
1 small clove garlic, crushed in a garlic press
½ teaspoon salt

For the mushrooms:
¼ cup (2 fl oz/60 ml) olive oil
Generous 2 tablespoons (35 g) unsalted butter
1 large shallot, finely diced
4 cloves garlic, crushed
2 teaspoons salt
10½ oz (300 g) shiitake mushrooms, stemmed, caps chopped into bite-size pieces
1½ lb (700 g) mushrooms (a combination of portobello, cremini/chestnut, or any variety), chopped into bite-size pieces
1½ tablespoons pure pomegranate molasses
2 teaspoons honey (see Note)
1 can (14 oz/400 g) chickpeas, drained and rinsed

For assembly:
½ cup (50 g) coarsely chopped toasted walnut pieces
Small bunch of dill fronds
Crushed chili flakes or pomegranate seeds (optional)

Preheat the oven to 350°F (180°C/Gas Mark 4). Arrange the pita bread pieces on a baking sheet. Bake, moving the bread around from time to time, until the squares are completely dry and crisp and starting to darken in color, 20–30 minutes. Remove and set aside. (This step can be done a couple of days in advance and the bread stored in an airtight container or a zipseal plastic food bag.)

Make the yogurt sauce:
In a bowl, stir together the yogurt, tahini, lemon juice, garlic, and salt. Set aside.

Prepare the mushrooms:
In a large frying pan, heat the olive oil and butter over medium-high heat. Add the shallot and fry, stirring, until translucent and starting to brown, 3–5 minutes. Add the garlic and 1 teaspoon of the salt and cook until fragrant, about 1 minute. Add the shiitake mushrooms and cook for 1 minute. Add the remaining mushrooms and remaining 1 teaspoon salt and cook until tender but retaining some bite, about 5 minutes. If the mushrooms release some liquid that is perfectly fine, you do not need to cook until it evaporates, only until the mushrooms are tender. Pour in the pomegranate molasses and honey, give one final good stir, then add the chickpeas and cook for 1 minute to heat through. Remove from the heat.

Assemble the dish:
This dish can be served on one large platter or on individual plates. Place the bread at the bottom of the serving platter/plates. Top with the mushroom mixture. Pour the yogurt sauce on top and sprinkle with the toasted walnuts and dill. If desired, sprinkle with chili flakes or pomegranate seeds. Serve immediately to retain the crunchiness of the bread.

Note: Ideally, this is made with pure pomegranate molasses that does not have any added sugar. But if you are making this with a brand that happens to have sugar, leave out the honey.

Shiitake Mushroom Fatteh with Walnuts, Dill, and Pomegranate Molasses

Fish Nayeh with Preserved Lemon, Bulgur, and Herbs

Every few weeks on a Friday morning, my family would make its way to the coastal town of Yaffa, where a fisherman named Abdo would be waiting near the beach with the freshest catch of the day. My mother would decide what dish to make with the fish and my father would request just one thing: an appetizer of raw fish. Most often it was a mild mackerel that my mother dressed simply in salt, lemon, and olive oil. As I traveled more, I saw the myriad ways in which different cultures consumed raw and cured fish, from sashimi and ceviche to crudo and poke. I also learned that *sìkbaj*, the vinegar-marinated dishes of the ancient Persian court, were the precursors to the acid-marinated raw fish dishes we enjoy today. Harking back to that history, the flavoring of the fish here is an ode to the fragrances and ingredients of the Middle East.

Serves 2-4 as part of a spread

For the bulgur:

- ½ cup fine-grain (#1) or medium-grain (#2) bulgur (see Note)
- ½ cup (4 fl oz/120 ml) hot water
- 2 tablespoons fresh lemon juice
- 2 tablespoons extra-virgin olive oil
- Scant ½ teaspoon salt
- ¼ teaspoon ground cumin
- ¼ teaspoon freshly ground black pepper

For the fish:

- 9 oz (250 g) freshly caught or very fresh skinless white fish fillets, such as snapper, bream, sea bass, or halibut (local and fresh is more important than variety)
- 1 tablespoon finely chopped preserved lemon rind
- ¼ teaspoon salt
- 1 tablespoon fresh lemon juice
- 1 tablespoon olive oil

For assembly:

- 2 tablespoons finely chopped fresh parsley, plus a few extra leaves for garnish
- 1 sprig fresh mint, leaves picked, finely chopped, or ½ teaspoon ground dried mint
- 1 scallion (spring onion), thinly sliced
- 1 very small tomato, seeded and finely diced
- 1 fresh red or green chili, very finely diced
- Extra-virgin olive oil, for drizzling
- 2 tablespoons pine nuts, toasted or fried, for garnish

Prepare the bulgur:
In a small bowl, soak the bulgur in the hot water until the water has been fully absorbed. Add the lemon juice, olive oil, salt, cumin, and pepper and refrigerate until completely cooled.

Prepare the fish:
Wash the fish and pat dry, then cut into ½-inch (1.5 cm) cubes. In a bowl, combine the fish, preserved lemon, salt, lemon juice, and olive oil and toss to combine. Refrigerate to marinate while you prep the rest of the ingredients.

To assemble:
Stir the parsley, mint, and scallion (spring onion) into the cooled bulgur and transfer to a serving platter.

Remove the fish from the refrigerator, add the diced tomato and chili and toss to combine. Spread the fish over the bulgur. Drizzle with olive oil and garnish with the toasted pine nuts. Serve immediately.

Note: Supermarket bulgur might be different from what you purchase in a Middle Eastern grocery store (Middle Eastern grocery stores will sell bulgur labeled from #1 to #3 coarseness and preparation will vary accordingly). So if you do not have #1 or #2 bulgur on hand, prepare the bulgur you have according to package directions. You want it soft but with a bite (think al dente pasta) and completely cool.

Fish Nayeh with Preserved Lemon, Bulgur, and Herbs

Fava Beans in Olive Oil with Garlic, Cilantro, and Lime

This dish is common across the Levant where fresh fava (broad) beans, both skin and seeds, are chopped and sautéed in a pan with a generous amount of olive oil until they are completely cooked and tender, then flavored with garlic and cilantro (coriander). I was never particularly fond of the dish, with the overcooked flavor of the fava beans a little too overpowering for me. But I have since tried it a few different ways and when I make it with only the beans and not the skins and keep them bright green and al dente, I find the dish exquisitely refreshing and flavorful. It's delicious in season, but most often I find myself making it with frozen fava beans or even baby lima beans (butter beans). It's wonderful as a topping for Labaneh (page 40), tossed in with pasta, as a side to roast meats, or if you're like me, simply mopped up with bread.

Serves 4 as part of a spread

- 3 tablespoons olive oil
- 2 large cloves garlic, finely chopped
- ½ teaspoon salt
- 2 cups (9 oz/250 g) fresh or frozen fava (broad) beans or lima beans (butter beans) (see Note)
- ½ cup (½ oz/15 g) packed cilantro (coriander) leaves, finely chopped
- 1 tablespoon fresh lime or lemon juice

In a frying pan, heat the olive oil over medium heat. Add the garlic and salt and cook until fragrant and turning golden around the edges, about 30 seconds.

Add the fava (broad) beans, tossing to combine, then cover and cook until just cooked through but still bright green, 3–5 minutes.

Add the cilantro (coriander) and lime juice, give one final toss to coat everything evenly, and remove from the heat. Serve warm or at room temperature.

Note: the frozen variety will already be blanched, and you can use directly from frozen. If you are using fresh fava beans, you will either need to blanch them for a couple minutes (you can then peel them if you want the color to be bright green) or you can use them without blanching, but you will need to cook them a bit longer and add a few splashes of water.

Fava Beans in Olive Oil with Garlic, Cilantro, and Lime

Okra in Lemon-Cilantro Sauce

When people ask me about the differences between Palestinian, Lebanese, Syrian, or any other Arab cuisine, I often point to the fact that our food is similar, but that specific techniques and dishes might differ from one area to the next. An example of this is the Lebanese way of finishing off tomato-based stews with fried garlic and cilantro (coriander) versus Palestinians, who rarely use cilantro and rely on onions sautéed at the beginning or garlic tempered at the end. The inspiration for this dish came from that fact. I decided to forgo the tomato sauce, in which okra is traditionally cooked, and highlight the garlic and cilantro tempering flavors instead. It turned out to be delicious and substantially lighter than the traditional version. This okra dish works perfectly as part of a mezze, as a side to meats, or even as a simple vegetarian meal served with bread.

Serves 4

1½ lb (700 g) fresh okra
6 tablespoons olive oil
1 teaspoon salt
5 cloves garlic, finely chopped
1 large red or green chili (Anaheim or jalapeño), finely chopped
1 very small tomato, seeded and finely diced (optional)
½ cup (½ oz/15 g) finely chopped fresh cilantro (coriander) leaves
1 teaspoon crushed chili flakes or Aleppo pepper
¼ cup (2 fl oz/60 ml) fresh lemon juice (about 2 lemons)

Preheat the oven to 450°F (230°C/Gas Mark 8).

Wash the okra, pat dry, and trim away the stem ends.

In a bowl, toss the okra with 2 tablespoons of the olive oil and ½ teaspoon of the salt. Arrange on a sheet pan in a single layer. Roast in the oven, tossing periodically, until the okra starts to brown and blister in parts and develops a nice seared aroma, 15–20 minutes. The time may differ slightly if your okra is quite large or exceptionally small, so keep an eye on it and adjust accordingly. Remove from the oven and set aside.

In a large frying pan, heat the remaining 4 tablespoons olive oil over medium heat. Add the garlic, chili, and remaining ½ teaspoon salt. Cook until fragrant but not browned, 2–4 minutes. Add the tomato (if using), cilantro (coriander), and chili flakes and cook for another minute.

Tip in the roasted okra, tossing to evenly combine, then pour in the lemon juice along with 2 tablespoons water. Give one final stir, then remove from the heat and serve.

Okra in Lemon-Cilantro Sauce

Spiced Kebabs with Preserved Lemon Dill Yogurt

You would be hard-pressed to find a cuisine today that does not involve some version of a kafta or meatball, but the very first reference to finely minced well-seasoned balls of lamb meat dates back to a recipe in a tenth-century Arabic cookbook in which they were cooked and glazed in saffron and egg yolk. Although much has changed in terms of food since then, the ubiquitous kafta remains a rustic food prepared across cultures in similar ways. In Arab cuisine it is, at its most basic, ground meat mixed with onion and spices. Other additions like herbs and nuts also abound, but it is the shaping and cooking styles that are countless. From balls and discs to sausage shapes or flattened out in a pan, from fried or baked with tahini to simmered in tomato sauce or grilled over coals, where we call it "kebab." The kebabs in this recipe are roasted in a home oven, but the texture is wonderfully browned and crisp on the outside but juicy and fluffy within. The flavor in this recipe takes inspiration from springtime in the Middle East when dill and cilantro (coriander) are plentiful, creating a unique combo that is delicious with a side of rice or roast potatoes or, if you're like me, wrapped up in my Unleavened Flatbread (page 30). I also often serve it with Dill, Mint, and Cranberry Almond Salad (page 104) to make the best use of all the dill I greedily buy when it is in peak season.

Makes about 15 kebabs

For the yogurt:

- ¾ cup (8 oz/225 g) Greek yogurt
- ¼ rind of a large preserved lemon (or 1 full rind of a miniature lemon)
- Small handful of fresh dill
- Salt

For the kebabs:

- 1½ lb (700 g) ground (minced) beef, lamb, veal, or a combination
- 2 oz (60 g) pita bread or white bread with crusts removed
- 1 small onion
- 1 small clove garlic, peeled (optional)
- Small handful (10 g) of fresh cilantro (coriander)
- Small handful (10 g) of dill
- 1½ teaspoons salt
- 1½ teaspoons Nine-Spice Mix (page 27), baharat, or Lebanese 7-spice blend
- 1 teaspoon Aleppo pepper (optional)
- 1 tablespoon olive oil

For serving:

- Orzo Rice (page 33) or Unleavened Flatbread (page 30)

Prepare the yogurt:

In a mini food processor, combine the yogurt, lemon rind, and dill and pulse until smooth and evenly combined. Taste for salt, this will depend on how salty the preserved lemons you used are, and add a pinch more if necessary. (This can be done up to a day in advance. Refrigerate until ready to use.)

Make the kebabs:

Preheat the broiler (grill) to high, set a rack above the middle of the oven, and lightly grease a sheet or roasting pan.

Place the meat in a large bowl and set aside.

In a food processor, combine the bread, onion, garlic (if using), cilantro (coriander), dill, salt, spice mix, Aleppo pepper (if using), and the olive oil and pulse to a fine paste.

Add the mixture to the meat in the bowl and mix with your hands until fully incorporated. Shape the meat into about 15 fat sausages and arrange them on the sheet pan. Flatten slightly with your hand, then use the side of your finger to make three diagonal indentations atop each sausage.

Transfer to the oven and broil until the tops are browned and you see some oil released and bubbling around the edges, 10–15 minutes.

To serve:

Remove from the oven and allow to sit for 10 minutes before serving. Serve with rice or flatbread and the preserved lemon yogurt on the side.

Spiced Kebabs with Preserved Lemon Dill Yogurt, Orzo Rice

Shrimp with Artichoke, Turmeric, and Preserved Lemon

Shrimp (prawns), *rubyan* in Arabic, feature quite a bit in medieval Arabic cookbooks: as dried pastes to add flavor, as relishes and condiments, as pickles, as stuffing for pastries, or as stand-alone meals cooked in myriad ways. Here I pair them with artichokes, which always remind me of my father sitting in our garden with a small knife, snipping away at a beautiful green flower until nothing was left but a yellow-tinged round heart. We would stuff, fry, or stew artichokes because they are a wonderful canvas for other flavors with a delicate texture uniquely their own. Native to the Mediterranean and first cultivated for food by the Arabs, the name of this thistle is actually derived from the Arabic language. You don't need to spend time preparing your own, though, because they are found abundantly in the frozen and jarred aisles nowadays making this fragrant dish a breeze to prepare. This meal is perfect on its own or paired with your favorite starch, from rice and couscous to mashed potatoes and pasta.

Serves 4

- 2 tablespoons olive oil, plus more as needed
- 1 lb (454 g) peeled and deveined shrimp (prawns)
- 1½ teaspoons salt
- 1 teaspoon ground turmeric
- ¼ teaspoon freshly ground black pepper
- 2 cups (7 oz/200 g) artichoke hearts (see Note)
- 3 large cloves garlic, finely minced
- ½ lemon, very thinly sliced
- ½ cup (4 fl oz/120 ml) half-and-half (single cream)
- 1 tablespoon finely chopped preserved lemon rind
- 1 sprig fresh za'atar, thyme, or oregano, leaves picked

In a large frying pan, heat the olive oil over medium heat. Add the shrimp (prawns), salt, turmeric, and pepper and cook just until the shrimp are cooked through, 3–5 minutes depending on size. Transfer to a plate and set aside.

To the same pan, add the artichokes and fry, tossing periodically, until browned in a few places, 3–5 minutes. Transfer to the same plate as the shrimp.

If the pan appears dry, add another tablespoon of olive oil, then add the garlic and lemon slices and cook just until fragrant, about 1 minute.

Return the shrimp and artichokes and any accumulated juices to the pan. Add the half-and-half (single cream), give them a quick toss to combine, and cook just until the cream bubbles up, only 1–2 minutes more.

Remove from the heat, mix in the preserved lemon, sprinkle with the za'atar leaves, and serve immediately.

Note: You can use fresh, frozen, jarred/canned artichoke hearts for this recipe. If you are using frozen hearts, thaw and set on a paper towel to absorb any liquid; otherwise, it will thin out the sauce. If using canned or jarred, look for a brand with as few added ingredients as possible, and drain very well and pat dry with paper towels.

Shrimp with Artichoke, Turmeric, and Preserved Lemon

Flounder with Olives, Pistachios, and Lemon

It is only in serving fish with condiments that it becomes delicious, or so the first-known Arabic cookbook *Kitab al-Tabikh* claims. The book includes countless suggestions on how to prepare fish and what condiments to serve it with. Many of the ingredients mentioned are hard to source, however, and the cooking process is complicated for today's cook. But one description drew my eye and I decided to tinker with it. It was not even a recipe, but a few lines included in the book from a poem by Ibn al-Mahdi, an Abassid prince and poet, in which he describes a delicious fish dish he ate. So this recipe draws inspiration from those lines and attempts to re-create a royal dish in a way fit for today's cooking and consumption. Below I have included an additional sauce option also based on descriptions from *Kitab al-Tabikh*.

p.96

Serves 4

For the sauce:
½ cup (½ oz/15 g) tightly packed fresh parsley leaves, finely chopped
20 pitted green olives (I usually use Castelvetrano or Manzanilla), finely chopped
½ cup (2 oz/55 g) pistachios, finely chopped or coarsely ground
1 clove garlic, crushed in a garlic press or grated on a Microplane
2 tablespoons extra-virgin olive oil
Grated zest of 1 unwaxed or organic lemon
2 tablespoons fresh lemon juice

For the fish:
Vegetable oil, for frying
4 thin skinless white fish fillets (see Note), 4–5 oz (120–150 g) each
Salt and freshly ground black pepper
Flour, for dredging
2 tablespoons (1 oz/30 g) unsalted butter, chopped into 8 small cubes

Pomegranate-Walnut Sauce:
1 cup (3½ oz/100 g) walnuts, toasted
½ cup (150 g) pomegranate jam (or any other sour berry jam like blueberry, currant, or sour cherry)
1 tablespoon pomegranate molasses
1 tablespoon fresh lime juice
1½ teaspoons apple cider vinegar
¾ teaspoon salt
½ teaspoon ground coriander
¼ teaspoon ground black pepper

Make the sauce:
In a bowl, combine the parsley, olives, pistachios, garlic, olive oil, lemon zest, and lemon juice and mix to combine. Set aside, covered, until ready to use.

Cook the fish:
In a large nonstick frying pan, add enough oil to coat the bottom of the pan and heat over medium heat.

Pat the fish dry with paper towels and sprinkle with salt and pepper on both sides. Dredge in flour, then pat between your hands to shake off any excess flour. When the oil is shimmering, add the fillets in a single flat layer (do this step in batches if your pan is small), and cook until golden and crispy around the edges, 2–3 minutes. Flip the fish and top each fillet with 2 cubes of butter. Cook until crisped and browned, another 2–3 minutes. If your fillets are thinner or thicker, you may need to adjust the time, so keep an eye on them and cook until browned to your liking.

Remove and transfer to serving plates. Top each fillet with the sauce and serve immediately.

Note: I most often use flounder for this recipe, because the mild taste is a good canvas for the bold flavor of both this sauce and the pomegranate-walnut variation, but any white fish could work including tilapia, bream, branzino, sea bass, etc. You could also use a skin-on fillet of fish, but if you do, skip the flour dredging and cook it as directed in Pan-Fried Branzino with Tahini-Onion Sauce (page 218).

—

Variation: Pomegranate-Walnut Sauce
Sweet *sibagh*, or sauces, were very common with fish in medieval times. Another delicious sauce with this fish is a pomegranate-walnut one. In a small saucepan, combine the walnuts, jam, pomegranate molasses, lime juice, vinegar, salt, coriander, pepper, and 3 tablespoons of water and bring to a simmer over low heat, stirring occasionally until the sauce has thinned out. If the sauce is still too thick, (this will depend on the kind of jam you have used), add 1 tablespoon of water at a time until you reach your desired consistency.

Seared Scallops with Garlic, Red Chili, and Preserved Lemon

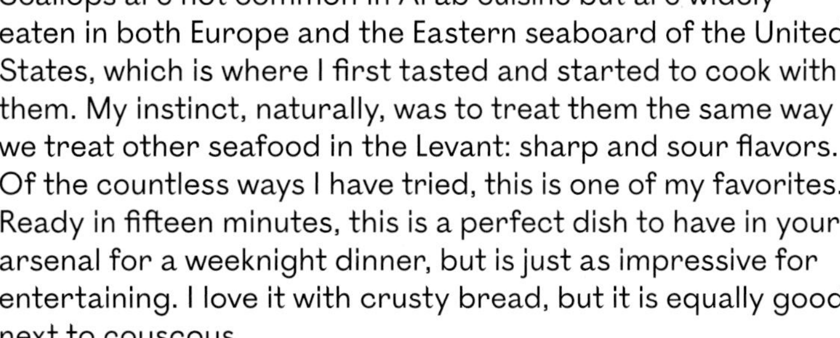

Scallops are not common in Arab cuisine but are widely eaten in both Europe and the Eastern seaboard of the United States, which is where I first tasted and started to cook with them. My instinct, naturally, was to treat them the same way we treat other seafood in the Levant: sharp and sour flavors. Of the countless ways I have tried, this is one of my favorites. Ready in fifteen minutes, this is a perfect dish to have in your arsenal for a weeknight dinner, but is just as impressive for entertaining. I love it with crusty bread, but it is equally good next to couscous.

p.97

Serves 2–4

I lb (450 g) dry-packed sea scallops, side muscle removed
Salt
Olive oil
6 large cloves garlic, finely chopped
3–4 fresh red chilies, seeded and finely chopped
¼ cup (2 fl oz/60 ml) fresh lemon juice
½ cup (1 oz/25 g) packed fresh parsley leaves, finely chopped
2 teaspoons finely chopped preserved lemon rind
Crusty bread or couscous, for serving

Pat the scallops dry and season with a good pinch of salt on each side. In a frying pan large enough to fit the scallops without overcrowding, pour enough olive oil to very generously coat the bottom, and place over medium heat. When shimmering, place the scallops into the pan and cook, undisturbed, for 1–2 minutes.

Add the garlic and chilies around the scallops, sprinkle with ½ teaspoon salt, and continue to cook until the garlic is fragrant but not browned, about 3 minutes. Flip the scallops over and cook for another 1–2 minutes.

Add the lemon juice, parsley, and preserved lemon and cook for 30 seconds more just to warm everything. Serve immediately with bread or couscous.

Flounder with Olives, Pistachios, and Lemon

Seared Scallops with Garlic, Red Chili, and Preserved Lemon

Seafood Stew with Preserved Lemon, Apricots, and Olives

The Moroccan chicken, olive, and preserved lemon tagine is known the world over. And for good reason—it's an absolutely delicious dish. Over the years, I have made it countless times and played around with it quite a bit before settling on a version I adore. But it struck me as odd, given how Arabs generally eat their fish plain with copious amounts of freshly squeezed lemon, that preserved lemon and fish were not as celebrated a duo. So after numerous experiments, this stew emerged an undisputed winner. Taking inspiration from different tagines, fish stews, and cooking techniques, this dish is unique and deeply layered with flavor. Savory, sweet, sour, and pungent, it keeps you coming back for more. Although the combination below is my preferred one, feel free to experiment with other kinds of seafood like clams, squid, or your favorite kind of fish fillets. Crusty bread and couscous both make wonderful accompaniments.

Serves 4–6

2–3 cloves garlic, peeled
2-inch (5 cm) knob fresh ginger
1 medium shallot, peeled
Handful loosely packed cilantro (coriander) leaves and tender stems, plus more for garnish
1 teaspoon salt
½ teaspoon ras el hanout
Generous pinch of saffron threads
2 tablespoons olive oil
12–14 dried apricots, roughly chopped
1–2 tablespoons finely chopped preserved lemon rind
1½ lb (700 g) firm white fish fillets (such as halibut or monkfish), cut into 2–3-inch (5–7.5 cm) pieces
24 mussels, scrubbed and debearded
12 jumbo shrimp (prawns), tail-on
Two 6-inch squids, sliced into rings, heads kept whole if using
15 green olives of choice
Juice of 1 lemon
Crusty bread or couscous, for serving

In a food processor, combine the garlic, ginger, shallot, cilantro (coriander), ½ teaspoon of the salt, the ras el hanout, and saffron and process until finely chopped.

In a wide braiser (sauteuse), heat the olive oil over medium heat until shimmering. Add the garlic mixture and cook, stirring regularly, until fragrant and starting to brown, 5–7 minutes. Gradually pour in 2½ cups (20 fl oz/550 ml) water to deglaze the pan, scraping the browned bits at the bottom as you go. Bring to a boil, add the remaining ½ teaspoon salt, then reduce the heat and simmer for 5–7 minutes.

Add the dried apricots and preserved lemon to the simmering broth and continue to cook for another 5–7 minutes to allow the flavors to meld.

Spread the fish fillets in a single layer in the broth, cover, and cook for 2 minutes. Add the mussels, shrimp (prawns), squids, and olives and simmer, covered, until they are just cooked through and the mussels open wide, about 5 minutes. Discard any mussels that do not open.

Remove from the heat, add the lemon juice, and garnish with cilantro leaves. Serve with crusty bread or couscous.

Seafood Stew with Preserved Lemon, Apricots, and Olives

Roots + Shoots + Leaves

On the steps leading down from Damascus Gate into the Old City of Jerusalem sat a woman, her face leathered by the life of the soil. She called out to me. "Habeebti," she said, "I picked them this morning, I'll give you a good price." I peered into her large, blue plastic bags—wild dandelion and chard. This woman had not only woken up before dawn to forage this harvest, she had crossed miles and military checkpoints to sell it, at a somewhat fair price, even in the face of the unfairness of her life. I handed her the money. She swept the edge of a white headscarf over her shoulder and tucked the notes into her chest. "Allah yirda aleiki," she said, asking God to bless me. But I was already blessed—I had grown up enjoying this bounty throughout my life.

If you travel across the Middle East, you will see wide-ranging landscapes, from vast, empty deserts and lush pastures to long coastlines and rocky mountains. The guaranteed commonality is that whatever the land produces, our people have found a way to consume it. Grapevines are valued for their leaves as much as their fruits and the olive groves are foraged for the dandelion weeds before the olives. Wild plants like borage, mallow, sage, and za'atar are picked from the mountains in season, and those who have the access and time to pick them will bring them to markets to sell.

Arabs across the region have found countless ways to consume this abundance, from stuffing and rolling to fermenting and sautéing. In this chapter, roots, shoots, and leaves take center stage showing how they can stand on their own in cases like salads (see Dandelion Salad with Scallions and Pomegranates, page 107) and sautés (see Broccoli Rabe with Caramelized Onions, page 110) or vastly complement the flavors of other ingredients like meat (see Grape Leaf Braised Short Ribs, page 116) or provide a wonderful canvas for other flavors (see Potato Kafta Pie, page 118).

The history of roots and leaves in the Middle East is fascinating. Many of our most popular root vegetables—think carrots and beets—are actually native to the region and its immediate surroundings. Beets are mentioned as growing in the Hanging Gardens of Babylon, while carrots, originally grown for their seeds and leaves before evolving into the sweet crunchy food we enjoy today, are native to present-day Iran. Green leaves, for lack of a better term, are also stars in the cuisine. While herbs and greens in the West are often relegated to the realm of flavoring or possibly salads and minor components of stews, in the Arab kitchen they are the stars. Tabbouleh is essentially a giant bowl of parsley. *Khubeizeh* (see Swiss Chard Khubeizeh, page 113) is traditionally a giant amount of mallow (I use chard now that I've moved abroad) dotted with pearly orbs of dough and flavored with browned onion.

While many of these ingredients might seem too plain or too bitter to stand on their own, I think the secret to making them delicious is in the methods of preparation, specifically, in the contrast of flavors and textures that allows each recipe to surpass its individual elements and become a final dish that truly sings. Tart grape leaves break through the richness of beef ribs; sweet carrots contrast with sharp garlic, chilies, and lemon; and pomegranates brighten up bitter dandelion.

In the spirit of cooking from root to leaf, take these recipes as a blueprint for how you can enhance whatever produce you have access to. Bought some beets with the leaves? Use them in place of the chard for your stew. There are dandelions at your farmers' market but no broccoli rabe (rapini)? Cook them with the caramelized onions instead. Sweet potatoes in peak season? Swap them in for the potatoes in the kafta pie and have a mix of sweet and savory. It's more about the method and flavor profile than the exact ingredient you choose to cook with. So let your imagination run as wild as the roots and leaves in this chapter.

Arugula Mint Salad with Tomato and Labaneh Drops

When I was growing up, arugula (rocket) grew in our garden and we ate it raw next to labaneh in the morning or put it on the staple plate of scallions, lemons, and green chilies we enjoyed at lunch. In more recent years, we have started to use it in salads like this recipe here. The tradition of salads was popularized during the Roman Empire when various raw greens were doused with salt and olive oil. Even the word "salad" is derived from *sal*, the Latin word for salt. Arugula, which has surged in popularity in the Western world in recent years, is a plant native to the Mediterranean that has been enjoyed in our diets since ancient times. Here I combine it with mint, a sweet but pungent contrast to arugula's peppery character, and add labaneh and tomatoes for a salad that is a wonderful combination of flavors and textures.

Serves 4–6

¾ cup (3 oz/85 g) labaneh, preferably homemade (page 40)
½ teaspoon salt
Olive oil, for greasing
5 oz (140 g) arugula (rocket) or mixed greens including arugula, if you find arugula alone too strong
10–12 sprigs fresh mint, leaves picked and roughly torn
3 tablespoons fresh lemon juice
2 tablespoons extra-virgin olive oil, plus more for drizzling
1 pint (10 oz/275 g) cherry or grape tomatoes, halved or quartered lengthwise
Flaked sea salt, for sprinkling (I use Maldon)
1 tablespoon salted roasted sunflower seeds (optional)

To prepare the labaneh balls, line a sieve with paper towels. Scoop the labaneh into the sieve and allow to sit for about 1 hour at room temperature, until some of the liquid has drained and it is drier and easier to roll. Stir in the salt. The labaneh should be salty and tangy, reminiscent of feta, so taste at this point and add more salt to your liking.

Line a flat plate with parchment or plastic wrap (clingfilm) and lightly oil with olive oil. With lightly oiled hands, roll the labaneh into balls the size of marbles and set on the plate. Cover with plastic wrap and refrigerate until ready to use.

To assemble the salad, combine the arugula (rocket) and mint in a large salad bowl. Add the lemon juice and extra-virgin olive oil and gently toss (preferably with your hands). Top with the sliced tomatoes and sprinkle with the sea salt flakes (do this to taste because the labaneh is salty and the sunflower seeds are as well). Distribute the labaneh balls on top and sprinkle with the sunflower seeds (if using). Drizzle some olive oil on top and serve.

Note: If you do not have labaneh, you can substitute with a good-quality sheep or goat feta cut into small cubes.

Arugula Mint Salad with Tomato and Labaneh Drops

Dill, Mint, and Cranberry Almond Salad

One of the things people love most about Arab restaurants is the countless small plates that come out to the table—leaving one utterly full and satisfied—all before the main course has even been served. My cousin's husband is the chef of one such restaurant overlooking the Mediterranean Sea in Akka. While he keeps up the tradition of serving numerous salads and appetizers before mains—of mostly fresh-caught fish from the sea the restaurant overlooks—he experiments quite a bit with the salads he serves. The family members are the taste testers for these endeavors, so at every gathering there is anticipation about what new salad he will bring our way. This is a salad he made for us one summer when dill was in season in the Galilee. Although it is the dill seed that is most often used in Arab cooking, the dill weed is the star of this dish and deservedly so.

Serves 4–6

3 large bunches of dill (about 7 oz/200 g), tough stems discarded, finely chopped
6 sprigs fresh mint, leaves picked and finely chopped
1 Granny Smith apple, finely diced
½ cup (2 oz/60 g) dried cranberries
3 tablespoons fresh lemon juice
3 tablespoons extra-virgin olive oil
½ teaspoon sugar
¾ teaspoon salt
½ cup (45 g) sliced (flaked) almonds, toasted

In a large bowl, combine the dill, mint, apple, and cranberries.

In small bowl, whisk together the lemon juice, olive oil, sugar, and salt until fully combined.

Pour the dressing over the salad and gently toss everything to combine. Top with the flaked almonds. Serve immediately.

Note: This salad, unsurprisingly, has a very forward dill flavor, so if you are not that keen on eating dill in such large quantities, you can replace about two-thirds of the dill quantity with mixed greens (roughly 4 oz/120 g). You will still get the fresh burst of flavors but in a more nuanced way.

 Carrot Salad with Cumin and Chili (1) p. 106; Dill, Mint, and Cranberry Almond Salad (2)

Carrot Salad with Cumin and Chili

Originating in what is roughly present-day Iran and first cultivated for their leaves and seeds instead of their roots, carrots have been on quite a journey to obtain the form and sweetness we recognize today. There are several varieties cultivated in the Middle East, from orange to red and purple, and they are used in salads and stews, and, of course, as with everything in the Arab world, are also stuffed. Across the world, many cultures have taken to using carrots in salads, from Tunisian *houria* and *Koryo-Saram morkovcha* to Indian *kosambri* and Polish *surówka z marchewki*. In the Middle East, carrots, like most vegetables, are often simply dressed with lemon, olive oil, and salt. I've enhanced this simple raw salad with the flavors of garlic, chili, and cumin.

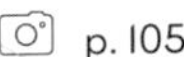
p. 105

Serves 4 as part of a spread

1 lb (455 g) carrots (orange or multicolored)
1 or 2 green chilies, like jalapeño or Hatch chili, finely chopped
1 clove garlic, minced
3 tablespoons fresh lemon juice
2 tablespoons extra-virgin olive oil
1 teaspoon salt
¼ teaspoon ground cumin

Peel the carrots and using a julienne peeler or sharp knife, cut them into matchsticks. Put in a bowl. Add the chilies, garlic, lemon juice, olive oil, salt, and cumin and toss until evenly combined and all the carrot slices are coated in the dressing. Taste and adjust the seasoning if necessary. Transfer to a serving platter and serve immediately.

Dandelion Salad with Scallions and Pomegranates

This salad is an acquired taste, so don't be surprised if the first time you try it you find the bitter flavor too strong. In the Levant, dandelion greens tend to be foraged from around olive trees after the first rain. They are extremely bitter and require blanching before using. The most popular ways of eating them are either by mixing with tahini or by sautéing with caramelized onions. The first time I tasted the dandelion greens that grow in Europe and the US, it was refreshing to find their bitterness more nuanced and eating them raw an option. I learned this salad from my mother-in-law who emigrated from Jordan to the United States over fifty years ago—it is a staple on her dinner table and the perfect accompaniment to almost any grain-based meal.

Serves 4

1 large bunch dandelion greens (about 12 oz/350 g), tough stems removed, finely chopped
1 teaspoon salt
4 scallions (spring onions), thinly sliced
3 tablespoons fresh lemon juice
1 tablespoon extra-virgin olive oil
½ teaspoon Aleppo pepper (optional)
4 tablespoons pomegranate seeds

Put the dandelion greens in a colander and sprinkle with the salt. Set aside for 15 minutes to release some of their bitter juices. Gently squeeze the greens and transfer to a bowl.

Add the scallions (spring onions), lemon juice, olive oil, Aleppo pepper (if using), and pomegranate seeds and toss to combine. Transfer to a serving bowl and serve.

Mustard Greens and Labaneh

In the Levant, there is a wild green that grows along the roadsides in late winter and early spring known as *hwaìrneh*, or "hedge mustard." My mother would finely chop this very sharp and peppery plant and mix it with labaneh. It was and still is one of my favorite ways to eat this green. It's actually quite a common preparation for many sharp and bitter greens that grow wild in the Middle East. The same variety is not easily accessible here in the West, but mustard greens have an almost identical flavor profile, so since living abroad I have been using them in its place. This dip is delicious eaten with bread, but is also great as a side to grilled meats.

Serves 4 as part of a spread

- 5 oz (140 g) mustard greens (about 1 small bunch including stems)
- ½ teaspoon salt
- 1 small green chili, such as jalapeño, finely diced
- ¾ cup (3 oz/85 g) labaneh, preferably homemade (page 40; see Note)
- Extra-virgin olive oil, for drizzling
- Aleppo pepper, for garnish

Finely chop the mustard greens, including the stems, and set in a colander. Sprinkle with the salt and let sit for 15–30 minutes. Squeeze the greens between your hands to release excess water.

Transfer the greens to a bowl, add the diced chili and labaneh, and mix until evenly combined. The prepared dip will keep in an airtight container in the refrigerator for up to 3 days.

To serve, spoon into a serving plate, drizzle with olive oil, and sprinkle with Aleppo pepper.

Note: Labaneh varies drastically from one brand to the next in moisture content, texture, and saltiness. The homemade labaneh suggested here (see recipe on page 40) is salty and sour, more reminiscent of feta and goat cheese in flavor than cream cheese. You certainly could use store-bought labaneh, just keep in mind the sour/salty flavor profile you are looking for and adjust the seasoning accordingly. (Alternatively, you could use Greek yogurt in place of the labaneh, but the texture will be looser and you will definitely need to increase the salt in the recipe and add a squeeze of lemon.)

Broccoli Rabe with Caramelized Onions

Growing up, my family would trek through the mountains and valleys surrounding Jerusalem foraging for the greens of the season. We would pick borage and cyclamen leaves for stuffing, za'atar and sage for drying, and various greens for sautéing or baking. *Hìndbeh*, or dandelion greens, were a favorite at home, mostly prepared with caramelized onions and lemon. The exact variety we foraged is not readily available abroad, so over the years I have prepared this dish with escarole, chicory, and kale. But one of my favorite preparations uses broccoli rabe (rapini), whose intense bitterness is a wonderful contrast to the sweetness of the fried onions. Leftovers also make a wonderful canvas for fried eggs. Simply reheat, make some wells, and crack an egg into each, then cook, covered, to desired doneness.

Serves 4 as part of a spread

- 2 large bunches broccoli rabe (rapini)
- 4 tablespoons olive oil
- 1 large onion, sliced into thin half-moons
- Salt
- 1 teaspoon crushed chili flakes, or more to taste, plus more for garnish
- 1 small lemon

Remove and discard any tough or dry stems from the broccoli rabe (rapini). Coarsely chop the leaves and very finely slice the stems.

In a large frying pan, heat the oil over medium-high heat. Add the onion, sprinkle with salt, and cook, tossing regularly, until golden and starting to crisp up, about 15 minutes. When ready, transfer a large spoonful to a plate lined with paper towels to use as garnish (leave the rest of the onion in the pan).

Add the chili flakes to the onion and stir until combined. Add the broccoli rabe leaves and stems, and toss to combine. Sprinkle with salt to taste (I usually start with ½ teaspoon and adjust at the end if necessary).

Reduce the heat, cover, and cook, tossing occasionally, until the greens have completely wilted and come together with the onion. This could take 15–30 minutes, depending on how tender the variety you have is.

Meanwhile, with a vegetable peeler or sharp knife, peel the zest off the lemon, leaving the spongy white pith intact, and cut into cubes.

Remove the broccoli rabe from the heat, taste, and adjust the seasoning. Transfer to a shallow bowl, spoon the fried onions into the center, sprinkle with some chili flakes, and arrange the lemon cubes around the platter.

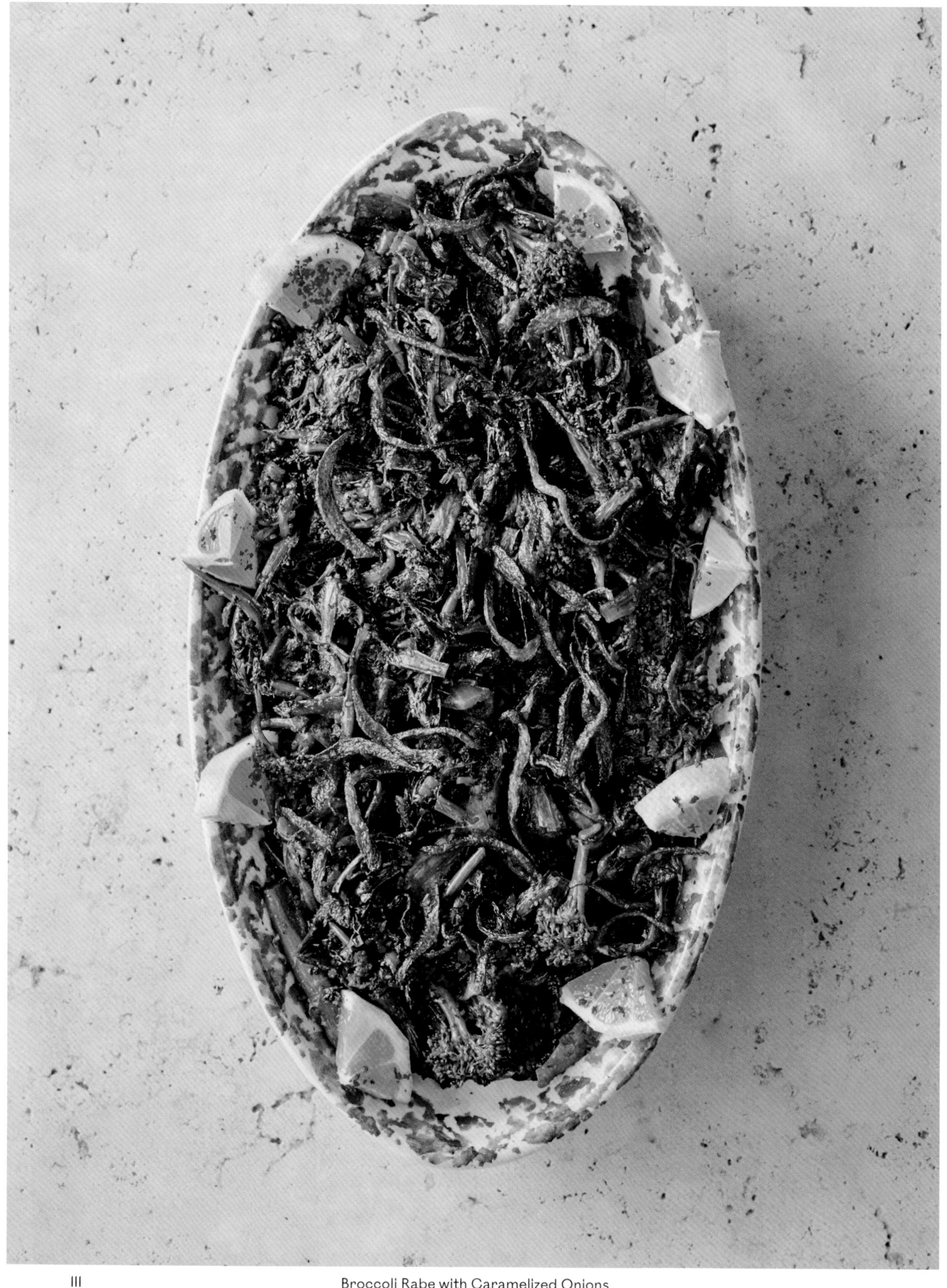

Broccoli Rabe with Caramelized Onions

Roasted Beets with Grilled Halloumi and Parsley Walnut Gremolata

By and large, the most common way beets are eaten across the Middle East is in salad form: They are roasted and then mixed with olive oil, lemon, parsley, and usually some garlic as well. A love-it-or-hate-it dish—because of the beets' earthy, almost soil-like flavor—I decided to play around with it to see if there was a way to elevate the standard fare. There were many failed attempts—from roasted wedges with yogurt, to paper-thin slices wrapped around cheese like ravioli, to raw grated, and many more—but this was finally a winner. The salty cheese was the perfect foil for the beets' sweetness, while the parsley and lemon zest provided a welcome brightness to both the walnut and beets' woody astringency. The flavor components hark back to the traditional Arab beet salad, but the arrangement and additional ingredients lend it a more interesting flair.

---

p. 114

Serves 4–6

1¼ lb (550 g) beets (about 2 medium)

For the gremolata:
- ½ cup (1¾ oz/50 g) walnut pieces, toasted and finely chopped
- ½ cup (¾ oz/20 g) tightly packed fresh parsley leaves, finely chopped
- Grated zest of 1 organic or unwaxed lemon
- ¼ teaspoon salt
- 2 cloves garlic, very finely diced or crushed in a garlic press
- 2 tablespoons extra-virgin olive oil

For assembly:
- 2 tablespoons fresh lemon juice
- ¼ teaspoon salt
- 9 oz (250 g) halloumi cheese, sliced into ten ⅓-inch (1 cm) slabs

Preheat the oven to 450°F (230°C/Gas Mark 7). Trim the beets and wash thoroughly. Wrap each beet individually in aluminum foil and roast until a skewer or sharp knife easily penetrates the flesh, 45–60 minutes. Remove and set aside until cool enough to handle. Once the beets are cooled, peel the skin off with a peeler or by rubbing off with your fingers. Use gloves to avoid staining your hands. Cut the beets into large bite-size cubes and set aside.

Make the gremolata:
In a bowl, combine the walnuts, parsley, lemon zest, salt, garlic, and olive oil and mix until incorporated. Set aside.

To assemble:
Toss the beets with the lemon juice and salt and arrange in a serving bowl.

Heat a griddle or grill pan over medium heat until hot. Arrange the halloumi pieces on the pan and cook until you see grill marks and the halloumi releases easily, about 3 minutes. Flip and cook until the other side releases easily as well, 2–3 minutes.

To serve, top the beets with the halloumi and spoon the gremolata on top.

Swiss Chard Khubeizeh

Khubeizeh is an extremely old and rustic Palestinian dish made with mallow. But mallow is not that easy to come across in the West, so since living abroad I've taken to making it with Swiss chard instead. I also use *fregola sarda* or giant/pearled couscous in place of the traditional hand-rolled drops of dough, making this an extremely easy and quick dish to prepare. Do not skip the crisp onions; they are the backbone of this dish and the dominant flavor thread throughout. My favorite way to eat this dish is with a spoon, like a thick soup, with some Shattah Chili Paste (page 22) and a squeeze of lemon. But if I really want to indulge in carbs, I'll scoop the whole thing, greens and grains, with bread.

---

p. 115

Serves 4 as an appetizer

2 big bunches of Swiss chard (1½–1¾ lb/700–800 g)
1½ teaspoons salt
Generous ½ cup (3½ oz/100 g) fregola sarda or giant/pearled couscous
¼ teaspoon freshly ground black pepper
1 medium onion, finely chopped
¼ cup (2 fl oz/60 ml) olive oil

For serving:
Shattah Chili Paste (page 22) or your favorite chili paste
Lemon wedges

Rinse the Swiss chard leaves and set aside to drain. Remove and discard the stem and tough midrib from each leaf, and finely chop the chard leaves.

In a medium pot, combine the chopped chard leaves, 3 cups (24 fl oz/700 ml) water, and 1 teaspoon of the salt. Bring to a boil over medium heat, then add the fregola sarda and black pepper and cook in gently boiling water until the pasta is fully done, 15–20 minutes depending on the variety.

Meanwhile, in a frying pan, combine the onion, olive oil, and the remaining ½ teaspoon salt and set over medium heat. Cook, stirring occasionally, until the onion is very well browned and starting to crisp, 15–20 minutes.

When the chard and fregola are cooked, pour the onion and its oil into the pot and simmer for another 1–2 minutes to meld the flavors. The consistency should be that of a thick soup. You will see a little bit of liquid, but the chard and fregola should not be swimming in broth. Bear in mind that it will also thicken as it sits.

To serve:

Ladle the stew into shallow bowls and place 1 teaspoon of chili paste and a lemon wedge on the side.

Roasted Beets with Grilled Halloumi and Parsley Walnut Gremolata

Grape Leaf Braised Short Ribs

One of my favorite parts of a pot of stuffed grape leaves is the meat lining the bottom—crispy in parts, but mostly melt-in-your-mouth-tender and rife with flavor. Yet I don't always have the patience (or desire) to spend several hours wrapping a whole pot of grape leaves, so I found this way to braise meat that yields the best part of the whole dish with a fraction of the effort. While you could use the jarred variety of grape leaves, I would urge you to get your hands on fresh leaves (frozen is fine), because they have an acidic flavor and capacity to break apart the tough meat tissue that the jarred variety does not. It's not that difficult to find these leaves: From spring through summer, anywhere you see wild grapevines you can find the leaves. Just taste the leaf first and make sure it has a somewhat sour flavor. You can also freeze the leaves for use throughout the year. The dish works just as well with other juicy cuts, especially beef cheeks or veal shanks as well as lamb shanks.

Serves 4–6

1¾ lb (795 g) bone-in short ribs or veal shanks
1¾ lb (795 g) boneless beef short ribs or beef cheeks
3 bay leaves
2 tablespoons olive oil
1 tablespoon pomegranate molasses
1 tablespoon soy sauce
2 teaspoons salt
1 teaspoon Nine-Spice Mix (page 27), baharat, or Lebanese 7-spice blend
½ teaspoon ground cumin
½ teaspoon freshly ground black pepper
30–40 fresh grape leaves

Place the meat in a large bowl and add the bay leaves, oil, pomegranate molasses, soy sauce, salt, spice mix, cumin, and black pepper and mix until evenly and fully coated. Cover and refrigerate overnight to marinate.

Preheat the oven to 500°F (260°C/Gas Mark 10).

Line a roasting pan large enough to snugly fit your chosen cuts of meat with half of the grape leaves. Remove the meat from the refrigerator and place on top of the grape leaves. Cover entirely with the remaining grape leaves so no pieces of meat are visible. Place a layer of parchment paper over the roasting pan, then tightly cover with a layer of aluminum foil.

Transfer the pan to the oven and immediately reduce the temperature to 400°F (200°C/Gas Mark 6). Roast for 30 minutes.

Reduce the heat to 280°F (140°C/Gas Mark 1) and roast until the meat is fork-tender, another 2–3 hours. The meat should release enough juices to keep it moist and give you nice pan juices at the end, but check once during the cooking time and if the pan is dry, add a few tablespoons of water, cover tightly again, and return to the oven until done.

The meat can be served directly from oven to table, but if preferred, you can transfer it to a serving platter and pour all the pan juices on top.

Potato Kafta Pie

I love this dish because it's a full meal in a single pan, exceptionally easy to prepare in advance, and the result is as delicious as it is beautiful. My grandmother often made kafta—the Levantine minced meat with onion, herbs, and spices—spread out in a roasting pan and baked. At times she topped it with diced tomatoes, onions, and peppers, and other times she layered thinly sliced potatoes on top as well. Another dish she often made was *kubbet batata*, a mixture of diced meat and onions sandwiched between two layers of mashed potatoes—a distant cousin of cottage pie, if you will. Here I have taken inspiration from both those meals and combined my favorite bits of each into a single, winning dish.

Serves 4–6

For the mashed potatoes:
1½ lb (700 g) red-skinned or yellow potatoes (4 small to medium), peeled and cut into large even chunks
1 tablespoon coarse sea salt
⅓ cup (2¾ fl oz/80 ml) whole milk
2 tablespoons (1 oz/30 g) unsalted butter
¼ teaspoon freshly ground black pepper
Fine salt

For the meat layer:
1¼ lb (550 g) coarsely ground (minced) beef, lamb, veal, or a combination
2 oz (60 g) pita bread or white bread, roughly torn
1 small tomato, quartered
1 small onion, quartered
1 clove garlic, peeled
1 green chili (optional)
1 tablespoon chopped fresh flat-leaf parsley
1 tablespoon olive oil
2 teaspoons salt
2 teaspoons Nine-Spice Mix (page 27), baharat, or Lebanese 7-spice blend

For finishing:
2–3 medium tomatoes, thinly sliced
Olive oil, for drizzling
Salt
½ teaspoon dried za'atar leaves or dried oregano (optional)

Make the mashed potatoes:
In a large pot, combine the potatoes and water to generously cover. Add the coarse salt and bring to a boil, uncovered, over medium-high heat. Cook until tender, 15–20 minutes.

Drain and allow to steam-dry in the pot for a few minutes. Add the milk, butter, and pepper to the potatoes and mash until very smooth. Taste and adjust the salt to your liking. I usually add about ½ teaspoon fine salt. Set aside.

Make the meat layer:
Preheat the oven to 450°F (230°C/Gas Mark 8).

Place the meat in a large bowl and set aside.

In a food processor, combine the bread, tomato, onion, garlic, chili (if using), parsley, olive oil, salt, and spice blend and pulse to a coarse paste. Pour the mixture over the meat in the bowl and mix with your hands until evenly incorporated.

Spread the meat mixture in an 8-inch (20 cm) square or round or oval ovenproof baking dish and spread the meat across the bottom and about 1 inch (2.5 cm) up the sides. The meat will shrink when cooked, so to ensure you end up with a layer that covers the bottom of the dish, it is important to take it up the sides before cooking. With your finger, make a few dimples in the center of the meat; this also helps with shrinkage.

Transfer the dish to the oven and bake until the meat is cooked through and starting to brown around the edges, 20–25 minutes. Remove from the oven and spread the mashed potatoes in an even layer on top. Return the dish to the oven and bake for 5–10 minutes to warm the potatoes through.

To finish:
Remove the dish from the oven and set the oven to broil (grill). Layer the sliced tomatoes on top of the potato layer. Drizzle some olive oil on top and sprinkle with salt and za'atar (if using). Return the dish to the oven and broil until the tomatoes are starting to brown around the edges, about 5 minutes.

Let stand for 5 minutes before serving.

Potato Kafta Pie

Herb, Garlic, and Chili Stuffed Chicken Thighs

Little goes to waste in traditional Arab households, especially when it comes to butchering livestock, and my family is no exception. Around the holidays, my mother often made a dish of spleen stuffed with the most piquant garlic and herb filling. As a child, I hated spleen because I found it too minerally, but I would always take a piece of bread and mop up the delicious stuffing that had fallen out into the pan. Here I replicate that filling but with milder, and more easily accessible, chicken thighs for the best of both worlds. The potatoes are optional, but I love the crispiness and flavor that come from cooking them alongside the chicken and its rendered fat. The stuffing works just as well with other cuts of meat, such as flank steak or chicken breast, and of course, with lamb offal.

Serves 4–6

For the chicken:
8 bone-in, skin-on chicken thighs
1½ teaspoons salt
1 tablespoon olive oil

For the stuffing:
6 cloves garlic, crushed in a garlic press
3 fresh red chilies, finely diced
2 jalapeño peppers, finely diced
½ cup (½ oz/15 g) packed fresh cilantro (coriander) leaves, finely chopped (see Note)
¼ cup (¾ oz/25 g) walnut pieces, finely chopped
3 tablespoons olive oil
1 tablespoon fresh lemon juice
½ teaspoon ground cumin
½ teaspoon salt
¼ teaspoon freshly ground black pepper

For assembly:
1 lb (450 g) potatoes (3 small to medium), cut into wedges
Salt and freshly ground black pepper

Prepare the chicken:
Pat the chicken thighs dry with paper towels and trim off any straggly bits. Sprinkle all over with the salt. Drizzle with the olive oil, rub all around, and refrigerate for at least 30 minutes and up to overnight.

Preheat the oven to 425°F (220°C/Gas Mark 7).

Make the stuffing:
In a bowl, combine the garlic, both chilies, the cilantro (coriander), walnuts, olive oil, lemon juice, cumin, salt, and black pepper and mix to combine.

Gently loosen the skin from the thigh meat with your fingers to make a pocket, but make sure the skin is still connected to the meat. Divide the stuffing evenly among the thighs and place it in the pocket between the skin and the meat, pulling the skin so it covers the chicken and stuffing.

To assemble:
Put the potato wedges in a 9 × 13-inch (23 × 33 cm) roasting pan and sprinkle lightly with salt. Nestle the thighs between the potato wedges and use any drippings or remaining oil to rub on the potato wedges. Top everything with a few twists of pepper.

Transfer to the oven and roast until the meat is cooked through, the skin is crisp to your liking, and the potatoes are crisped and browned, 45 minutes to 1 hour.

Let rest for 5 minutes, then transfer to a platter or individual plates and serve.

Notes: You can replace the cilantro with 2 tablespoons crushed dried herbs, such as za'atar, oregano, marjoram, thyme, dill, etc. If you do, reduce the salt in the stuffing to ¼ teaspoon.

Herb, Garlic, and Chili Stuffed Chicken Thighs

Coriander + Cumin + Cardamom

Through an archway of ancient Jerusalem stone, I strolled in with my mother, the clack of our shoes loud against the cobblestone pathways early in the morning. We had just walked down from the Holy Sepulcher and made a right to enter Souk el Attarine in Jerusalem's Old City. At first glance, it looked like painters' palettes propped against walls with artists by their side, but a closer look revealed mounds of spices in countless shades and textures. The smell that wafted as we walked down the cobbled road would have left no room for doubt, even with our eyes closed. We were in the presence of a powerful story that spoke of history, trade, migration, and of a land as old as this history itself. We were in the Old City's spice market.

Spices are powerfully enchanting. Shrouded in legend and mystical tales, they formed the basis of trade in antiquity, led to countless wars, and inspired sailors and merchants to undertake voyages of discovery. Spices found their way to the Middle East some four thousand years ago. They were some of the first items to cross the globe on trade networks and the reason the Maritime Silk Roads—the sea routes connecting East and West—were often called the "Spice Routes."

In ancient times, the Arab world was a center of trade for fragrant resins, gums, and spices. From the rise of Islam all the way through the Middle Ages, the spice trade was fragmented among diverse, predominantly Muslim merchants. Merchants withheld the true source of spices they sold and spread fantastical tales to discourage competitors, inspiring famous legends like Sinbad and the Seven Seas. Between the tenth and fifteenth centuries, Venice gained a strong hold on the spice trade throughout Europe. By the end of the fifteenth century, sailors from other parts of Europe were embarking on spice expeditions, which eventually led to imperial expansion and culminated in European domination over much of the world. This is but a very simplistic view, for the story of spices is much more complex, with tomes needed to cover its intricacies. Spices tell a tale of globalization from ancient times, of tiny seeds worth more than gold traveling from one end of the world to the other, and that story continues into the present day.

In the Middle East, countless spices are used in cooking and even prescribed for cures and health benefits. The recipes in this chapter feature different kinds in multiple variations, but I've chosen coriander, cumin, and cardamom as the anchors—cumin with its citrusy zest when toasted, cardamom with its elusive earthy flavor, and coriander with its sweet floral notes—because cumin and coriander are two spices native to the Middle East, and cardamom, although native to India, is one of the most widely used in Arab cuisine, especially in drinks like coffee and in desserts.

Whether used together in recipes like Makmoora (page 138), separately in desserts like Cardamom Halaweh Oum Ali (page 142), or to complement other spices in meat dishes like Halloumi-Stuffed Kofta Meatballs (page 136), these three offer a diverse and aromatic combination of flavors in our food. The surest way to ensure you experience the best these flavors have to offer is to buy your spices whole and grind at home as needed.

Sujuk—Spicy Cured Sausage

This spicy dry sausage is eaten across the Balkans, Central Asia, and the Middle East, where almost all cultures have adopted some variation of its Turkish name *sucuk*. Curing was a way to preserve meats before refrigeration, and is found in recipes across the globe. In the Middle East, *sujuk*, as it's called, is most often purchased from a butcher where the meat has been spiced, dried, and then encased in intestines—delicious, but not the easiest or most practical thing to do at home. That's why this recipe offers the same flavors of *sujuk*, but with a much easier preparation. It's almost entirely hands off—the only hard thing about it is being patient as you wait for it to be ready. It is delicious fried next to eggs, in a grilled cheese sandwich, and in place of any other sausage you may use. There are a few recipes in this book that use it, but get creative yourself, because the flavor of this sausage will give a real kick to any dish you add it to.

Makes about 1 pound (450 g) sausage

- 1 lb 2 oz (500 g) ground (minced) beef or lamb
- 5–6 cloves garlic, minced
- 1 teaspoon salt
- 1 teaspoon ground cumin
- ½ teaspoon cayenne pepper or chili powder
- ½ teaspoon ground coriander
- ½ teaspoon ground fenugreek (or curry powder as long as fenugreek is on the ingredients list)
- ½ teaspoon sweet paprika
- ½ teaspoon smoked paprika (optional)
- ½ teaspoon Nine-Spice Mix (page 27), baharat, or Lebanese 7-spice blend

Lay flat a cheesecloth (muslin) or flour sack towel (any cloth that is breathable) and set aside.

In a bowl, combine the meat, garlic, salt, and all of the spices and knead until fully incorporated. Flatten the meat mixture into a rectangle roughly 8 × 4 inches (20 × 10 cm) and place on the prepared cloth.

Carefully wrap the cloth around the meat, making sure it will stay in place and no meat is exposed. Put the bundle on a wire rack set over a plate and place in the back of your refrigerator for 1 week. You want air to circulate around the meat so it dries and never gets damp.

After a week, the meat will have dried and the spices fermented, giving it the unique *sujuk* flavor. At this point, the meat can be used as called for in a recipe or it can be sliced and frozen in ready-to-use portions.

Fried Basturma Spiced Rolls

Basturma is heavily spiced, salt-cured, and air-dried beef hailing back to Byzantine times and found in most Ottoman cuisines today. Growing up in Jerusalem, we used to buy it thinly sliced from butchers and grocers. My absolute favorite part was the spice paste around the beef, a highly seasoned mixture of fenugreek, garlic, paprika, and cumin. I often crave that flavor, but making *basturma* at home—while possible—is highly time-consuming and involved. So I decided to take my favorite part, the spice mixture, and try to apply it to different ingredients and methods of cooking. After many trials, from roasts and kebabs to cauliflower and potatoes, only one dish was good enough to satisfy, perhaps even surpass, my nostalgic craving. It was these perfectly seasoned, savory, and crisp spiced beef rolls. I fry them for maximum flavor, but they are perfectly delicious baked as well.

Makes about 30 rolls

8 oz (225 g) ground (minced) beef or lamb or a combination
2 teaspoons olive oil
1 teaspoon salt
1 teaspoon ground fenugreek
1 teaspoon garlic powder
1 teaspoon paprika
½ teaspoon freshly ground black pepper
½ teaspoon ground cumin
2 thin Lebanese pita breads (5 oz/140 g total), or four 9-inch/23 cm flour tortilla wraps
Vegetable oil, for deep-frying

In a medium bowl, combine the ground meat, olive oil, salt, and all the spices and mix until fully combined.

With the tip of a sharp knife, cut around each pita so you end up with a total of 4 flat, round pieces of bread. If you are using tortillas, you can skip this step.

Take one-quarter of the meat mixture and spread evenly over one piece of bread, reaching all the way to the edges. Roll the pita tightly into a log. Repeat with the remaining 3 pieces of bread and meat.

With a sharp knife, slice the uneven ends off and discard, then slice each log crosswise into roughly 1-inch (2.5 cm) discs. The rolls can be frozen at this point for later use or fried immediately.

Line a plate with paper towels. Pour 3 inches (7 cm) vegetable oil into a deep pot or wok and heat to 350°F (180°C), or until a morsel of bread dropped into the oil immediately rises to the surface and bubbles.

Working in batches so as not to crowd them, fry the rolls until golden brown, about 5 minutes. Remove with a slotted spoon to the paper towels to drain. Transfer to a platter and serve.

Note: If you choose to bake instead of fry these rolls, lightly brush with olive oil and bake in a preheated 450°F (230°C/Gas Mark 8) oven until browned and crisp, about 20 minutes.

Fried Basturma Spiced Rolls

Sambusak with Spiced Lamb and Pine Nuts

"You who asked me about the most delicious dish. You have asked, indeed, the person to answer your wish." So starts a poem by Ishaq al-Mawsili, an eighth-century Persian musician of the Abbasid court, before he describes a recipe for one of the oldest dishes on record to have originated in the Middle East—the *sambusak*. This stuffed fried dough traveled the Silk Road all the way to medieval Europe, Africa, Central Asia, and even India, where today it is known as "samosa." You'd be hard-pressed to find a culture anywhere in the world today that does not enjoy some variation of these savory dumplings. One of the earliest recorded recipes for *sambusak* is in the tenth-century Arabic *Kitab al-Tabikh*, but it is more of a blueprint than a recipe as we know recipes today. This is my contemporary take on that blueprint.

Makes about 50 sambusaks

For the filling:
2 tablespoons olive oil
1 very small onion, finely diced
10 oz (300 g) ground (minced) lamb or beef or a combination
Scant 1 teaspoon salt
1 teaspoon Nine-Spice Mix (page 27), baharat, or Lebanese 7-spice blend
¼ teaspoon ground coriander
¼ teaspoon ground ginger
¼ teaspoon freshly ground black pepper
2 scallions (spring onions), green parts only, finely chopped
Small handful cilantro (coriander), finely chopped
1–2 sprigs fresh mint, leaves picked and finely chopped
¼ cup (35 g) pine nuts, fried or toasted

For the dough:
4 ¼ cups (1 lb 2 oz/500 g) all-purpose (plain) flour
4 tablespoons fine semolina
1 teaspoon salt
1 teaspoon baking powder
½ teaspoon baking soda (bicarbonate of soda)
½ cup (4 fl oz/120 ml) vegetable oil
¼ cup (2 oz/60 g) yogurt
4 tablespoons distilled or cider vinegar
Vegetable oil, for deep-frying
Yogurt sprinkled with sumac, for serving (optional)

Make the filling:
In a frying pan, heat the olive oil over medium-high heat. Add the onion and fry, stirring, until translucent and starting to brown, 3–5 minutes. Add the meat, salt, spice blend, coriander, ginger, and pepper and cook, breaking up any lumps, until any released water has evaporated and the meat is nicely browned, 6–8 minutes.

Remove from the heat, add the scallions (spring onions), cilantro (coriander), mint, and pine nuts, and mix to combine. Set aside to cool.

Make the dough:
In a large bowl, stir together the flour, semolina, salt, baking powder, and baking soda (bicarb). Add the oil, yogurt, vinegar and ⅔ cup (5 fl oz/150 ml) water and start kneading. Depending on the flour variety you use, you may need to add a couple tablespoons of water at a time to bring the dough together. If the mixture feels sticky, let rest for 5 minutes, then knead again. Repeat once or twice until you have a pliable but robust dough. Put into a bowl, cover with plastic wrap (clingfilm), and set aside to rest for 15 minutes.

Divide the dough into 2 equal portions. Leave one covered in the bowl and roll out the other on a floured surface, as thinly as possible. Using about a 3-inch (7.5 cm) round cookie cutter, cut out rounds of dough. Place about 1 teaspoon of the meat filling into each round, leaving a very small border around the perimeter. Fold over into a half-moon shape and, using a fork, crimp the edges shut for a nice design and to ensure the filling won't fall out. Repeat until all the rounds are filled.

Gather the scraps, knead into a ball, and set aside to rest while you work on the second ball of dough. Repeat until you run out of filling. At this point, the parcels can be fried right away or frozen for later.

If freezing, freeze in a single layer on a parchment-lined sheet or plate, then transfer to an airtight container and freeze for up to 3 months.

If frying, line a plate with paper towels. Pour 3 inches (7 cm) oil into a deep-fryer or heavy Dutch oven (casserole) and heat to 350°F (180°C), or until a morsel of dough in the oil immediately rises to the surface.

Working in batches, deep-fry the parcels until a deep golden color, about 5 minutes. Drain on the paper towels and serve immediately.

Sambusak with Spiced Lamb and Pine Nuts

Arayes Pita Burgers

This dish was not supposed to make it into the book. But I prepare it often at home (usually when testing recipes for the first time) to guarantee that if a tested recipe fails, my daughters still have something healthy, filling, and easy to eat. Without exception, every time I make it they ask, "Are you going to put this one in the book?" In the end I figured I had to. *Arayes* are a very traditional Levantine dish made by stuffing pita with seasoned ground meat then grilling it. I simplify here by cooking in a panini press. I also opt for very small pita breads, which lend the final dish a hamburger-like shape, but you could just as well use larger ones and slice into quarters after grilling.

Makes eight 4-inch (10 cm) pita burgers

- 1 small tomato, seeded and very finely chopped
- 1 small onion, very finely chopped
- 1 green chili pepper, minced
- Small handful of fresh flat-leaf parsley, minced
- 11 oz (300 g) ground (minced) beef or lamb or a combination
- 1 teaspoon olive oil
- 1 teaspoon salt
- ½ teaspoon crushed chili flakes (optional)
- ¼ teaspoon ground allspice
- ⅛ teaspoon freshly ground black pepper
- ⅛ teaspoon ground cumin
- 8 mini (4-inch/10 cm) pita breads
- Olive oil, for brushing
- Yogurt, to serve (optional)

In a medium bowl, combine the tomato, onion, chili, and parsley. Add the meat, olive oil, salt, and all the spices and mix with your hands until thoroughly combined.

Using a sharp knife, cut halfway around the edge of each pita to make a pocket. Divide the meat mixture among the pitas and evenly spread it inside. Gently press to close.

Generously brush each bread with olive oil on both sides. Place the stuffed pitas in a panini press and cook on medium-high heat until the meat is fully cooked and the bread has nicely browned and crisped up, 5 minutes. To make cleanup easier you could line the panini press with parchment paper and top the pita breads with another piece of parchment before grilling. (Alternatively, if you don't have a panini press, wrap each pita in foil and bake in a 400°F/200°C/Gas Mark 6 oven until the meat is cooked through and the bread is crispy, 15–20 minutes.) Serve immediately with yogurt on the side (if using).

Note: The meat mixture will keep for a full day in the refrigerator, so you can prepare in advance and cook on demand, but once the pitas are stuffed they need to be cooked immediately or the bread will become soggy.

Lamb Dumplings with Garlic Yogurt, Tomatoes, and Pine Nuts

From Europe to Central Asia, the Middle East and Africa, all the way to the Far East and South America, if there is one dish that almost every culture across the world has a version of it is the dumpling. In the Arab world, the two most common versions are *shushbarak*, adopted from the Persian and Ottoman empires, and *mantì*, embraced from Turkish and Armenian cuisines. The oldest diaspora of Armenians outside Armenia is actually thought to be in Jerusalem. Even the Old City of Jerusalem is split into four quarters: Muslim, Christian, Jewish, and Armenian. These cross-cultural influences have inevitably led to countless dumpling variations. My recipe here is a cross between *shushbarak* and *mantì* served, nontraditionally, with a refreshing tomato relish on top.

Serves 4–6

For the dough:
2 ⅓ cups (300 g) bread (strong) flour (or all-purpose/plain)
2 tablespoons olive oil
½ teaspoon salt

For the filling:
6 oz (170 g) ground (minced) lamb or beef or a combination
½ onion, finely grated
2 teaspoons olive oil
½ teaspoon salt
¼ teaspoon freshly ground black pepper
¼ teaspoon ground cumin

For the yogurt sauce:
1 cup (9 oz/250 g) yogurt
1 clove garlic, crushed in a garlic press
½ teaspoon salt

For the tomato relish:
1 teaspoon dill seed, or a very small bunch of fresh dill or cilantro/coriander
½ teaspoon salt
1 jalapeño pepper, seeded
9 oz (250 g) tomatoes (about 2 medium or 1 pint cherry tomatoes)
1 teaspoon fresh lemon juice

For finishing:
Salt
1 tablespoon olive oil
¼ cup (1 ¼ oz/35 g) pine nuts, toasted or fried, for garnish

Make the dough:
In a large bowl, combine the flour, olive oil, and salt. Pour in ⅔ cup (5 fl oz/150 ml) water and knead until fully incorporated. If the dough seems dry, do not add more water as it will make rolling and stuffing much harder; just set it aside for a few minutes and come back and knead again. (Alternatively, in a stand mixer fitted with the dough hook, combine the ingredients and mix on medium speed until the dough comes together.) Cover the dough and let rest for 30 minutes.

Meanwhile, make the filling:
In a small bowl, combine the meat, grated onion, olive oil, salt, pepper, and cumin and mix to incorporate. Refrigerate until ready to use.

Make the yogurt sauce:
In a small bowl, stir together the yogurt, garlic, and salt. Set aside.

On a floured surface, roll the dough to roughly ⅛ inch (3 mm) thick. Using a 2-inch (5 cm) round cookie cutter or an inverted glass, cut as many rounds as you can out of the dough. Gather up the scraps and set aside. To stuff the dumplings, place ¼–½ teaspoon of the filling into the middle of each round and fold in half to make a half-moon. Take the ends of the half-moon and press together to form a hat shape. If you still have some filling left, you can reroll the scraps of dough, cut out more rounds, and continue until the filling is done. At this point, the dumplings can be frozen for a couple of months, refrigerated for 1 day, or cooked immediately.

Make the tomato relish:
With a mortar and pestle, pound the dill seed and salt until the dill seeds have broken apart and become more fragrant. In a food processor, combine the dill seed mixture, jalapeño, tomatoes, and lemon juice and pulse until you have a fine salsa consistency. Set aside.

To finish:
Bring a pot of salted water to a boil and add the olive oil. When boiling, gently add the dumplings and cook until they rise to the surface, 3–5 minutes. Lightly stir with a fork while cooking to avoid them sticking to the bottom of the pot. Remove from the heat and drain.

To serve, spoon the yogurt sauce into a large shallow bowl or individual bowls, and slightly spread around. Place the dumplings on the yogurt and top with the tomato relish and pine nuts. Serve immediately.

Lamb Dumplings with Garlic Yogurt, Tomatoes, and Pine Nuts

Spiced Mushroom and Halloumi Stuffed Kebab Domes

Grilling over fire is the oldest form of cooking known to man, and probably the reason eating meals and sharing food is as we know it today. From Argentinian *asado* and Korean barbecue to Japanese *yakitori* and Arabic *mashawi*, every culture has its own way of cooking over live flame. But all share the connection to our ancient roots, to a primal way of cooking, which to this day gives us a sense of pleasure —if not for the flavor of the food, then for the gathering of people it precipitates. *Ma'ajuqa* is a mushroom and cheese filled kebab and one of the most famous grilled meats in Aleppo, Syria. While few of us these days fire up a grill and barbecue on a regular basis, this version of kebab domes is just as perfect in a home oven.

Serves 4

For the stuffing:
- 14 oz (400 g) mushrooms, thinly sliced
- 2 tablespoons olive oil
- 2 cloves garlic, minced
- ½ teaspoon salt
- ½ teaspoon fresh thyme leaves or crushed dried za'atar leaves
- 2 tablespoons pine nuts, toasted
- 4½ oz (125 g) Akkawi, Nabulsi, halloumi, or low-moisture mozzarella cheese, grated

For the meat:
- 1 lb (450 g) ground (minced) beef
- 1 tablespoon olive oil, plus more for greasing
- 1 egg, whisked well
- 1 oz (30 g) crustless bread, ground into fine breadcrumbs in a food processor (if unavailable, use ¼ cup/30 g store-bought dried breadcrumbs, but the fresh crumbs yield a softer meat texture)
- 1½ teaspoons salt
- ¼ teaspoon freshly ground black pepper
- ½ teaspoon ground allspice
- ½ teaspoon ground coriander
- ½ teaspoon paprika
- ¼ teaspoon ground cumin

Make the stuffing:
In a large dry frying pan, cook the mushrooms over medium-high heat until they release their water and it evaporates, about 10 minutes.

Add the olive oil, garlic, and salt and continue to cook, stirring occasionally, until the garlic is fragrant and the mushrooms are starting to brown, 3–5 minutes. Remove from the heat, add the thyme and pine nuts, and set aside to cool. Once cool, stir in the grated cheese.

Prepare the meat:
In a bowl, combine the meat, olive oil, egg, breadcrumbs, salt, pepper, and spices and mix until evenly incorporated. Divide into 8 equal portions.

To shape the kebab domes, invert two medium round dinner plates, where the raised circle on the bottom is 5–6 inches (12–15 cm) across, and place a piece of plastic wrap (clingfilm) or parchment paper on each plate and grease with some oil. The plates help you shape the meat into identical rounds, but also maintain that shape as you attach the two sides together.

Take a portion of meat and place in the center of the inverted plate. Using your hands, flatten the patty until it just fills the circle on the bottom of the plate. Repeat with the second plate.

Spoon one-quarter of the mushroom mixture onto one of the patties. Using the paper or plastic under the second patty, lift the meat and flip onto the patty with the stuffing. Peel off the paper and use oiled hands to seal the edges and smooth out the dome. Transfer to a well-oiled baking sheet. Repeat with the remaining meat and mushroom stuffing until you have 4 kebab domes. At this point the kebab domes can be cooked immediately or refrigerated for several hours until ready to use.

Preheat the oven to 550°F (290°C/Gas Mark 10) or as high as your oven will go.

Transfer the kebabs to the oven and bake until nicely browned and you see some oil bubbling around the edges, about 10 minutes. Let stand for a few minutes before serving.

Spiced Mushroom and Halloumi Stuffed Kebab Domes

Halloumi-Stuffed Kofta Meatballs

I have a soft spot for the ubiquitous kofta, *polpette*, *albondiga*, or meatball, which by any other name would taste just as delicious. Thought to hail from Persia but found in almost every cuisine in the world, the origins of this versatile treat can be attributed to a desire to stretch small portions of meat (which was expensive and labor-intensive to prepare) to create something sustaining and flavorful. This recipe was originally intended to be cooked in a tomato and pomegranate molasses sauce and served with rice, and the result was indeed utterly delicious. But one of the days I tested the recipe, I had not eaten breakfast and I stole two meatballs as soon as they came out of the oven before going into the sauce. As much as I wanted this to be a recipe for a stew, the meatballs were just too good not to stand on their own. So serve them as canapés, appetizers, or even as a main with a side salad.

Makes 30 meatballs

- 1½ lb (700 g) ground (minced) beef, veal, lamb, or a combination
- 7 oz (200 g) white Arabic cheese, such as Akkawi, Nabulsi, or halloumi
- 3½ oz (100 g) white bread, such as pita, baguette, ciabatta, or whatever you have on hand
- 1 small onion, quartered
- 1 small tomato, quartered
- 1 small green chili pepper, such as jalapeño, serrano, or Anaheim
- 2 small cloves garlic, peeled
- Small bunch of parsley
- Very small bunch of cilantro (coriander)
- 1 egg
- 1 tablespoon olive oil, plus more for brushing
- ½ teaspoon salt
- ½ teaspoon freshly ground black pepper
- 1½ teaspoons Nine-Spice Mix (page 27), (or baharat, or Lebanese 7-spice blend)
- 1 teaspoon ground cumin
- 3–4 tablespoons pine nuts, toasted

Preheat the oven to 500°F (260°C/Gas Mark 10). Line a baking sheet with parchment paper.

Put the meat in a large bowl and set aside.

Take three-quarters (5¼ oz/150 g) of the cheese and cut into 30 even cubes. Set aside.

In a food processor, combine the remaining cheese (1¾ oz/50 g) and the bread and pulse into crumbs. Add the onion, tomato, chili, garlic, parsley, cilantro (coriander), egg, 1 tablespoon oil, the salt, pepper, and the spices and pulse to a paste. Pour the mixture over the meat and mix gently with your hands until evenly incorporated. The meat mixture will be quite sticky, so it helps to grease your hands with oil as you shape the meatballs.

Divide the meat into 30 equal portions (the size of golf balls, about 2 tablespoons; use an ice cream scoop if easier). Make a hole in the center of each portion with your thumb and insert 1 cheese cube and 2–3 pine nuts. Seal the meat tightly around the cheese, roll into a ball, and place on the lined baking sheet. Press 1 pine nut in the top of each meatball and brush the meatballs with olive oil.

Transfer to the oven and bake until the meat is cooked through and the outsides have browned nicely, 10–15 minutes. Remove from the oven and serve immediately.

Variation: To make the tomato sauce referenced in the headnote: In a saucepan, combine 1 jar (24 oz/680 g) passata or 2 cans (14 oz/400 g each) crushed tomatoes, 1½ cups (12 fl oz/355 ml) water, 1 tablespoon tomato paste (purée), 2 minced cloves garlic, and 1½ teaspoons salt. Bring to a boil, then reduce the heat and simmer, covered, for 45 minutes. Uncover, add 1 tablespoon butter (15 g) and 1 tablespoon pomegranate molasses and cook for another minute until the butter has melted. Taste for salt and adjust seasoning. Add the meatballs, cover, and cook for another 3–5 minutes. Serve with rice.

Mushroom Shawarma with Parsley Tahini

The Turkish town of Busra is credited with giving birth to the meat roasted on a vertical revolving spit famously known as *doner kebap*. This iconic street food—one of the most famous across the Middle East—entered the Arabic kitchen via the Ottoman Turks and is called *shawarma*, a rendering of the Turkish word *cevìrme*, which means "turning" or "revolving." It is, at its most basic, slices of meat stacked on a rotating skewer, roasted and then shaved into bread with various condiments. There are many ways to replicate the flavor at home without the spit. But to forgo the meat entirely? In truth, it felt almost irreverent to do a vegetarian version of this dish. But there was a mushroom farmer in Pennsylvania who brought his produce to the market outside our building every Saturday and I couldn't resist trying. Not only was it a real triumph of flavors, you actually didn't miss the meat. You can use any variety of mushrooms you want, but the meatier varieties, like shiitake, maitake, and portobello hold up best for this kind of dish, where you want not only flavor but texture as well. It's not a mistake to put the mushrooms in the pan first without oil. This allows them to release all their liquid and brown evenly in the oil once you do add it.

Serves 2–4

For the tahini sauce:

4 tablespoons tahini
2 tablespoons fresh lemon juice
2 tablespoons yogurt
1 small clove garlic, peeled
Handful of fresh parsley leaves
¼ teaspoon salt

For the mushroom shawarma:

1 lb (450 g) portobello mushrooms (about 4 large), cut into large bite-size slices
7 oz (200 g) shiitake mushrooms (about 10 large), stems discarded, caps thinly sliced
2 tablespoons olive oil
1 teaspoon salt
1 teaspoon garlic granules
1 teaspoon Nine-Spice Mix (page 27), baharat, or Lebanese 7-spice blend
1 teaspoon curry powder (with fenugreek in the ingredients list)
¼ teaspoon chipotle powder
¼ teaspoon smoked paprika
1 small onion, thinly sliced
2 cloves garlic, crushed
1 tablespoon fresh lemon juice

For serving:

Flatbread, homemade (page 30) or store-bought
Chopped cucumbers and tomatoes
Pickles (optional)

Make the tahini sauce:
In a mini food processor, combine the tahini, lemon juice, yogurt, garlic, parsley, and salt with 3 tablespoons water and pulse until smooth with small specks of parsley seen throughout. Taste for salt, adjust the seasoning, and set aside.

Make the mushroom shawarma:
Place all the mushrooms in a large dry frying pan over high heat. Cook, stirring regularly, until the mushrooms have released their water and it has evaporated, about 10 minutes.

Add the olive oil, salt, garlic granules, spices, and onion and cook, tossing regularly, until the mushrooms and onions are evenly coated in spices and starting to brown, another 4–5 minutes. Tip in the crushed garlic and continue to cook for another minute until fragrant. Add the lemon juice, giving one final toss to combine, and remove from the heat. Taste and add more salt if necessary.

To serve:
Spread the tahini sauce on a flatbread and add the shawarma. If desired, top with the chopped vegetables and pickles and roll up.

Makmoora

I first came across this dish while working in microfinance in Jordan where we visited poor communities throughout the country. Later, I came across a class of dishes in the tenth-century *Kìtab al-Tabìkh* called *maghmumat* (the plural of *maghmuma*). Both *makmoora* and *maghmuma* mean "enclosed" or "covered" in Arabic and are dishes of different cooked meats and vegetables covered, sometimes layered, with pastry, then baked. Similar to game and pot pies, I don't know why those dishes have taken the world by storm while these Arab precursors have sunk into oblivion. What I do know: This is one delicious dish that deserves to be made time and time again. After all, the evolution of a cuisine is sometimes as simple as recovering its forgotten gems.

Serves 6–8

For the dough:
- 1⅔ cups (7 oz/200 g) all-purpose (plain) flour
- Generous ½ cup (2 oz/60 g) whole wheat (wholemeal) flour
- 2 teaspoons nigella seeds
- 2 teaspoons unhulled sesame seeds
- ¾ teaspoon salt
- ¼ teaspoon ground turmeric
- 1 tablespoon olive oil, plus more for coating

For the filling:
- 1 lb 10 oz (750 g) boneless, skin-on chicken breasts or thighs
- 1 lb 10 oz (750 g) onions (about 2 very large), finely chopped
- ½ cup (120 ml) olive oil
- 2½ teaspoons salt
- ½ teaspoon freshly ground black pepper
- 1 teaspoon ground cinnamon
- 1 teaspoon ground cumin
- 1 teaspoon ground turmeric
- ½ teaspoon ground cardamom
- ½ teaspoon ground coriander
- ½ teaspoon curry powder
- A few twists/grates of nutmeg
- ¼ cup (1¼ oz/35 g) pine nuts, toasted
- ¼ cup (1 oz/30 g) coarsely chopped toasted walnuts

For assembly:
- Olive oil, for greasing, brushing, and stretching
- Yogurt, for serving (optional)

Preheat the oven to 400°F (200°C/Gas Mark 6).

In a stand mixer fitted with the dough hook, combine both flours, both seeds, the salt, turmeric, olive oil, and ¾ cup (6 fl oz/175 ml) water. Mix on medium speed until you have a soft ball of dough. Divide into 3 portions: one weighing about 7 oz (200 g) and two around 5 oz (140 g) each. Generously coat the balls with oil, cover with plastic wrap (clingfilm), and set aside to rest for at least 45 minutes.

Place the chicken in a baking dish and bake until just cooked through, 15–20 minutes. Remove and set aside until cool enough to handle, then shred into small bite-size pieces.

Meanwhile, in a large frying pan, combine the onions, olive oil, and 1 teaspoon salt and cook over medium to medium-low heat until they are completely soft.

Add the shredded chicken, 1½ teaspoons salt, the pepper, and all the spices and stir to combine. Cook for another 1–2 minutes to help the chicken absorb the flavors. Remove from the heat, add the pine nuts and walnuts, and set aside.

Preheat the oven to 350°F (180°C/Gas Mark 4). Line an 8-inch (20 cm) round nonstick cake pan with parchment paper and grease with olive oil.

Take the large ball of dough and stretch it out, oiling your hands as often as necessary, to a roughly 12-inch (30 cm) round. Place the rolled dough in the cake pan with the extra dough hanging over the sides. Brush with olive oil. Take half of the filling and spread over the dough.

Take another ball of dough and flatten out to a thin 8-inch (20 cm) round. Place the dough in the cake pan over the filling, brush with olive oil, and top with the remaining filling. Stretch the final piece of dough to 8 inches (20 cm), place on top, and brush with olive oil. Bring the overhanging dough in over this layer and brush again with olive oil.

Cut an 8-inch (20 cm) round of parchment paper and place over the dough. Tightly seal the pan with aluminum foil. Transfer to the oven and bake for 2 hours. Then remove the foil and paper and cook until crisped and slightly darker in color, 10–15 minutes. Remove from the oven and let rest for a few minutes.

Place the serving platter over the pie and flip, so the top is at the top again. Serve on its own or with a side of yogurt.

All-Spice Chicken and Potatoes with Garlic and Green Chili Sauce

When my mother-in-law's father emigrated from Jordan to the United States in the mid-1960s, he had never before cooked a meal for himself. When she joined him in the United States a couple of years later to finish high school, she found he now had several delicious dishes in his arsenal. This recipe is the one she says reminds her of her father the most. The ingredients may look simple, but together they become a fragrant dish reminiscent of many different Arab meals. Perhaps that nostalgia was what led my mother-in-law's father to come up with this dish that is full of Arab flavors but decidedly not a traditional one. I love it with a side of rice, but it is just as good all on its own or with some crusty bread to mop up the delicious juices.

Serves 4–6

8 boneless, skinless chicken thighs (about 2 lb/900 g total)
2 teaspoons fresh lemon juice
2 teaspoons olive oil
2 teaspoons salt
¼ teaspoon freshly ground black pepper
½ teaspoon ground allspice
½ teaspoon ground cinnamon
½ teaspoon ground coriander
¼ teaspoon ground cumin
¼ cup (2 fl oz/60 ml) vegetable oil
4 medium potatoes (about 2 lb/900 g total), peeled, halved lengthwise, and cut into ½-inch (1.5 cm) slices
10 cloves garlic, finely chopped
2–4 green chilies (such as jalapeño or Anaheim), finely chopped
1 cup (8 fl oz/250 ml) chicken stock or water
White rice or bread, for serving

Trim the chicken of any straggly bits, then season with the lemon juice, olive oil, 1 teaspoon of the salt, the pepper, and all the spices (see Note). Set aside to marinate at room temperature while you cook the potatoes (or up to overnight in the refrigerator).

In a large Dutch oven (casserole), heat the vegetable oil over medium heat. When hot, add the potatoes in a single layer and fry until a nice golden brown, flipping once, 5–10 minutes on each side. Timing will depend on the potato variety, size of pot, and strength of heat. Transfer the fried potatoes to a plate lined with paper towels. Reserve the oil in the pot.

Set the same pot over medium-high heat. Add the chicken thighs in a single layer and fry until a nice golden brown, about 5 minutes on each side. With the chicken still in the pot, add the garlic and chilies and cook, stirring from time to time, for 1–2 minutes until fragrant.

Return the fried potatoes to the pot and pour in half the chicken stock. Bring to a boil, then reduce the heat and simmer with the lid slightly ajar. While simmering, very gradually add the remaining ½ cup (4 fl oz/120 ml) chicken stock. Continue to cook over low heat until cooked through, about 30 minutes.

Taste and add as much of the remaining 1 teaspoon salt as necessary. If you used water in place of stock, you will likely need to use all of it; otherwise, it will depend on the saltiness of the stock you use. Serve immediately with rice or bread.

Note: If you do not have the individual spices listed here, you can use 2 teaspoons Nine-Spice Mix (page 27), baharat, or Lebanese 7-spice blend.

All-Spice Chicken and Potatoes with Garlic and Green Chili Sauce

Cardamom Halaweh Oum Ali

Croissants are perfect all on their own. A croissant soaked in milk and cream then baked into a bread pudding, perhaps a bit more luxurious. But croissants mixed with dates, soaked in halaweh and cardamom-flavored milk, and topped with plenty of nuts? Well, even the word "royal" falls short for that. *Oum Ali* (it means "Ali's mother," but controversy surrounds the origins of the name) is an Egyptian version of bread pudding that forgoes the eggs entirely. Most cultures have some version of bread pudding, likely born of the need to use up stale bread. This nontraditional version uses French croissants instead of bread and flavors the custard with *halaweh* (halva)—an ancient Arab sweet first mentioned in the early tenth-century Arabic *Kitab al-Tabikh*—before topping the creamy concoction with nuts and baking. A truly decadent dessert, it is best served warm and eaten soon after preparation.

Serves 8–10 (can be halved)

- 6 all-butter croissants (about 12 oz/340 g), see Note
- 12 Medjool dates, pitted and chopped
- 3 cups (24 fl oz/750 ml) whole milk
- 1 cup (8 fl oz/250 ml) heavy (double) cream
- 4½ oz (125 g) halaweh (halva)
- ½–¾ cup (125–150 g) sugar, to taste (see Note)
- 1 teaspoon ground cardamom
- 1 teaspoon vanilla extract
- ½ cup (2 oz/55 g) pistachio pieces, lightly toasted
- 1 cup (3½ oz/100 g) sliced (flaked) almonds, lightly toasted

Preheat the oven to 400°F (200°C/Gas Mark 6).

Tear the croissants into large bite-size pieces and arrange in an approximately 10-inch (25 cm) round, oval, or square glass baking dish. Scatter the chopped dates evenly over the croissants.

In a blender, combine the milk, cream, *halaweh*, sugar, cardamom, and vanilla and blend until smooth and fully incorporated. Pour the milk mixture over the croissants and allow to sit for 5 minutes to absorb some of the liquid.

Sprinkle with the pistachios and almonds. Transfer to the oven and bake until it's puffed up and bubbling, and the peaks are a golden brown, 20–30 minutes.

Remove from the oven, leave to cool for about 10 minutes, and serve warm.

Notes: All-butter croissants, the ones you would buy from a coffee shop or bakery, are the best choice here. Buy them the day before you make this dessert and leave them out overnight to dry. If you can only get them the day of, halve them horizontally and lightly toast in the oven until starting to crisp. (Alternatively, you can bake puff pastry sheets at home until crisp and use once cool, or use stale brioche/challah, or in a pinch, even palmier cookies.)

The *halaweh* and dates add sweetness to this dish, so I usually opt for only ½ cup (100 g) sugar, but if you prefer your desserts sweeter, add a little more, but not more than ¾ cup (150 g).

Cardamom Halaweh Oum Ali

Date and Cardamom Coffee Tiramisu

The Italians can't agree on who invented this iconic dessert, but at least all non-Italians can agree it hails from The Boot. It is one of those dishes whose list of ingredients invariably begs the question: *How can something so simple taste so good?* And yet, it truly does. Savoiardi biscuits soaked in alcohol-spiked coffee, layered with cream, and dusted with cocoa somehow become much more than that in our mouths. I'm usually of the mindset, especially when it comes to such iconic dishes, "If it ain't broke, don't fix it." So this is in no way a better version of the classic. Rather, it is a variation of it that uses traditional Arabic cardamom coffee (because that's what we usually drink at home), adds a bit more texture to the cream with chopped dates, and tops it with bright green crushed pistachios instead of cocoa powder. It's indeed a pick-me-up dessert—Arabian style—not only for the coffee but for the vividness of the colors and flavors as well.

Serves 6–10

- 2 cups (16 fl oz/475 ml) freshly brewed strong dark coffee
- 2–4 tablespoons rum or Cognac, to taste
- ¼ teaspoon ground cardamom
- 16 oz (450 g) mascarpone cheese
- 1½ cups (12 fl oz/355 ml) heavy (double) cream
- ½ cup (3½ oz/100 g) sugar
- 1 teaspoon vanilla extract
- 1 cup (5 oz/150 g) pitted dates, finely chopped
- 10½ oz (300 g) ladyfingers (sponge fingers) or savoiardi (about 36)
- ½ cup (2½ oz/70 g) pistachios, finely ground

In a bowl, stir together the coffee and rum, using as little or as much as you like. Stir in the cardamom and set aside to cool as you prepare the remaining ingredients.

In a stand mixer fitted with the whisk (or in a large bowl with a hand mixer), combine the mascarpone, cream, sugar, and vanilla and whip on medium-high speed until the cream has thickened and the whisk leaves behind tracks that don't disappear, 2–3 minutes. Gently fold in the chopped dates until evenly combined and set aside.

To assemble the cake, briefly dip the ladyfingers (sponge fingers), one at a time, into the coffee mixture until just soaked but not soggy. Line the bottom of a 9 × 7-inch (23 × 18 cm) rectangular dish with two rows of 6 ladyfingers each. Spread one-third of the mascarpone/cream mixture over the ladyfingers. Repeat with a second layer of coffee-dipped ladyfingers and top with another third of the cream mixture. Repeat with the remaining ladyfingers and top with the final layer of remaining cream. Sprinkle with the crushed pistachios. Cover and refrigerate for at least 4 hours, or overnight before serving.

Note: I most often use a deep 6-cup (1.4-liter) glass dish that measures 9 × 7 inches (23 × 18 cm) and end up with exactly three layers. However, you can use a round 9- or 10-inch (23 or 25 cm) cake pan, individual serving bowls, or a larger square or rectangular dish for a thinner cake. If you plan to remove the cake from the dish it is assembled in to serve, line the dish with plastic wrap (clingfilm), leaving a 3-inch (7.5 cm) overhang on all sides. You can then invert a plate over the tiramisu, flip it and remove the wrap, then invert your serving platter and flip back, pistachio-side up, and serve.

Za'atar + Sumac

The least understood yet most recognized ingredient of the Middle East has to be za'atar. Za'atar has been a staple in Arab cuisine since the Middle Ages, and evidence points to it having been used as far back as Ancient Egypt. Contrary to what some may think, za'atar is not thyme or a mixture of different dried herbs and spices. Za'atar is an actual plant native to the Levant, most closely related to oregano. In season, it is foraged and the leaves picked and used in various ways. When I was a child, every spring my family would take trips to the mountains surrounding Jerusalem to pick za'atar leaves. We used some in salads and bread, then dried the rest for use throughout the year. The most recognized item sold as za'atar in the West is the condiment, traditionally made by drying the herb's leaves and then crushing and mixing them with sesame seeds and sumac to form a mixture enjoyed with bread and olive oil. But the leaves are also used fresh in salads or folded into pastries. Today, I also use za'atar as a way to add flavor to foods and give them an Arab flair like Za'atar and Halloumi Scones (page 151) or Za'atar Schnitzel (page 154).

Sumac, a component of the za'atar blend we have come to know and love in the West, has its own fascinating history. Prevalent in medieval Arabic cookbooks, there are entire sections dedicated to dishes made with either its juice or its powder. *Summaqiyat* is a whole category of stews made with sumac, but there are plenty of other dishes in which it is used to flavor chicken, lamb, and even pickles. Its uses today seem to have become less varied, although there are still a few places, like Gaza, where *sumaqiya* is one of the most recognized local dishes. Generally perceived as Middle Eastern, there are in fact many species of sumac that are native to North America where it was gathered and put to multiple uses by native Americans and continues to be foraged across the continent today.

Sumac is a flowering plant whose berries are used in cooking. They are dried, ground, and then sifted. The sifting is important because it gets rid of the inner seed, which is bitter, and leaves the skin, which is a beautiful crimson color with a sour flavor. What is sold in stores is at times not sifted, mixed with salt, or even worse, a combination of citric acid and food coloring. So the best advice I can give is to choose a trusted brand with no additional ingredients, or if you have access to the plant, pick and dry your own, then grind and sift.

Both za'atar and sumac are what I like to call "flavor makers" because they brighten up dishes and give them depth. This chapter includes numerous recipes featuring these ingredients—but take them as a blueprint. Za'atar can be used to flavor pastries and breads, but don't settle for the options I have given here. Experiment with your favorite loaf, or your preferred pastry for a new twist. Sumac can be used in place of lemon juice or pomegranate molasses or anytime you want something sour. Use it in salad dressings or to marinate chicken before grilling. The recipes here will, I hope, get you familiar with the flavor notes of these two magical ingredients. From there, what you can do with them is boundless.

Ka'ak Crackers with Za'atar and Nigella Seeds

Almost all cultures across the world can claim a cracker to their cuisine, from Italian *taralli* and Japanese *arare*, to Indian mathri, and Swedish *knäckebröd*. The Arab version is called *ka'ak*, although the word itself can mean anything from cakes to cookies to crackers and even breads. More often than not, however, *ka'ak* have a distinctive ring shape and their first recorded mention is in medieval Arabic cookbooks. In fact, those books are where the first record of bagel making—the distinct process of boiling bread before baking it—is referenced. Here I have opted for the more basic form, akin to crackers, but flavored with za'atar and nigella seeds. For an easier and faster process, I also roll them out and cut into triangles instead of shaping each individually. While the ingredients list might seem simple, the flavor is anything but.

Makes about 2 pounds (900 g)

- Generous 3 cups (14 oz/400 g) all-purpose (plain) flour
- Scant 1 cup (3½ oz/100 g) whole wheat (wholemeal) flour (or use more all-purpose)
- 4 tablespoons za'atar blend
- 2 tablespoons nigella seeds
- 2 tablespoons unhulled sesame seeds, lightly toasted
- 1 teaspoon salt
- 1 teaspoon baking powder
- 7 tablespoons (3½ fl oz/100 ml) olive oil
- 7 tablespoons (3½ fl oz/100 ml) vegetable oil

In a large bowl, combine both flours, the za'atar blend, both seeds, the salt, and baking powder and mix well. Add both oils and mix with your hands until the mixture resembles wet sand. Add most of ½ cup (4 fl oz/120 ml) water and knead until the dough comes together. Gradually add more water until you have a pliable dough. Set aside to rest for 15–20 minutes.

Preheat the oven to 350°F (180°C/Gas Mark 4).

Place the dough on a sheet of parchment paper and roll into a large square or rectangle roughly ⅛ inch (3 mm) thick.

Transfer the dough and parchment paper to a baking sheet (see Note). Use a knife or pizza cutter to cut the dough into small triangle, square, or diamond shapes or even strips—it's a matter of preference.

Transfer to the oven and bake until the crackers are a light golden brown, about 30 minutes. Timing may vary depending on size and thickness, so start checking at 25 minutes and don't hesitate to keep in longer if you prefer a darker finish. Remove from the oven and let cool for about 10 minutes before transferring to a wire rack to cool completely.

The crackers can be stored in an airtight container at room temperature for up to 3 weeks—if you can resist finishing them off before then!

Note: If your baking sheets are not large enough to accommodate the full quantity, you can divide the dough in half and bake on two sheets, switching racks and rotating the sheets front to back halfway through baking.

Za'atar Deviled Eggs

Stuffed eggs go as far back as Roman times, making their way to Andalusia by the thirteenth century, expanding all over Europe by the fifteenth century, and reaching the United States by the nineteenth. Called by different names from mimosa eggs to dressed eggs to deviled eggs, this interesting concoction seems to never have gained a strong foothold in the Arab world. But I've always loved eating boiled eggs with labaneh and za'atar, so I imagined they would make a wonderful combination in this classic dish, and indeed they do.

Makes 12 deviled eggs

6 hard-boiled eggs
4 tablespoons Greek yogurt (see Note)
2 teaspoons za'atar blend, plus more for garnish
2 tablespoons extra-virgin olive oil
Scant ½ teaspoon salt
Freshly ground black pepper

Peel the hard-boiled eggs and halve lengthwise. Scoop out the egg yolks and transfer to a bowl or the bowl of a mini food processor. Arrange the whites on a serving platter.

Add the yogurt, za'atar blend, oil, salt, and pepper to taste to the yolks. Either mash with a fork until fully mixed and smooth or process in the food processor into a smooth paste.

Using a spoon, fill the cavities of the egg whites with the yolk mixture. (Alternatively, for a prettier presentation, place the yolk filling in a piping bag fitted with a star or flower tip/nozzle and fill the whites.) Sprinkle each deviled egg with a pinch of za'atar and serve immediately.

Note: I use Greek yogurt in the recipe for consistency because store-bought labaneh can vary in saltiness and texture, but if you have a preferred labaneh brand you trust, you can substitute and slightly reduce the salt.

Za'atar and Halloumi Scones

Next to our house in London was a quaint little bakery that sold the most delicious scones—both savory and sweet. It also happened to be right next to the hospital where I gave birth, so I think I ate my weight in scones those first few days. A classic British food first referenced by a Scottish poet in the 1500s, it is no wonder the best scones I have ever eaten were from that bakery in London. One of my favorite flavors was chive and Cheddar, and while I still adore that classic combo, there is something entirely different and uniquely piquant about this za'atar and halloumi version. These scones are perfect with some fresh tomatoes and olives for breakfast, as a snack on their own, as a side to soups, or next to salads as I have them here. They also freeze very well; simply reheat in the oven before eating.

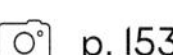

p. 153

Makes 12 scones

- 2¼ cups (9½ oz/270 g) all-purpose (plain) flour
- 1½ teaspoons baking powder
- 1 teaspoon salt
- 9 tablespoons (4½ oz/125 g) cold unsalted butter, cut into cubes
- 3 oz (85 g) feta cheese
- 3 oz (85 g) halloumi cheese, grated
- Small handful of fresh za'atar, thyme, or oregano leaves, or a combination, finely chopped (or in a pinch, 2 tablespoons za'atar blend)
- 3 eggs
- ½ cup (4fl oz/120 ml) whole milk

Preheat the oven to 350°F (180°C/Gas Mark 4). Line a baking sheet with parchment paper.

In a large bowl, combine the flour, baking powder, and salt. Tip in the cold cubes of butter and cut into the flour using a fork, pastry blender, or your fingertips until the mixture resembles oats but you can still see some pea-size flecks of butter.

Finely crumble the feta cheese. If the feta is too watery, set on paper towels for a few minutes after crumbling. Add the feta, grated halloumi, and za'atar to the flour and mix to combine.

In a separate bowl, whisk together the eggs and milk until fully combined and the mixture is a pale yellow and lightly frothy. (I often use a hand blender to do this quickly.) Pour the egg mixture over the flour and mix with a spatula until blended.

Using an ice cream scoop, drop heaping spoonfuls onto the lined baking sheet. You will end up with around 12 scones. Bake until golden brown around the edges but still soft in the center, 20–25 minutes. Serve immediately or transfer to a wire rack to cool before storing.

Scones are best eaten the day they are made.

Vegetable Salad with Sumac and Garlic Dressing

I once called my father from university complaining about a stupid question I was asked in an interview. "They wanted to know what salad ingredient I'd be," I cried to him in frustration over an interview system that left me baffled and dejected. "I would have said garlic," he replied, "It's the strongest and most noticeable flavor in any salad." His answer shocked me because I never thought of garlic as an ingredient in a salad, but when he said it, I realized how right he was (and I was annoyed to not have thought of the answer myself). How had this humble ingredient, which featured so prominently in my childhood salads, escaped me? The star of this salad is indeed the garlic dressing, but it draws inspiration from the various salads I grew up with: parsley from tabbouleh, radish and mixed greens from fattoush, tomatoes and scallions from farmers' salad, and the grated halloumi cheese reminiscent of the way I enjoyed it often next to fresh vegetables. Play around with whatever produce you have that's freshest, but do not compromise on the stars in the dressing—use fresh garlic and freshly squeezed lemon juice, and the best olive oil and sumac you can find.

Serves 4–6

For the dressing:

5 tablespoons extra-virgin olive oil
4 tablespoons fresh lemon juice
1 teaspoon pomegranate molasses
2 large cloves garlic, crushed in a garlic press
1½ teaspoons salt

For the salad:

4 oz (120 g) mixed greens or baby lettuces
1¾ oz (50 g) fresh parsley (about 1 large bunch), coarse stems removed, finely chopped
1 large tomato, cut into ¾-inch (2 cm) cubes
2 mini cucumbers, cut into ¾-inch (2 cm) cubes
1 orange or yellow bell pepper, cut into ¾-inch (2 cm) squares
4 or 5 radishes, halved and thinly sliced
5 oz (150 g) halloumi cheese, coarsely grated
2 teaspoons sumac

Make the dressing:
In a small screw-top jar, combine the olive oil, lemon juice, pomegranate molasses, garlic, and salt. Tightly seal and shake until fully combined and emulsified.

Prepare the salad:
In a very large bowl, combine the greens, parsley, tomato, cucumbers, bell pepper, and radishes and gently toss with your hands to combine.

Pour the dressing over the vegetables and lightly mix with your hands to evenly coat. Transfer to a serving bowl, top with the grated cheese, and sprinkle with the sumac.

Za'atar and Halloumi Scones (1) p. 151; Vegetable Salad with Sumac and Garlic Dressing (2)

Za'atar Schnitzel

It feels almost too clichéd to include za'atar fried chicken in this book and call it Arab, but give this dish a chance. I grew up hearing my mother tout the benefits of za'atar for intelligence, and to this day she checks in and asks if I've fed my daughters za'atar. In an ironic twist of fate, I'm a cookbook author whose daughters don't like food much. But I've found a way to get them to eat za'atar: I put it in their schnitzel! While this may be a very child-friendly dish, I challenge you to find an adult who won't want a plate for themselves, too. There's a reason, after all, that this dish of Austrian origin has a variation in most of the world's cuisines from Japanese *tonkatsu* and Persian *kotlet* to Colombian *chuleta* and South American *milanesa* (yes, borrowed from the Italians) to of course good ol' Southern fried chicken. The soy sauce may feel out of place to you, but it's actually not far-fetched. Medieval Arabs used to make a condiment called *murrì* from lumps of barley injected with mold spores, allowed to ferment for forty days, and then ground and mixed with water and salt before fermenting for another forty days. It tastes almost exactly like soy sauce and was often used to flavor meat dishes.

Serves 4

3 boneless, skinless chicken breasts (6–7 oz/170–200 g each)
1 teaspoon olive oil
1 teaspoon soy sauce
1 teaspoon fresh lemon juice
½ teaspoon finely crushed dried za'atar, oregano, or marjoram
½ teaspoon salt
¼ teaspoon garlic granules
A few twists of black pepper
Pinch of paprika
1 egg
1 heaping cup fine unseasoned breadcrumbs
1 tablespoon za'atar blend
Vegetable oil, for frying

Clean the chicken breasts of any gristle, fat, or sinew and cut each breast into 4 strips.

In a shallow bowl, combine the chicken, olive oil, soy sauce, lemon juice, za'atar leaves, salt, garlic granules, black pepper, and paprika. Toss to coat evenly. (This step can be done immediately before cooking or up to a day in advance and the chicken left to marinate in the mixture.)

To bread the chicken, crack the egg on top of the chicken and mix well to coat evenly. If this feels strange, it is, but it works perfectly and saves you dirtying another plate.

In another shallow bowl, spread the breadcrumbs and za'atar blend and stir to combine. Taking one piece of chicken at a time, dip the chicken into the breadcrumb mixture to coat. Turn it over and, with the palm of your hand, firmly pat the chicken to ensure the breadcrumb mixture sticks well. This patting also flattens the chicken to an even thickness. Repeat once or twice for each piece until fully coated. Continue until all the chicken pieces are done.

Line a plate with paper towels. Pour ¾ inch (2 cm) of vegetable oil into a large frying pan. Place over medium-high heat until a pinch of breadcrumbs bubbles up right away.

Working in batches to avoid overcrowding the pan, add pieces of chicken with enough room between them to make flipping easier. Cook until golden brown all over, 3–4 minutes on each side. Drain the chicken on the paper towels while you cook the remaining pieces.

Squid Shawarma with Sumac Onions and Amba Chili Tahini

Don't be deterred by the long ingredients list. This is a simple meal to prepare with ingredients, which if you cook Arabic food, are almost always on hand. It is not traditional, as shawarma is most often made with lamb or chicken, but I love making it with squid because it's quicker and healthier. The garnishes I suggest are discretionary, and you might choose to forgo all and just drizzle tahini on top. Or you could fill your sandwiches with a cabbage salad and sliced avocados or with Toum Sauce (page 32), tomatoes and pickles, or serve the squid alongside rice or potatoes instead. You could use pita bread and stuff it or flatbread and roll it. The variations are endless, but this kind of meal—a well-spiced protein stuffed into bread with flavorful garnishes—is a staple for us at home. Give it a try and you'll see why.

Serves 4

For the squid:
- 1 lb 2 oz (500 g) cleaned squid, tubes cut into rings (see Note)
- 2 tablespoons olive oil
- 1 tablespoon fresh lemon juice
- 1 teaspoon salt
- ½ teaspoon garlic granules
- ½ teaspoon mild curry powder (fenugreek, cumin, and coriander included)
- ½ teaspoon paprika (or hot chili)

For the sumac onions:
- 1 small red onion, sliced into thin half-moons
- 2 tablespoons finely chopped fresh parsley leaves
- 1 teaspoon sumac
- 1 teaspoon extra-virgin olive oil
- Pinch of salt

For the chopped salad:
- 3 tomatoes, finely chopped
- 2 mini cucumbers, finely chopped
- 1 small bell pepper, finely chopped
- 3 small cucumber pickles, finely chopped
- 1 tablespoon finely chopped fresh parsley leaves
- 1 tablespoon fresh lemon juice
- 1 tablespoon extra-virgin olive oil
- ½ teaspoon salt

For the amba chili tahini:
- Amba Tahini (page 24)
- ½ teaspoon Shattah Chili Paste (page 22), or more to taste
- Salt

For assembly:
- 2 tablespoons olive oil
- Pita bread or flatbread (homemade, page 30)

Prepare the squid:
In a medium bowl, combine the squid, olive oil, lemon juice, salt, garlic granules, and spices and gently mix until fully coated. Allow to sit in the refrigerator while you prepare the remaining elements.

Make the sumac onions:
In a bowl, stir together the onion, parsley, sumac, olive oil, and salt. Cover and set aside.

Prepare the chopped salad:
In a large bowl, toss together the tomatoes, cucumbers, bell pepper, pickles, parsley, lemon juice, and olive oil. Add the salt right before serving.

Make the amba chili tahini:
In a bowl, stir together the amba tahini and chili paste until evenly incorporated. If you prefer a runnier drizzling consistency, add water a tablespoon at a time and mix well until you reach the desired consistency. Taste and adjust salt and lemon to your liking.

To assemble:
In a large frying pan, heat the olive oil over high heat until shimmering. Add the squid and cook, tossing frequently, until opaque and cooked through, 2–3 minutes. Do not overcook to avoid making tough.

Remove from the heat and transfer to a plate. Serve with bread, the sumac onions, chopped salad, and amba chili tahini so each person can make their own sandwich.

Note: You can swap out the squid for a firm-fleshed white fish, such as tilapia, monkfish, mahi mahi, or halibut, sliced into thin strips. If you do, I recommend baking the fish rather than pan-frying to avoid breaking up the fish, which is more delicate. Simply preheat the oven to broil (grill), line a baking sheet with parchment paper, spread the fish in a single layer without crowding, and broil until opaque throughout and browned around the edges, about 10 minutes. Keep an eye on the fish because timing may vary considerably depending on the size of the strips, the kind of fish, the size of oven and the distance from the heat.

Squid Shawarma with Sumac Onions and Amba Chili Tahini

Msakhan Fatteh

Msakhan, a dish of *taboon* bread (a Palestinian clay oven bread) topped with slow-cooked onions, sumac, and roast chicken, is one of the most traditional and recognized dishes in the Palestinian kitchen. It's a labor of love, not only for the time it takes to prepare, but for the gathering it compels, with people often sitting communally around a large platter of *msakhan* tearing the bread apart with their hands. *Fatteh*, on the other hand, is a method of cooking common across the Middle East where stale bread is topped with various meats and dressings (see page 82, 160, and 212). So this recipe deconstructs the components of classic *msakhan* and puts them back together as a *fatteh*, resulting in a dish that is as delicious as the original but also more surprising and easier to eat. Always the first dish to disappear from my dinner party tables, this is one recipe worth coming back to time and time again.

Serves 4–6

3 large, thin Lebanese pita breads (about 3 oz/85 g each), cut into ¾-inch (2 cm) squares (about 4 cups), or flour tortilla wraps in a pinch

For the yogurt sauce:
1 lb 2oz (500 g) yogurt (regular, Greek, or a combination)
4 tablespoons fresh lemon juice
2 tablespoons tahini
1 large clove garlic, crushed in a garlic press
½ teaspoon fine salt

For the chicken and onions:
1½–2 lb (700–900 g) boneless, skinless chicken breasts (about 3)
1 tablespoon coarse sea salt
1 bay leaf
3–5 allspice berries
½ cup (4 fl oz/120 ml) olive oil
2¼ lb (1 kg) onions (about 3 very large), sliced into thin half-moons
1 tablespoon plus 1 teaspoon fine salt
3 tablespoons sumac
1 teaspoon ground cumin
½ teaspoon Nine-Spice Mix (page 27), baharat, or Lebanese 7-spice blend
6 tablespoons pine nuts, toasted or fried

For assembly:
2 tablespoons pine nuts, toasted
Very small handful of fresh parsley, finely chopped
Sumac
Extra-virgin olive oil, for drizzling

Preheat the oven to 350°F (180°C/Gas Mark 4).

Arrange the pita bread squares on a baking sheet. Bake until the squares are dry and crisp and starting to darken in color, moving them around with a wooden spoon from time to time, about 15 minutes. (This step can be done several days in advance and the pita chips stored in an airtight container or a zipseal plastic food bag.)

Make the yogurt sauce:
In a bowl, whisk together the yogurt, lemon juice, tahini, garlic, and salt until fully combined. Refrigerate until ready to assemble.

Prepare the chicken and onions:
In a large saucepan, combine the chicken, coarse salt, bay leaf, allspice berries, and water to cover. Bring to a bare simmer over medium heat, then reduce the heat to low and cook until the chicken is fully cooked and registers 165°F (74°C) on an instant-read thermometer, 15–20 minutes. Remove from the heat, discarding the broth, and wash any scum off the chicken breasts. Set the chicken aside, covered, until cool enough to handle. Once cooled, pull the chicken into very thin shreds.

Meanwhile, in a large frying pan, heat the olive oil, onions, and 1 tablespoon of the fine salt over medium-low heat. Cook, stirring periodically, until the onions have softened and cooked completely, 30–40 minutes. Toward the end, add in 2 tablespoons of the sumac, the cumin, and spice blend and stir to incorporate.

When the onions are fully cooked, add the shredded chicken, the remaining 1 tablespoon sumac, and 1 teaspoon fine salt and cook, stirring regularly, for another 3–5 minutes to meld the flavors. Add the pine nuts and toss to mix through.

To assemble:
Place the toasted bread at the bottom of a large serving platter with raised edges. Top the bread with the chicken and onion mixture. Pour the yogurt sauce evenly on top, smoothing out with a spoon if necessary. Sprinkle with the toasted pine nuts, parsley, sumac, and a drizzle of olive oil. Serve immediately to retain the crunchiness of the bread.

Caramelized Butternut Squash Fatteh with Za'atar

Fall in New England is beautiful, from the red and orange leaves dotting the horizon and the smell of cinnamon and nutmeg in the air to the gourds and pumpkins that pop up in markets and on windowsills. These fall crops, native to North America, provide a ray of warmth in a cold geography. While I've used pumpkins and squash in salads and stews, simply roasted, and even in desserts, my Arab roots rear their head every once in a while, and I can't resist making a *fatteh*. Probably born out of poverty as a way to bulk up meals and not let bread go to waste, *fatteh* relies on stale (now we use toasted) bread as a base for a variety of meats or vegetables topped with sauce and garnish. But even the wealthy used to eat this way as evidenced by the numerous dishes referenced in medieval Arab cookbooks called *thareed*, basically pieces of bread soaked in meat, vegetable, or legumes and their broth. This dish takes that classic concept but applies a seasonal and local twist to it.

Serves 4–6

9 oz (250 g) pita bread, cut into ¾-inch (2 cm) squares (about 4 cups)

For the butternut squash:
- 1 medium butternut squash (about 1¾ lb/750 g), peeled and cut into bite-size cubes (about 5 cups)
- 1 large red onion, cut into 16 wedges
- 3 tablespoons olive oil
- 1 teaspoon salt
- ¼ teaspoon freshly ground black pepper

For the yogurt sauce:
- 1⅓ cups (10½ oz/300 g) yogurt
- 3 tablespoons tahini
- 2–3 tablespoons fresh lemon juice, to taste
- 1 small clove garlic, crushed in a garlic press
- ¾ teaspoon salt

For serving:
- 1 tablespoon za'atar blend
- Aleppo pepper or crushed chili flakes, for sprinkling
- Pomegranate seeds, for garnish (optional)

Preheat the oven to 350°F (180°C/Gas Mark 4).

Arrange the pita bread squares on a baking sheet. Bake until the squares are completely dry and crisp and starting to darken in color, moving the bread around from time to time, about 15 minutes. Remove and set aside. (This step can be done a couple of days in advance and the pita chips stored in an airtight container or a zipseal plastic food bag.)

Roast the butternut squash:
If the oven is still on, increase the temperature to 450°F (230°C/Gas Mark 8); or preheat the oven. Line a baking sheet with parchment paper.

In a bowl, toss together the butternut squash, onion wedges, olive oil, salt, and pepper and spread on the baking sheet. Try to keep the onions hidden between the squash as they cook faster and you do not want them to burn. Roast for 30 minutes, moving the vegetables around once during cooking.

Meanwhile, make the yogurt sauce:
In a bowl, combine the yogurt, tahini, lemon juice, garlic, and salt and stir until smooth.

To serve:
Place the bread on a serving platter. Top with the roasted squash and onions and toss gently to distribute evenly. Pour the yogurt sauce on top and sprinkle with the za'atar blend, Aleppo pepper, and pomegranate seeds (if using). Serve immediately.

Caramelized Butternut Squash Fatteh with Za'atar

Grains + Pulses

Grains and pulses are the cornerstones of Arab cuisine. I think that more than any other ingredient, they recount the history of the region and of its people's connection to the land. From the earliest domesticates, one can see how intimately the people of the region relied on what the land had to offer and the meaning the land bore to its population past the sustenance it provided. People sowed the land and harvested it with their sweat and blood. In return, the land sustained generations throughout time. The land was, and remains, synonymous with culture and family history, an extension of identity and a symbol of life.

By the time my parents were old enough to remember, my family did not harvest its own wheat or legumes, but my grandparents had plenty of stories to recount. What remains alive in my memory is what we did with the land's bounty. In spring we picked green wheat, smoked it, then cracked it to make freekeh. The hard winter wheat berries we boiled until almost bursting, then sun-dried and cracked them to make bulgur. Multiple times throughout the year, my grandmother would coat the bulgur in wheat flour, rolling her hands around a giant wooden bowl until she had tiny pearls called *maftool*. Bread was prepared too often to recount.

Wheat has been harvested in the present-day Middle East since the dawn of history. That is why some of the oldest and most traditional recipes coming out of the region rely on wheat and its ensuing products. It wasn't until the time of Islamic rule over the region (around the tenth century) that rice cultivation became widely established, with the Arabs spreading its cultivation to Europe and the most far-flung outposts of the Islamic world, as far north as present-day Russia and as far south as East Africa. In the cookbooks *Kìtab al-Tabìkh* (tenth century) and *Kìtab al-Wusla ìla al-Habìb* (thirteenth century), you start to see rice featured in recipes, yet it was still not a staple food, but an ingredient reserved for the wealthy. This is not surprising given that cookbooks were historically records of foods eaten in palaces or commissioned by the wealthy to record specific dishes. That is why there is a saying in Arabic "*el ìz lal rìz*" or rice is for splendor. In fact, until just a few decades ago, rice was often consumed more in urban centers while wheat was the staple food of the countryside.

Legumes are also intricately woven into the fabric of human history and are as old as agriculture itself. Lentils are thought to be the oldest pulse crop known to man, with most varieties native to the Middle East or Central and East Asia. In spite of being one of the most nutritious ingredients in the Arab diet, lentils, and beans in general, are associated with poverty. Meat signals wealth and respect to guests. I still remember menu tasting for my wedding in the United States, when the wedding planner proudly brought out an elaborate fish dish served atop stewed lentils. My mother-in-law gawked at him, "We can't disrespect our guests; no lentils at the wedding!"

Although legume dishes were mostly born of necessity or poverty, they are still some of the Middle East's most loved and recognized meals, and in my opinion, some of its most delicious ones. They are definitely among its healthiest. This chapter explores some of the Middle East's classics in new renditions. From Split Pea Falafel (page 185) and Vegetarian Kubbeh Niyeh (page 164) to Maftool Salad (page 168), the dishes here herald back to the Middle East's ancient history but give a glimpse of an exciting and evolving culinary future.

Vegetarian Kubbeh Niyeh

Although Christianity originated in the Middle East, today it accounts for only 5 percent of the Arab world's population. Lent, a forty-day period of fasting before Easter, is one of the reasons there are vegetarian takes on classic nonvegetarian dishes in our kitchens, and Christians and Muslims alike often refer to them as *siyamì*, which means "fasting" or Lenten dishes. This vegetarian take on *kubbeh nìyeh* (a bulgur and lamb tartare) is called by other names as well—such as "widow's kubbeh" or "trickster kubbeh" or "fake kubbeh"—all of which hark back to the conditions of poverty and shortage of meat that also gave rise to vegetarian meals across the Middle East. It's perfect on its own as part of a spread, but I also love to roll bites of it in lettuce leaves.

Serves 4–6 as part of a spread

- 1 cup (6 oz/175 g) very fine (#1) bulgur
- 1 cup (250 ml) very hot water
- 1 medium tomato, halved
- 1 medium onion, halved
- 1 tablespoon pomegranate molasses
- 1 tablespoon tomato paste (purée)
- 1 tablespoon paprika
- 1 teaspoon salt
- ½ teaspoon ground cumin
- ¼ teaspoon freshly ground black pepper
- 1 green or red chili, finely chopped (optional)
- ½ cup (1 oz/25 g) coarsely ground lightly toasted walnuts
- ¼ cup (60 ml) extra-virgin olive oil, plus more (optional) for drizzling
- 2 tablespoons finely chopped fresh parsley
- 1 teaspoon dried ground mint, or 1 tablespoon finely chopped fresh mint leaves, plus fresh leaves for garnish
- Lettuce leaves, for serving (optional)

In a large bowl, combine the bulgur and hot water, wait until fully absorbed, then set aside or refrigerate until completely cooled.

In a food processor, combine the tomato, onion, pomegranate molasses, tomato paste (purée), paprika, salt, cumin, and black pepper and process until smooth. Add this mixture to the bulgur, mix well, then set aside for 5–10 minutes for the bulgur to absorb most of the liquid from the mixture. Knead well with your hands until it comes together in a paste-like consistency. Taste to see if the bulgur is still more than al dente, and if it is, add a tablespoon of water, mix well and set aside for another 5–10 minutes, then knead again. You want to feel the texture of the bulgur in your mouth, but you do not want the wheat to feel hard or dry. You will probably have to knead the bulgur for a total of 5–10 minutes.

Once you reach the desired consistency, add the chopped chili (if using), walnuts, olive oil, parsley, and mint and mix to combine.

To serve, spoon the mixture into a serving bowl or onto a platter, arranging as desired; drizzle with more olive oil if desired and garnish with fresh mint leaves. (Alternatively, spoon portions of it into lettuce leaves, arrange on a platter, and serve.)

Lentil Bulgur Salad with Marinated Beet

Overlooking the shores of the sea of Galilee, where the ancient city of Magdala once stood, now stands Magdalena, a restaurant named for the ancient city and birthplace of Mary Magdalene. Yousef Hanna, or "Zuzu" as he's commonly known to his friends, a Palestinian from the small Galilean town of Rameh, opened Magdalena half a decade ago. It was his fourth restaurant, but the first to stray from traditional Arabic food and venture into contemporary, upscale cooking that pairs traditional Palestinian recipes with modern techniques and cosmopolitan inspiration. This salad is similar to one I had at his restaurant soon after it opened, and the flavors are still fresh in my mind five years later. It takes inspiration from two Arab classics, tabbouleh and *mjadarah*, and pairs them with the contrasting zing of pickled beets and crunch of toasted nuts.

Serves 4–6

½ cup (3 oz/90 g) medium-grain (#2) bulgur
½ cup (120 ml) hot water
1½ cups (12 oz/340 g) beluga lentils (or French green/Puy or brown lentils)
½ cup (120 ml) fresh lemon juice
5 tablespoons extra-virgin olive oil
3 tablespoons good-quality pomegranate molasses
1 tablespoon honey (omit if there is sugar in your pomegranate molasses)
2 teaspoons salt
½ teaspoon sugar
¼ teaspoon freshly ground black pepper
1 medium beet (about 9 oz/250 g), peeled and cut into very thin matchsticks or coarsely grated
1 cup (2 oz/50 g) finely chopped fresh flat-leaf parsley
4 scallions (spring onions), thinly sliced
½ cup (1½ oz/50 g) coarsely chopped lightly toasted walnut pieces
¼ cup (1½ oz/50 g) pine nuts, lightly toasted

In a large bowl, combine the bulgur and hot water and allow to soak while you prepare the rest of the salad.

In a saucepan, combine the lentils with plenty of water. Set over medium heat and bring to a boil. Reduce the heat, cover, and simmer gently until the lentils are almost done but still have a little bite, 15–20 minutes. Remove from the heat, drain, and set aside to cool.

Meanwhile, in a medium bowl, mix together the lemon juice, olive oil, pomegranate molasses, honey (if using), salt, sugar, and pepper. Add the beet, toss to combine, and set aside for at least 10 minutes to marinate.

To assemble, add the lentils to the bulgur and toss gently. Pour the beet and its soaking liquid over the lentils and bulgur. Add the parsley, scallions (spring onions), walnuts, and pine nuts and toss to combine. It can be served immediately but is best after a couple of hours so all the flavors to meld.

Lentil Bulgur Salad with Marinated Beet

Maftool Salad with Preserved Lemon, Pistachios, and Currants

Maftool means "rolled" in Arabic and refers to the way flour is rolled around small bulgur grains to arrive at these beautiful caviar-size pearls of wheat. It is a perfect pairing with chickpeas, usually served alongside a delicately sweet butternut squash and onion chicken stew. As much as I love that traditional Palestinian dish, the summer months call for something lighter and more refreshing. That's where the idea for this salad came from. Brightened up with fresh herbs and preserved lemon, it feels nutritious and filling without weighing you down. If you can't find *maftool*, *fregola sarda* is the closest substitute for taste and texture, but giant/pearled couscous could also work in a pinch.

Serves 4

For the maftool:
2 tablespoons olive oil
1 cup (6 oz/170 g) maftool
1 teaspoon salt
1 can (14 oz/400 g) chickpeas, rinsed and drained

For the dressing:
1 cup (20 g) packed fresh parsley and cilantro (coriander) leaves and tender stems
1 tablespoon finely minced preserved lemon rind
3 tablespoons fresh lemon juice
1 tablespoon extra-virgin olive oil
½ teaspoon salt
¼ teaspoon freshly ground black pepper
1 teaspoon Aleppo pepper or crushed chili flakes
1 teaspoon crushed dried mint
½ teaspoon ground cumin

For assembly:
¼ cup (1¼ oz/35 g) pistachios, walnut pieces, or slivered almonds, toasted
¼ cup (1 oz/28 g) dried currants, dried cranberries, or raisins

Cook the maftool:
In a medium pot, heat the olive oil over medium heat. Add the *maftool*, tossing to coat, and stir for about 5 minutes to lightly toast. Add 1 cup (8 fl oz/250 ml) water and the salt, cover, and bring to a simmer. Reduce the heat and continue to cook, stirring periodically, until the *maftool* is tender, 15–20 minutes. The cooking time and liquid may vary depending on the brand of *maftool*, so check regularly. If the liquid is entirely evaporated and the *maftool* still has a bite, add a couple tablespoons of water at a time and continue to cook. Remove from the heat, add the drained chickpeas, and set aside to cool.

Meanwhile, make the dressing:
In a small blender or food processor, combine the fresh herbs, preserved lemon rind, lemon juice, 1 tablespoon water, the olive oil, salt, black pepper, Aleppo pepper, mint, and cumin and process until finely minced and combined.

To assemble:
Once the *maftool* is cool, pour the dressing and half of the pistachios and currants on top and toss to combine. Transfer to a platter, garnish with remaining pistachios and currants, and serve. The salad will keep in the refrigerator for a couple days.

Maftool Salad with Preserved Lemon, Pistachios, and Currants

Lentil and Vegetable Soup with Preserved Lemon

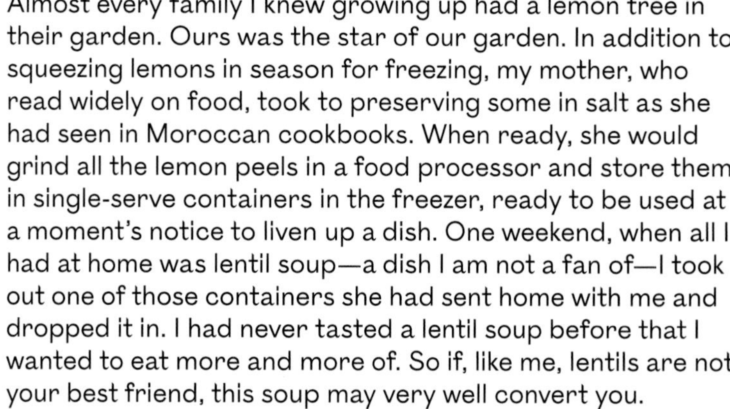

Almost every family I knew growing up had a lemon tree in their garden. Ours was the star of our garden. In addition to squeezing lemons in season for freezing, my mother, who read widely on food, took to preserving some in salt as she had seen in Moroccan cookbooks. When ready, she would grind all the lemon peels in a food processor and store them in single-serve containers in the freezer, ready to be used at a moment's notice to liven up a dish. One weekend, when all I had at home was lentil soup—a dish I am not a fan of—I took out one of those containers she had sent home with me and dropped it in. I had never tasted a lentil soup before that I wanted to eat more and more of. So if, like me, lentils are not your best friend, this soup may very well convert you.

Serves 6–8

- 2 tablespoons olive oil
- 1 onion, finely chopped
- 3 medium carrots, finely chopped
- 4 stalks celery, finely chopped
- 4 cloves garlic, minced
- 1½ teaspoons salt, plus more to taste
- ½ teaspoon ground cumin
- ¼ teaspoon freshly ground black pepper
- 8 oz (225 g) beluga or French green (Puy) lentils (a generous 1 cup), picked over and rinsed
- 1½ cups (about 2½ oz/70 g) packed fresh spinach or chard, chopped
- 2 tablespoons fresh lemon juice
- 2 tablespoons finely minced preserved lemon rind (see Note)
- 1 tablespoon Shattah Chili Paste (page 22) or harissa (optional)

In a Dutch oven (casserole), heat the olive oil over medium-high heat. Add the onion, carrots, and celery and cook, stirring regularly, until the vegetables have softened and started to brown around the edges, 6–8 minutes. Add the garlic, salt, cumin, and pepper and cook until the garlic is fragrant but not browned, another 2–3 minutes.

Pour in 5 cups (40 fl oz/1.25 liters) water and deglaze any bits stuck to the bottom of the pot. Add the lentils, stir to combine, and bring to a boil. Reduce the heat and simmer vigorously until the lentils are tender but still hold their shape, 20–30 minutes depending on the variety.

Stir in the chopped spinach and cook for another minute or so to wilt the leaves. Add the lemon juice, preserved lemon, and chili paste (if using). Stir to combine, taste and adjust salt to your liking. (I usually end up adding another ½ teaspoon or so.) Remove from the heat and serve.

Note: The most flavorful part of preserved citrus is the rind. What I generally do at home is pick a variety of lemon with a thick rind, and once it has been preserved and is ready for consumption, I discard the flesh and seeds, grind the rind in a food processor, and store in ice cube trays in the freezer.

Lentil and Vegetable Soup with Preserved Lemon

Kubbeh Dumpling and Chickpea Soup in Roast Chicken Broth

This is the dish we always eat the day following a roast chicken dinner. I make the most delicious stock with the roasted bones and leftover chicken and then turn it into a full meal with kubbeh dumplings and chickpeas. The kubbeh dumplings are meatless and in Arabic are often referred to as "trickster kubbeh" because they look like normal kubbeh but have no meat. Although I make this with roast chicken broth, you could skip that step and use any chicken or vegetable stock you prefer. What really imparts the flavor to this dish is the finishing with onions, paprika, and coriander (or with garlic, mint, and lemon; see Note).

p. 174

Serves 4–6

For the chicken:
1 tablespoon olive oil
2 teaspoons fresh lemon juice
1 teaspoon soy sauce
2 teaspoons fine salt
1 teaspoon garlic granules
1 teaspoon paprika
1 teaspoon Nine-Spice Mix (page 27), baharat, or Lebanese 7-spice blend
1 teaspoon sumac
1 teaspoon dried za'atar leaves or oregano, finely crushed
1 whole chicken, or 3 lb (1.5 kg) chicken backs, necks, and wings, or leftover bones and skin from a raw chicken carcass
1 small onion
1 carrot
2 cloves garlic, peeled
2 bay leaves
1 tablespoon coarse sea salt

For the kubbeh dumplings:
1 cup (6 oz/175 g) very fine (#1) bulgur
1 cup (8 fl oz/250 ml) very hot water
½ cup (3 oz/85 g) fine semolina
Scant 1 teaspoon fine salt
½ teaspoon tomato paste (purée)
½ teaspoon ground cumin
½ teaspoon paprika
¼ teaspoon freshly ground black pepper

For the soup:
1 can (14 oz/400 g) chickpeas, drained and rinsed
1 tablespoon olive oil
1 small onion, finely chopped
1½ teaspoons paprika
1½ teaspoons ground coriander

Prepare the chicken:
In a small bowl, combine the olive oil, lemon juice, soy sauce, fine salt, garlic granules, paprika, spice blend, sumac, and za'atar leaves and mix into a paste. Rub all over the whole chicken or chicken pieces.

Preheat the oven to 425°F (220°C/Gas Mark 7). Line a roasting pan with parchment paper.

Put the chicken in the pan, transfer to the oven, and roast until cooked through and the skin is crisped to your liking, about 1 hour. (If roasting a whole chicken, serve as desired, reserving all the skin, bones, and any leftover meat for the stock.)

In a large stockpot, combine all the roast chicken pieces, the onion, carrot, garlic, bay leaves, and coarse salt. Add 12 cups (3 quarts/liters) water and bring to a boil over high heat. Reduce the heat and simmer for at least 4 hours and up to 8. Strain through a fine-mesh or cloth-lined sieve and reserve until ready to use.

Make the kubbeh dumplings:
In a large heatproof bowl, combine the bulgur and water and mix. Set aside until the bulgur has absorbed the water and cooled, 10–15 minutes.

Add the semolina, fine salt, tomato paste (purée), cumin, paprika, and pepper and knead with your hands until you have a pliable dough that can be shaped without falling apart. Shape the dough into balls about the size of a small cherry. You should end up with 70–75 balls.

Make the soup:
In a soup pot, bring 9 cups (72 fl oz/2.25 liters) of the roast chicken broth to a gentle boil. Carefully drop in the kubbeh dumplings, add the chickpeas, and simmer until the kubbeh is cooked through and the soup has lightly thickened, about 10 minutes.

Meanwhile, in a frying pan, heat the olive oil over medium-high heat. Add the onion and fry, stirring regularly, until starting to brown around the edges, 3–5 minutes. Add the paprika and coriander and stir to combine.

Pour the pan contents over the soup and simmer 1–2 minutes to meld the flavors. Taste, adjust the seasoning if necessary, and serve.

Note: If you choose to finish the dish with garlic instead of onion, fry 4–6 cloves garlic in 1 tablespoon olive oil until fragrant but not browned, 1–2 minutes. Add 1 tablespoon crushed dried mint leaves and fry for 30 seconds, then put the entire contents into the soup. Add ¼ cup (60 ml) fresh lemon juice and serve.

Kubbeh Burgers with Labaneh and Tomato Relish

One of the most recognized dishes across the Levant, kubbeh comes in countless versions. From raw, stuffed, baked, and fried, to stewed, grilled, and poached in different broths, there are estimates of over sixty distinct kubbeh varieties in Aleppo alone. Growing up, we made only a few varieties at home with *kubbeh nìyeh* (a tartare, basically) being my father's favorite. Whatever was left over the next day my mother shaped into small patties and shallow-fried for the most delicious lunch. I often make them from scratch at home, and my daughters always call them hamburgers when I do, so the name stuck. We eat them without burger buns—the bulgur offers just the right amount of crunch and heft to not need bread—but we do lather them with labaneh and top with a homemade tomato relish for a truly unique "burger" experience.

---

p. 175

Serves 4–6

For the kubbeh:
- 10 oz (300 g) lean cut of beef, such as top round (topside), flank, or sirloin,
- 1¾ cups (9 oz/300 g) fine-grain (#1) bulgur
- 1¾ cups (14 fl oz/420 ml) hot water
- 1 small onion, halved
- 1½ teaspoons salt
- ½ teaspoon Nine-Spice Mix (page 27), baharat, or Lebanese 7-spice blend
- ½ teaspoon ground cumin
- 1 small sprig fresh marjoram, thyme, basil, or oregano, leaves picked (optional)
- ¼ teaspoon grated unwaxed or organic lemon zest (optional)

For the tomato relish:
- 10 oz/300 g (about 2 large or 3 medium) seasonal or heirloom tomatoes, very finely diced
- 1 green chili, seeded and finely chopped
- 3 sprigs fresh mint, leaves picked and finely chopped
- 1 clove garlic, crushed in a garlic press
- 1 tablespoon extra-virgin olive oil
- 1 tablespoon fresh lemon juice
- ½ teaspoon sumac
- ¼ teaspoon salt

For assembly:
- Vegetable oil, for shallow-frying
- Labaneh, preferably homemade (page 40), for serving

Prepare the kubbeh:
Clean the meat of any fat, sinew, or gristle. Cut into large cubes and place in the freezer to cool and firm up, about 1 hour. This makes processing the meat into a paste much easier. (Alternatively, if you have a very powerful food processor, you can forgo this step and add 1–2 ice cubes while processing the meat.)

Meanwhile, in a large bowl, combine the bulgur and hot water. Stir, then set aside until the bulgur has absorbed the liquid and cooled completely, about 1 hour.

In a food processor, combine the onion, salt, spice blend, cumin, herbs (if using), and lemon zest (if using) and process until finely ground. Add the meat and pulse until it's evenly combined and resembles a smooth paste. Tip the mixture into the large bowl of bulgur and knead until everything is evenly combined. The mixture can be refrigerated up to 1 day or used immediately.

Prepare the tomato relish:
In a bowl, gently stir together the tomatoes, chili, mint, garlic, olive oil, lemon juice, sumac, and salt. Set aside.

To assemble:
Scoop out portions of kubbeh the size of a golf ball and flatten into patties. You should end up with somewhere between 20 and 30 patties. Place on parchment paper until you are done with the entire mixture.

Line a plate with paper towels. Pour ¾ inch (2 cm) oil into a large frying pan and heat over medium heat until a drop of the kubbeh mixture bubbles up right away. Add several patties to the pan, leaving enough room between them to make flipping easier and cook until golden brown on both sides, about 2 minutes per side. Transfer the fried kubbeh to the paper towels to drain.

Kubbeh patties can be served hot, warm, or at room temperature. To serve, spread a dollop of labaneh on each patty and top with a spoonful of the tomato relish.

Kubbeh Dumpling and Chickpea Soup in Roast Chicken Broth

Kubbeh Burgers with Labaneh and Tomato Relish

Freekeh with Radish Green Pesto

In a culture heavily reliant on agriculture, rarely does part of a plant go to waste. When squash is cored for stuffing, the insides are sautéed with onions and spices. When cabbage is blanched for rolling, leftover leaves are turned into salad. When Swiss chard is stuffed, discarded stalks are mixed with tahini for a healthy spread. Radishes are no exception and their leafy green tops are often used in falafel mixes (see Split Pea Falafel, page 185) or combined with labaneh as a dip. I took a different path using the greens to make pesto. Rather than mixing the pesto with pasta, I folded it with one of the Arab world's most traditional grains—freekeh. The combination of smoky freekeh and this fresh, sharp pesto was sublime. I serve this dish family-style, but you could also serve it in individual bowls and have each person add as much or as little pesto as they like. If you can't find radish greens, you could replace with watercress or arugula (rocket). In a pinch, traditional basil pesto will do.

Serves 4–6

For the pesto:

- 1 clove garlic, peeled
- 4 tablespoons grated Parmesan cheese
- 3 tablespoons pistachios, lightly toasted
- ½ teaspoon salt
- 2½ oz (75 g) radish tops (from about 1 small bunch)
- Grated zest and juice of ½ lemon
- ⅓ cup (2⅔ fl oz/80 ml) light, fruity extra-virgin olive oil (or any olive oil whose taste you like, because the flavor here will be quite pronounced)

For the freekeh:

- 2 tablespoons (1 oz/30 g) unsalted butter or ghee
- 2 tablespoons olive oil
- 1 large onion, finely diced
- 1 teaspoon salt
- 2 teaspoons Nine-Spice Mix (page 27), baharat, or Lebanese 7-spice blend
- ½ teaspoon ground cumin
- 1 lb (450 g) freekeh
- 4 cups (32 fl oz/1 liter) chicken or vegetable stock, homemade or store-bought

For serving:

- Greek yogurt (optional)
- ⅓ cup (1¼ oz/35 g) pine nuts or slivered almonds, lightly toasted

Make the pesto:

In a mini food processor, combine the garlic, Parmesan, pistachios, salt, radish tops, lemon zest, and lemon juice and process until combined. Add the olive oil and process, adding a little more oil if necessary, until you have a smooth paste. Transfer to a bowl and cover with plastic wrap (clingfilm) touching the top until ready to use.

Make the freekeh:

In a large pot or Dutch oven (casserole), heat the butter and oil over medium heat. When shimmering, add the onion, salt, spice blend, and cumin; reduce the heat, and cook, stirring occasionally, until the onion has softened and is just starting to brown, 6–8 minutes. Add the freekeh and mix with a wooden spoon until well combined. Continue to cook, stirring occasionally, until lightly toasted and you can smell its nutty aroma, another 4–5 minutes.

Pour in the stock, give it one final stir, and bring to a boil. Reduce the heat, cover, and simmer gently over low heat, 35–45 minutes. Check on the freekeh from time to time, stir to make sure it is not sticking to the bottom, and add water as necessary. If the freekeh is still too al dente, add some more water and continue to cook over low heat until it is fully cooked. It does not need to be as soft as rice, but it should not feel like uncooked grains either. The consistency of cooked pearl barley is ideal. Taste and adjust the seasoning (this will depend on how salty the stock you are using is). Remove from the heat and place a large paper towel or thin tea towel between the pot and its lid (this will absorb any rising steam) and allow to sit covered for about 15 minutes.

Add about half the pesto to the freekeh and toss to combine. Taste and add more pesto to your liking. Any leftover pesto can be stored in an airtight container in the refrigerator for a couple of days or inthe freezer for several weeks.

To serve:

Transfer the freekeh to a large serving platter. If desired, place dollops of Greek yogurt on top and smidgens of pesto on the yogurt. Sprinkle with the toasted pine nuts and serve.

Freekeh with Radish Green Pesto

Rice-Stuffed Cabbage Pie

Long gone are the unhurried days of my childhood where I sat with my mother and aunts coring, rolling, stuffing, and cooking big pots of stuffed vegetables. As much as I miss those delicious dishes, it is the amity of that companionship I truly crave. So I rarely sit by myself at home and spend two hours wrapping a pot of grape or cabbage leaves—I wax nostalgic. That's why one morning, during a routine call when my mother asked what I would be cooking, I said, "I miss *malfoof* (stuffed cabbage), but I'm too tired to deal with it now." She told me the story of one of her best friends, Nadia, who on a trip to visit her son in France ended up layering the cabbage and rice in a tray instead of rolling it to save some time. "Why don't you try it?" she offered. So I ended up with this showstopper that tastes just as good as it looks with far less effort than the original dish.

Serves 4

- Generous 1 cup (8oz/225 g) short-grain rice
- Coarse sea salt
- 1 small to medium head green cabbage (about 2¼ lb/1 kg)
- 1 tablespoon olive oil, plus more for greasing
- 1 tablespoon (15 g) ghee or unsalted butter
- 1½ teaspoons fine salt
- 1 teaspoon Nine-Spice Mix (page 27), baharat, or Lebanese 7-spice blend
- 1 teaspoon ground cumin
- 2 cloves garlic, crushed in a garlic press
- 1 teaspoon tomato paste (purée)
- ½ lb (225 g) coarsely ground (minced) beef or lamb or a combination
- 1–1½ cups (240–355 ml) chicken or beef stock or water
- 2–3 lemons, cut into wedges
- Shattah Chili Paste (page 22) or crushed chili flakes (optional)

Rinse the rice until the water runs clear. Set aside in a bowl with water to cover and soak for 15–30 minutes, then drain and set aside.

Meanwhile, half-fill a pot (wide enough to hold the entire cabbage) with water, add 1 tablespoon of coarse salt for every 4 cups (1 liter) water, and bring to a boil. With the tip of a sharp knife, make an incision around the stem of the cabbage and pull out the core. Carefully slide the entire cabbage into the pot of boiling water. After a couple of minutes, as the leaves start to soften, use metal tongs to pull out one leaf at a time and set aside on a large platter until you are left with only the center. Remove and set everything aside.

In a large bowl, combine the drained rice, olive oil, ghee, fine salt, spice blend, cumin, garlic, and tomato paste (purée). Add the meat and mix with your hands until everything is well incorporated.

Preheat the oven to 400°F (200°C/Gas Mark 6). Grease a 3-inch-(7 cm) deep 8–9-inch (20–23 cm) round nonstick cake pan with olive oil. (Do not use a springform pan as water will leak out.)

Use the largest cabbage leaves you have, cutting and discarding any tough midribs, to line the bottom of the pan, leaving half of each leaf as an overhang. Place more leaves in the center to have an even and sturdy layer of cabbage leaves.

Add the rice and meat mixture evenly over the leaves. Cover with a few more leaves then fold the overhanging cabbage on top to cover.

Mix the stock with tomato paste; if you are using water, add ½ teaspoon salt and stir to dissolve. Taste and adjust the seasoning if necessary. With the tip of a sharp knife, make a few deep incisions into the top layer of cabbage to help the liquid penetrate the pie and cook the rice. Gently pour the stock over the cabbage until it almost reaches the top but the cabbage is not fully submerged.

Cover the pan tightly with a layer of aluminum foil. Transfer to the oven and bake until the water has evaporated and the edges, if you peek, are just starting to brown, 1 hour 10 to 1 hour 20 minutes. Remove from the oven and set aside for 10 minutes to rest.

To serve, remove the foil, place an inverted plate on the pan and flip over, lifting the cake pan to reveal a beautiful cake-shaped stuffed cabbage. Serve with plenty of lemon and chili paste (if using).

Ouzi Rice with Lamb, Peas, and Carrots

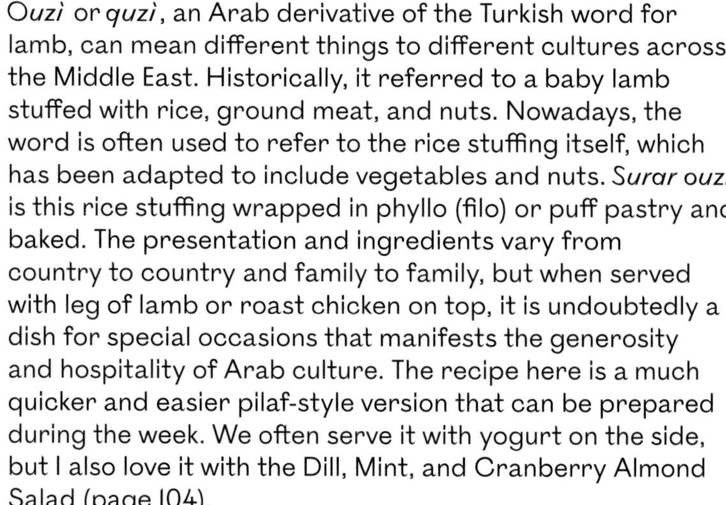

Ouzi or *quzi*, an Arab derivative of the Turkish word for lamb, can mean different things to different cultures across the Middle East. Historically, it referred to a baby lamb stuffed with rice, ground meat, and nuts. Nowadays, the word is often used to refer to the rice stuffing itself, which has been adapted to include vegetables and nuts. *Surar ouzi* is this rice stuffing wrapped in phyllo (filo) or puff pastry and baked. The presentation and ingredients vary from country to country and family to family, but when served with leg of lamb or roast chicken on top, it is undoubtedly a dish for special occasions that manifests the generosity and hospitality of Arab culture. The recipe here is a much quicker and easier pilaf-style version that can be prepared during the week. We often serve it with yogurt on the side, but I also love it with the Dill, Mint, and Cranberry Almond Salad (page 104).

Serves 6–8

For the meat:
2 tablespoons olive oil
2 tablespoons (30 g) ghee or unsalted butter
1 onion, finely diced
1 lb 2 oz (500 g) ground (minced) lamb, beef, or a combination
1 teaspoon Nine-Spice Mix (page 27), baharat, or Lebanese 7-spice blend
1 teaspoon salt
2 cups (10½ oz/300 g) frozen peas and carrots

For the rice:
2¼ cups (1 lb 2 oz/500 g) basmati rice, washed until the water runs clear, soaked for 15 minutes, and drained
4 cups (1 quart/1 liter) unsalted chicken stock (see Note)
1 tablespoon salt
½ teaspoon ground turmeric
½ teaspoon Nine-Spice Mix (page 27), baharat, or Lebanese 7-spice blend
1 cup (4 oz/110 g) slivered almonds and/or pine nuts, toasted or fried
Yogurt, for serving

Prepare the meat:
In a large frying pan, heat the olive oil and ghee over medium heat. Add the onion and cook, stirring occasionally, until translucent and starting to brown, 5–7 minutes. Add the meat, spice blend, and salt and cook, breaking up any lumps with a wooden spoon, until the water has evaporated and the meat is nicely browned, 10–12 minutes. Remove from the heat, add the peas and carrots, and set aside.

Make the rice:
In a large pot, combine the drained rice, stock, salt (see Note), turmeric, and spice blend and bring to a boil. Reduce to a lively simmer, cover, and cook for 5 minutes.

Add the meat and vegetable mixture to the rice, give it a good mix, and taste for seasoning. Cook until the rice is soft but firm to the bite and not so overcooked that it all sticks together, another 10–12 minutes. Check on it once or twice, and if the liquid evaporates entirely before the rice is cooked, add a few tablespoons of water. As a test, when you remove it from the heat, you should still be able to easily stir the rice with a spoon.

Remove from the heat, uncover, and place a thin tea towel over the pot, then securely close the lid again and allow to sit for 15 minutes.

To serve, uncover the pot and fluff the rice up with a large fork, then transfer to a serving platter and top with the toasted almonds. Serve with yogurt on the side.

Note: If your stock already has salt, start with 1 teaspoon salt on the rice, then taste as it cooks and add more to your liking.

Ouzi Rice with Lamb, Peas, and Carrots

Shrimp Sayadiyeh with Tomato Dill Tahini

"El ìz lal rìz" is a common saying across the Levant translating roughly to "rice is for the wealthy." Historically, rice was an expensive grain consumed only by the upper echelons of society, with everyone else relying on more accessible wheat grains and their products, such as freekeh, bulgur, and *maftool*. Today, it is one of the most prevalent ingredients across the region, and many traditional dishes, like the fish and rice *sayadìyeh*, are based on it. Here I take *sayadìyeh* back to the humble roots I imagine it could have had, and use bulgur instead of rice. I substitute shrimp (prawns) and shellfish stock for traditional fish because I find the sweet flavor complements the bulgur better. The list of ingredients might seem long, but it's quite simple, with many of the same ingredients used in different preparations. To make it faster, you could use store-bought seafood stock (see Note).

Serves 4–6

For the stock:
- 1½ lb (700 g) shellfish and fish heads or bones (see Note)
- 2 tablespoons olive oil
- 1 small bulb fennel, fronds removed, bulb and stalks roughly chopped
- 1 carrot, roughly chopped
- 1 onion, roughly chopped
- ½ teaspoon tomato paste (purée)
- 1 tablespoon arak, ouzo, Pernod (or water for alcohol-free version)
- 1 tablespoon allspice berries
- 1 tablespoon coriander seeds
- 1 teaspoon cumin seeds
- 1 teaspoon black peppercorns
- 1 tablespoon salt

For the bulgur:
- ⅓ cup (2½ fl oz/80 ml) olive oil
- 3 cups (1 lb/450 g) finely chopped onions (about 3 medium)
- 3 cups (1 lb/450 g) coarse-grind (#3) bulgur
- ½ teaspoon salt
- 1 teaspoon ground cumin
- 1 teaspoon ground coriander
- 1 teaspoon Nine-Spice Mix (page 27), baharat, or Lebanese 7-spice blend
- ¼ teaspoon ground turmeric

For the tahini sauce:
- 1 tomato, quartered
- 1 jalapeño pepper, seeded and coarsely chopped
- 1 large bunch of dill fronds
- 1 teaspoon salt
- 1 clove garlic, peeled (optional)
- 4 tablespoons tahini
- 2 tablespoons yogurt
- 2 tablespoons fresh lemon juice

Make the stock:
Rinse the shellfish and fish bones very well and set aside to drain.

In a large stockpot, heat the olive oil over medium-high heat. Add the fennel, carrot, onion, and tomato paste (purée). Cook, stirring regularly, until the vegetables have browned and started to catch in places, 5–10 minutes. Deglaze the pan with the arak, then add the shellfish and fish bones, whole spices, salt, and enough water to cover, about 6 cups (1.5 liters). Bring to a gentle boil, skimming any scum that rises to the surface, then reduce the heat to a simmer. Continue to simmer, covered, for 50 minutes. Line a fine-mesh sieve with cheesecloth (muslin) and strain the stock through it; discard the seafood and spices. (This step can be done up to 2 days in advance and the stock stored in the refrigerator until needed.)

Prepare the bulgur:
In a large pot, heat the olive oil over medium-high heat. Add the onions and cook, stirring regularly, until crispy and deep golden brown, about 25 minutes. The exact timing may vary depending on the heat, pot size, and onion variety, so keep an eye on them as they can quickly go from brown to burnt.

Add the bulgur and toss to combine and evenly coat. Add 5 cups (40 fl oz/1.2 liters) of the seafood stock, the salt, and spices. Bring to a boil and cook for 3–4 minutes, then reduce the heat and simmer until the bulgur is fluffy and no longer hard to the bite, 15–20 minutes. Check halfway through the cooking and if the liquid has completely evaporated but the grains are still hard to the bite, add more broth (or water if no more broth is left) and continue to cook, checking and adding more liquid as necessary. The amount of liquid will vary based on the grain itself and the strength of heat; mine can take anywhere from 5–7 cups (40–56 fl oz/1.25–1.75 liters). Place a tea towel under the lid, remove from the heat, and set aside, covered, while you prepare the remaining components.

Meanwhile, make the tahini sauce:
In a mini food processor, combine the tomato, jalapeño, dill, salt, and garlic (if using) and process until finely chopped. Add the tahini, yogurt, and lemon juice and pulse just until evenly incorporated. Transfer to a small serving bowl and set aside.

» continues overleaf

Shrimp Sayadiyeh with Tomato Dill Tahini

For the shrimp:
I lb (450 g) peeled and deveined shrimp (prawns)
I tablespoon olive oil
¼ teaspoon salt
¼ teaspoon freshly ground black pepper
½ teaspoon ground cumin
½ teaspoon ground coriander
¼ teaspoon ground turmeric

For serving:
¼ cup (I ¼ oz/35 g) pine nuts, toasted or fried
¼ cup (I ¼ oz/35 g) cashews, toasted or fried

Prepare the shrimp:
Sprinkle the shrimp (prawns) with the olive oil, salt, pepper, and spices and rub to evenly coat. Heat a cast-iron skillet or nonstick frying pan large enough to fit the shrimp in a single layer over high heat. When hot, add the shrimp in a single layer and cook until nicely browned and cooked through, about 2 minutes per side. Depending on the size of the shrimp, cooking time may vary slightly.

To serve:
Spread the bulgur on a large serving platter. Top with the shrimp and sprinkle with the pine nuts and cashews. Serve with the tahini sauce on the side for each person to drizzle over their own plate.

Notes: I usually use one small fish head—about I2 ounces (350 g); snapper, bream, or any white fish are good, but avoid very oily fish like salmon or trout—and about I2 ounces (350 g) of shellfish (whole shrimp, crayfish, lobster shells, or crab shells). But whatever combination you have will be fine, I just strongly advise that you include some kind of shellfish as it adds a distinct layer of flavor.

For a quicker alternative, use store-bought seafood stock and doctor it with the ½ teaspoon each arak, tomato paste (purée), and spices above and simmer for I5 minutes.

Split Pea Falafel

The first mention of falafel dates back to the fourth century to the Coptic community in Egypt. In Egypt, and across much of the Arab world, most people make falafel from either chickpeas or a combination of dried chickpeas and split fava (broad) beans. Dried split favas, however, are difficult to find outside of Middle Eastern grocery stores, so since living abroad I have experimented with other dried beans. My favorite is a version using split peas, because not only do the peas lend falafel a subtle sweetness, but they also give it a beautifully vivid green color. The recipe is generous, so you can halve it, but I recommend making the full batch and freezing half before adding the baking powder. This way, you have falafel paste ready on the fly any weeknight.

 p. 23

Makes about 60 falafel (depending on size)

For the falafel:
About 1 cup (3 oz/80 g) mixed greens: any combination of parsley, cilantro (coriander), garlic scapes, radish greens (tops), or watercress
4 scallions (spring onions), or 1 small onion, halved
2 cloves garlic, peeled
1 red or green chili (optional), seeded
2 teaspoons salt
2 teaspoons ground coriander
2 teaspoons ground cumin
9 oz (250 g) dried chickpeas, soaked overnight in water and drained (do not use canned)
9 oz (250 g) dried green split peas, soaked overnight in water and drained (do not use canned)
Vegetable oil, for deep-frying
2 teaspoons baking powder

For serving:
Pita bread
Amba Tahini (page 24)
Pickles (page 25 or 26)
Diced cucumber and tomatoes

Make the falafel:
In a food processor, combine the mixed greens, scallions (spring onions), garlic, chili, salt, coriander, and cumin and process until finely chopped. Add the drained chickpeas and split peas and continue to process, stopping and scraping down the sides of the bowl occasionally, until everything comes together in a coarse paste. You want it grainier than hummus texture to keep the falafel light and fluffy. Transfer the paste to a bowl. At this point, if not frying immediately, the mixture can be stored in the refrigerator for a couple of days or in the freezer for a couple of months.

When you are ready to cook the falafel, line a plate with paper towels. Pour 2–3 inches (5–7 cm) oil into a large wok or Dutch oven (casserole) and heat over medium-high heat to 350°F (180°C) or until a pinch of falafel mixture bubbles up to the surface right away.

Meanwhile, sprinkle the falafel mixture with the baking powder and mix well.

Working in batches, use a falafel scoop (see Notes) or ice cream scoop to drop walnut-size falafel balls one by one into the hot oil, taking care not to overcrowd the pan. (If you do not have a scoop, use your hands to roll the dough into balls; see Notes.) Fry until a deep golden brown, about 5 minutes. Remove from the oil with a slotted spoon and drain on the paper towels.

To serve:
Serve with pita bread, amba tahini, pickles, and diced vegetables.

Notes: Take care not to overwork or densely pack the falafel, otherwise the texture will not be fluffy. The less you handle it with your hands after mixing in the baking powder, the better.

Falafel scoops, sold online or at Middle Eastern grocery stores, are stainless-steel tools that you spoon falafel mixture into, shape into a dome with the spoon, and then use a thumb-operated lever to drop directly into the hot oil.

Nuts + Seeds

"*Tfadalu tfadalu*," the vendor said, putting out a tray of nuts and dried fruits as my mother and I passed by. But we continued on because the spice vendor we bought our nuts from was three shops down. He went to the back as soon as he saw my mother and returned with a few bags. "This is the first shipment of pine nuts we got from Turkey; I took most home and saved these bags for you. And this here are the pistachios. They look small but they are green like a young pea inside and so much sweeter." She thanked him and paid what I thought was an exorbitant sum of money at the time, and we continued on our way. It was only when I started cooking myself that I realized what a big difference the right ingredients make and how a Mediterranean pine nut can add such buttery sweetness and crunch to a dish, whereas its inferior counterpart offers bitterness instead. Or how the right pistachios taste sweet and turn the green of a grass field when ground instead of yellow-tinged.

But nuts, or *mukasarat* as we call them, are not just for cooking in the Middle East. They are consumed on a daily basis for snacks and served to any guest who walks through your door. Every couple of weeks growing up, we would go to a roastery and pick the kinds we wanted roasted and the level of saltiness. In my parents' kitchen there are always jars of peanuts, pistachios, mixed nuts, and watermelon seeds. We scoop them out into colorful bowls when guests come or eat them straight out of the jar for a midday nosh.

While nuts might not be the first ingredients you think of when you think of Arabic food, they are in fact the real markers of our cuisine, with many nuts native to the region. If you look through medieval Arabic cookbooks, the vast majority of dishes include nuts. They were used in all kinds of stews and soups and sauces as thickening agents; they were used as jewels to garnish; and they featured frequently in sweets as well.

Today, some of the most widely used nuts and seeds in the cuisine are pine nuts, almonds, walnuts, pistachios, and sesame and nigella seeds. Given how prominently they feature in the following recipes, I urge you to try and get your hands on the best you can find. For pine nuts, always try to source the Mediterranean (sometimes called European) pine nuts. They are substantially more expensive, but you only need a very small quantity to make a big difference to your cooking. For pistachios, opt for the Turkish, Persian, or Sicilian varieties. They might be smaller in size, but they make up for it in sweetness and brightness. Walnuts and almonds are more forgiving and consistent across brands, but always taste to make sure they are not rancid before you use them. As for sesame seeds, by and large, we use the unhulled variety. Make sure to look for seeds that are plump and on the lighter side rather than flat and dark and dry. Nigella seeds (not to be confused with black sesame, onion seeds, or black cumin) are strong and pungent, but they add a unique aroma and are used in small doses with other ingredients.

I've always found it interesting how something as small as a pine nut can transform a dish in such a large way. Sesame seeds do that to za'atar blends, nigella seeds to pastries, and pistachios to many desserts. I've often described dishes as being "more than the sum of their parts," and if there is a single ingredient responsible for that transformation, more often than not, it is a nut or a seed. In the following recipes, nuts and seeds elevate what might be a simple dish into something spectacular—whether it is enhancing a simple protein like the Pistachio-Stuffed Chicken Balls (page 193), deepening the flavor of a simple cookie like the Aniseed and Sesame Qurshalleh (page 202), or taking center stage as the main actor in a dessert like Pistachio Cake with Orange Blossom Ganache (page 208). The recipes here are a triumph of both flavor and texture.

Sweet Duqqa

Duqqa, derived from the Arabic verb meaning "to pound," is a condiment eaten across the Middle East. It can refer to different things—some people even refer to za'atar as *duqqa*—but it is usually made of spices, grains, nuts, and possibly herbs, all ground together. Every family has its own recipe, but it is generally a savory mix eaten with bread and olive oil. I've always loved eating it with a spoon straight out of the jar, so I decided to experiment with making a sweet version. The result is a fragrant and crunchy mix that works beautifully as a topping for ice cream, oatmeal/porridge, smoothie bowls, yogurts, or even some soups like pumpkin or carrot. And of course, it's perfect out of the jar with a spoon. One of my favorite ways to use this condiment is sprinkled over a couple scoops of vanilla ice cream topped with a few strawberries chopped and mixed with rose water. Don't feel too constrained by the ingredients I use, it will work just as well with different nuts (think macadamia, cashews, or walnuts) and different spices (such as cardamom or fennel seeds). The more you experiment with it, the more you'll come to see which version is your family's favorite.

Makes about 2 cups (8 ½ oz/240 g)

- ½ cup (2 ½ oz/70 g) unhulled sesame seeds
- ½ cup (2 ½ oz/70 g) pistachios
- ½ cup (2 ½ oz/70 g) whole or blanched almonds
- 2 tablespoons unsweetened shredded (desiccated) coconut
- 1 tablespoon coriander seeds
- 1 tablespoon sugar
- 1 teaspoon crushed rose petals (optional)

In a medium frying pan, dry-roast the sesame seeds over medium-low heat, stirring regularly, until they are slightly darker in color and fragrant and you start to hear a popping sound, about 5 minutes. Set aside on a plate to cool.

Add the pistachios to the same pan and dry-roast, stirring regularly, until fragrant, about 5 minutes. Set aside on a separate plate to cool. Repeat with the almonds, adding them to the plate with the pistachios.

Add the coconut to the same pan and dry-roast, stirring frequently, until fragrant and golden brown. This will happen very quickly, less than 1 minute, as the pan is hot. Transfer to the plate with the nuts to cool.

Add the coriander seeds to the pan and dry-roast until fragrant and lightly browned, another minute. Add to the plate with the nuts.

Allow the ingredients to cool completely, otherwise you could end up with a paste instead of a powder when you grind. In a food processor, combine the pistachios, almonds, coconut, coriander seeds, and half of the sesame seeds and pulse until coarsely ground.

Pour into a large bowl, add the remaining sesame seeds and rose petals (if using), and mix well with a spoon until combined. Transfer to a jar or airtight container where it will keep at room temperature for about 1 month.

Turmeric and Nigella Seed Easter Bread

Baking Easter bread is a common tradition among the Greek Orthodox community across the world. In the Levant, there is a sweet mahlab and mastic-flavored bread made specifically by the orthodox Christian community, but there is also a traditional anise-flavored bread made around Muslim and Christian holidays alike. This recipe took inspiration from both, creating a rich, sweet loaf (if you think somewhere between a brioche and a challah you wouldn't be far off), but flavored with turmeric and nigella seeds like numerous Arab pastries. The result is striking—a deep yellow-hued, braided (plaited) loaf, dotted with black seeds throughout, and complemented by a sweet flavor and tender crumb. Delicious with a cup of tea and salty white cheese (halloumi, Akkawi, etc.), it is equally good on its own, lathered with spreadable cheese, or in place of your usual dinner roll. So don't let the name deceive you, this Easter bread is perfect all year round.

Makes 1 large loaf

- 1 cup (8 fl oz/250 ml) whole milk
- 6 tablespoons (3 oz/85 g) unsalted butter
- ¾ cup (5¼ oz/150 g) sugar
- 1 teaspoon salt
- 5¾ cups (1 lb 10½ oz/750 g) bread (strong) flour
- 2 tablespoons nigella seeds, plus more for sprinkling
- 1 tablespoon ground turmeric
- 2¼ teaspoons action dry (fast-acting) yeast
- 3 eggs
- ½ teaspoon vanilla extract

In a saucepan, combine the milk, butter, sugar, and salt and heat over medium-low heat just until the butter is melted. Remove from the heat and set aside until cool, 15–30 minutes.

Meanwhile, in a stand mixer fitted with the dough hook, combine the flour, nigella seeds, turmeric, and yeast and mix on low speed until combined.

Once the milk mixture has cooled, add 2 of the eggs and the vanilla and whisk to combine. Pour the mixture and ¼ cup (2 fl oz/60 ml) water over the flour and knead with the dough hook until the dough is smooth and elastic and pulls away from the sides of the bowl. If the dough appears too stiff, add a tablespoon of water at a time and continue to knead.

Lightly grease the bowl and the dough with some oil, cover with a damp tea towel or plastic wrap (clingfilm), and set aside to rise until doubled in size, about 1 hour.

Line a baking sheet with parchment paper. Once the dough has risen, divide into 5 equal portions and stretch each piece into a rope 14–16 inches (35–40 cm) long. If the dough is too stiff, let rest for about 10 minutes and try again. Transfer the ropes to the prepared baking sheet and press together at one end. To braid (plait) the loaf, number the ropes 1, 2, 3, 4, 5 (after every move, renumber the ropes) and braid them by moving rope 1 over rope 3, then rope 2 over rope 3, then rope 5 over rope 2. Repeat until you reach the end of the dough, then pinch the ends together and tuck under the loaf. (Alternatively, you could do a simple three-roped braid instead.) Cover with a damp tea towel and set aside to rise until almost doubled in size, another hour.

Preheat the oven to 350°F (180°C/Gas Mark 4).

Beat the remaining egg and brush over the entire loaf. Sprinkle some nigella seeds on top. Bake until the loaf is a dark golden brown and sounds hollow when tapped, 45–55 minutes. Let cool about 30 minutes, then slice and serve.

The loaf will keep, tightly covered, for 2 days at room temperature. It can also be frozen for up to 1 month and reheated in the oven.

Roasted Beet Muhammara

Mezze plates coincide across the region, but *muhammara* —a dish whose primary components are Aleppo peppers and walnuts—is indisputably a Syrian dish originating in Aleppo. Although chilies and peppers are native to Central and South America, they started their journey across the world after the fifteenth-century Columbian Exchange, and today, most cultures across the Mediterranean and Middle East claim some kind of a chili dip or sauce to their cuisine, from North African harissa and Palestinian *shattah* (see page 22) to Turkish *acuk*, Georgian *adjìka*, and Yemeni *zhug*. My great-great-grandmother who came to Palestine from Syria as a bride brought her family's *muhammara* recipe along with her and it has remained a staple in our family ever since. Although it is easy to find roasted red peppers in any supermarket aisle nowadays, I prefer to use seasonal ingredients. So in the winter, I find myself using the season's sweetest treat—beets—in place of the peppers, and what a triumphant flavor combination it is.

---

p. 194

Serves 4 as part of a spread

- 1 medium (about 5 oz/150 g) beet
- 4 tablespoons olive oil, plus more for drizzling
- 4 tablespoons pomegranate molasses
- 1 tablespoon honey
- 1 tablespoon tahini
- ½ teaspoon salt
- ¼ teaspoon freshly ground black pepper
- ¼ teaspoon ground cumin
- 1½ cups (5 oz/150 g) walnut pieces, plus a few extra for garnish
- 1 tablespoon breadcrumbs
- Fresh parsley, dill, or cilantro (coriander) leaves, for garnish (optional)

Preheat the oven to 450°F (230°C/Gas Mark 8).

Remove any leafy tops from the beet, keeping the stems intact so no flesh is exposed, then wash and scrub thoroughly. Wrap the beet in aluminum foil and bake until a skewer or sharp knife easily penetrates the flesh, 45–60 minutes. Remove and set aside to cool.

When cool enough to handle, peel the skin off the beet with a peeler or by rubbing off with your fingers. Use gloves to avoid staining your hands, or simply scrub your hands with lemon when washing to remove the stains. Cut the beet in half to make processing easier.

Put the beet in a food processor and add the olive oil, pomegranate molasses, honey, tahini, salt, pepper, and cumin and process until smooth. Add the walnuts and breadcrumbs and pulse until the walnuts are coarsely chopped. You want this dip to retain some texture and not be completely smooth, so do not overpulse. Taste for salt and add more if necessary.

To serve, spread in a bowl, drizzle with olive oil, and garnish with walnuts and green herb leaves for a beautiful contrast of colors.

Pistachio-Stuffed Chicken Balls

The summer evening breeze, the fragrance of jasmine in the air, old Fairuz songs, and fresh baked bread carried around in straw baskets are but a few of the things that make dining at Fakhreldin restaurant in Amman a magical experience. But if there is one dish I remember more than any other from the summers I traveled to Jordan, it is these chicken balls. The first time I picked up a deep golden ball of fried goodness, I expected I would enjoy it (it was fried after all), but I had no idea of the delicious surprise that awaited me within. A moist chicken croquette oozing with a pistachio filling, it quickly became a favorite. Of course the restaurant did not want to reveal its recipe, but after countless attempts, I have finally managed to make at home the pistachio-stuffed chicken balls I would be willing to travel to eat. I like to grind my own dark chicken meat at home, but you can just as easily use store-bought ground (minced) chicken. If you do, make sure to pick dark meat with good fat content so the croquettes are juicy and not dry.

---

p. 195

Makes 20 croquettes

For the filling:
- 7 tablespoons (3½ oz/100 g) salted butter, at room temperature (if using unsalted, add ¼ teaspoon salt)
- ⅓ cup (2 oz/60 g) pistachios, finely ground
- Pinch of freshly ground black pepper
- A couple grates of lemon zest (optional)

For the chicken:
- 1 lb (450 g) ground (minced) chicken (fatty leg meat is best)
- ¼ cup (1 oz/30 g) fine unseasoned breadcrumbs
- 1 egg
- 1 tablespoon olive oil
- 1 teaspoon salt
- ½ teaspoon Nine-Spice Mix (page 27), baharat, or Lebanese 7-spice blend
- ½ teaspoon garlic granules or powder

For finishing:
- 1 egg, lightly whisked
- 1 cup (4½ oz/120 g) fine unseasoned breadcrumbs
- Vegetable oil, for deep-frying

Make the filling:
In a bowl, fold together the softened butter, pistachios, pepper, and lemon zest (if using) until evenly combined. Place on a piece of plastic wrap (clingfilm) and try to shape into a thin log about 8 inches (20 cm) long. If it is too difficult, just flatten it into a uniform shape. Wrap in the plastic and refrigerate until hardened.

Meanwhile, prepare the chicken:
In a bowl, combine the ground (minced) chicken, breadcrumbs, egg, olive oil, salt, spice blend, and garlic granules and knead just until evenly incorporated. Do not overmix to avoid a tough croquette. Shape into 20 balls about the size of golf balls, oiling your hands as you go along if the mixture feels too sticky. Place on a parchment-lined tray and refrigerate until ready to use.

Remove the butter from the refrigerator and slice into 20 discs or cubes, depending on how you shaped it. If the butter is still soft, place the cut pieces on a parchment- or plastic-lined plate and pop in the freezer until hardened, 20–30 minutes.

To stuff, take a chicken ball and flatten slightly in the palm of your hand. Place a portion of butter in the center, close the meat around it, and roll it back into a ball. Repeat until the butter and chicken are gone.

To finish:
Dip each ball lightly in the whisked egg, then roll it around in the breadcrumbs. Roll it between your palms to tightly set the breadcrumbs and get rid of excess crumbs.

Line a plate with paper towels. Pour 3 inches (7 cm) vegetable oil into a wok or Dutch oven (casserole) and heat over medium-high heat until it reaches 350°F (180°C), or a breadcrumb dropped in the oil immediately bubbles to the surface.

Working in batches to avoid overcrowding, drop the chicken balls one by one into the hot oil and fry until a deep golden brown, about 5 minutes. Remove with a slotted spoon and set on the paper towels to drain.

Serve immediately so the filling oozes out as you cut into the ball.

Roasted Beet Muhammara

Pistachio-Stuffed Chicken Balls

Pistachio, Radish Greens, and Sumac Stuffed Chicken Breasts

The first time I made this dish I was recently married and living in London. We had picked up a rack of lamb from the neighborhood butcher and I tried to get fancy with some staple ingredients I had in my pantry—and what Arab pantry doesn't have pistachio, sumac, and fresh herbs? The dish quickly became a regular on our rotation of meals. Recently, I discovered a recipe for pistachio and herb stuffed chicken in a thirteenth-century Arabic cookbook *Kìtab al-Wusla ìla al-Habìb*. So I tried a variation with chicken breast and found that the mild flavor of the chicken allowed the pistachio stuffing to truly shine, and the contrast of bright green against white was stunning. Feel free to experiment with the greens you use—each blend will yield a slightly different flavor profile, but all will be delicious. One of my favorite combinations is mint and cilantro (coriander).

Serves 4 (can easily be halved)

For the chicken:
- 4 boneless, skinless chicken breasts
- 2 tablespoons olive oil, plus more for frying
- 2 tablespoons pomegranate molasses
- 2 teaspoons salt
- ½ teaspoon freshly ground black pepper

For the pistachio stuffing:
- 1 cup (3½ oz/100 g) pistachios
- 1 cup (¾ oz/20 g) packed mixed green leaves: a combination of any combination of radish tops, mint, cilantro (coriander), watercress, or parsley
- 2 cloves garlic, peeled
- 1 tablespoon olive oil, plus more for frying
- 2 teaspoons fresh lime or lemon juice
- 1 teaspoon sumac
- 1 teaspoon grated Parmesan cheese
- Scant 1 teaspoon salt
- ¼ teaspoon freshly ground black pepper

Prepare the chicken:
With the tip of a sharp knife, make an incision horizontally in the fatter side of each breast to make a large pocket but without cutting through and keeping the breast intact. Place the chicken breasts in a bowl. Add the olive oil, pomegranate molasses, salt, and pepper and rub the chicken all over—inside and out—with the mixture. Cover and refrigerate for a couple of hours and up to overnight.

Make the pistachio stuffing:
In a mini food processor, combine the pistachios, mixed greens, garlic, olive oil, lime juice, sumac, Parmesan, salt, and pepper and process into a coarse paste.

Preheat the oven to 350°F (180°C/Gas Mark 4).

Dividing evenly, spoon stuffing into the breast pockets, using your hands or the back of a spoon to smooth it into an even layer. You can use toothpicks (cocktail sticks) to hold the edges of the breasts together if necessary.

In a large cast-iron skillet or ovenproof frying pan, heat a couple tablespoons of olive oil over medium heat. When the oil is hot but not smoking, add the breasts in a single layer and cook for 3–4 minutes per side, flipping only once when the chicken easily releases from the pan.

Transfer the pan to the oven and bake until a meat thermometer inserted into the thickest part of the breast registers 165°F (74°C), 10–15 minutes.

Remove from the oven and allow to rest for 5 minutes before serving.

Pistachio, Radish Greens, and Sumac Stuffed Chicken Breasts

Cauliflower, Almond, and Yogurt Salad

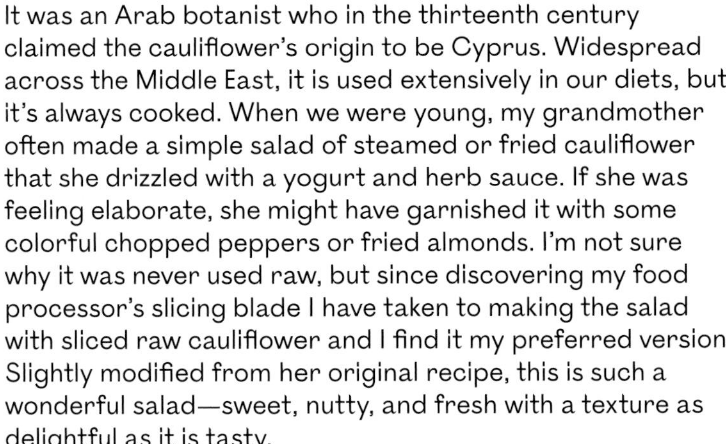

It was an Arab botanist who in the thirteenth century claimed the cauliflower's origin to be Cyprus. Widespread across the Middle East, it is used extensively in our diets, but it's always cooked. When we were young, my grandmother often made a simple salad of steamed or fried cauliflower that she drizzled with a yogurt and herb sauce. If she was feeling elaborate, she might have garnished it with some colorful chopped peppers or fried almonds. I'm not sure why it was never used raw, but since discovering my food processor's slicing blade I have taken to making the salad with sliced raw cauliflower and I find it my preferred version. Slightly modified from her original recipe, this is such a wonderful salad—sweet, nutty, and fresh with a texture as delightful as it is tasty.

Serves 4–6

- 1 medium head cauliflower
- ¼ cup (2½ oz/70 g) Greek yogurt
- ¼ cup (2 fl oz/60 ml) olive oil
- ¼ cup (2 fl oz/60 ml) apple cider vinegar
- 1 tablespoon honey
- 1 clove garlic, crushed in a garlic press
- Grated zest and juice of 1 large unwaxed or organic lemon
- ½ teaspoon salt
- 1 cup (20 g) loosely packed green herbs, finely chopped: any combination of dill, chives, parsley, or cilantro (coriander)
- 1 cup (3½ oz/100 g) sliced (flaked) almonds, toasted until golden brown

Divide the cauliflower into very large florets (or cut the head into quarters if your food processor is large enough). Using the slicing disc on your food processor or a mandoline, cut into thin slices. Some of it will come out riced like crumbs, that is fine. These crumbs will give the dressing more texture and help everything come together nicely. Transfer to a large bowl and set aside.

In a small bowl, whisk together the yogurt, olive oil, vinegar, honey, garlic, lemon zest, lemon juice, and salt until combined. Pour over the sliced cauliflower and toss to combine.

Transfer the cauliflower to a serving platter, top with the green herbs and toasted almonds and serve.

Mushroom and Cashew Salad with Lemon Parsley Dressing (1) p. 200; Cauliflower, Almond, and Yogurt Salad (2)

Mushroom and Cashew Salad with Lemon Parsley Dressing

Although mushrooms grow in most parts of the world and are eagerly gathered by locals as part of their diets, this was not always the case for Arabs. Today, however, with the widespread availability of mushrooms, Arabs have started to incorporate them into their diets, too. One of the most common ways is a salad in which button mushrooms are heavily dressed with lemon to retain their bright white color, then flavored with more common ingredients like parsley and scallions (spring onions) and olive oil. Almost every wedding I ever went to and every mezze restaurant I frequented in the Galilee had a plate of mushroom salad. It was basic: mushrooms, lemon, olive oil, and salt and often parsley and red chilies for color. So this salad, while certainly not an original Arab dish, takes inspiration from the flavors of the Middle East and elevates the most common of mushrooms into a dish that's as perfect on its own as it is a side to meats or fish.

---

p. 199

Serves 4–6

1½ lb (680 g) white button mushrooms
¼ cup (2 fl oz/60 ml) fresh lemon juice
¼ cup (2 fl oz/60 ml) olive oil
1 small red bell pepper, finely diced
2 scallions (spring onions), thinly sliced
4 tablespoons finely chopped fresh parsley
1½ teaspoons salt
⅓ cup (1¼ oz/35 g) cashew pieces or slivered almonds, toasted

Gently wash and dry the mushrooms. Trim the stems and cut the mushrooms into thin slices. Put the slices in a large bowl. Pour the lemon juice over the mushrooms and lightly toss until fully coated. Add the olive oil, bell pepper, scallions (spring onions), parsley, and salt and gently mix until evenly incorporated.

Put the mushrooms on a serving platter and top with the toasted cashews. Serve immediately or refrigerate until ready to serve.

Quick and Easy Bseeseh

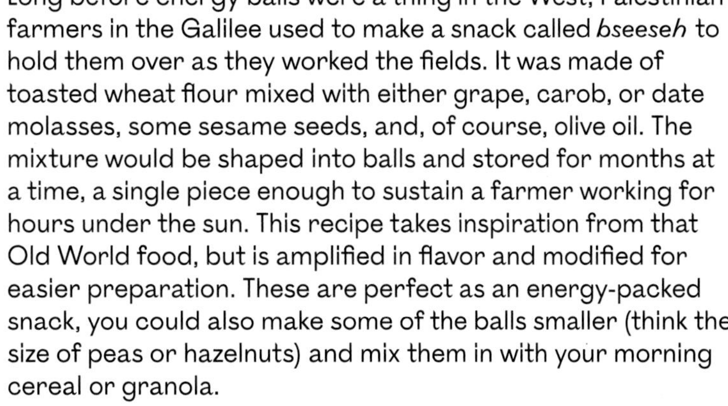

Long before energy balls were a thing in the West, Palestinian farmers in the Galilee used to make a snack called *bseeseh* to hold them over as they worked the fields. It was made of toasted wheat flour mixed with either grape, carob, or date molasses, some sesame seeds, and, of course, olive oil. The mixture would be shaped into balls and stored for months at a time, a single piece enough to sustain a farmer working for hours under the sun. This recipe takes inspiration from that Old World food, but is amplified in flavor and modified for easier preparation. These are perfect as an energy-packed snack, you could also make some of the balls smaller (think the size of peas or hazelnuts) and mix them in with your morning cereal or granola.

---

p. 203

Makes 25–30 balls

- 1 cup (5 ¼ oz/150 g) unhulled sesame seeds
- 14 oz (400 g) date paste (see Note)
- 2 tablespoons extra-virgin olive oil (choose one whose flavor you like)
- ¼ cup (1 oz/30 g) pistachios (or any other nut you like), coarsely ground
- ½ teaspoon ground cinnamon

Line a large plate with parchment or wax (greaseproof) paper and set aside.

In a large frying pan, dry-roast the sesame seeds over medium heat, stirring constantly, until aromatic and toasted, 7–10 minutes. You'll know they are toasted when you start to hear some seeds popping and smell the nutty aroma of sesame and notice the color darken slightly. Remove from the heat, transfer to a plate, and set aside to cool completely.

In a large bowl, combine the date paste, olive oil, pistachios, cinnamon, and cooled sesame seeds. Mix with your hands until thoroughly combined. Wearing disposable food gloves is the easiest way to do this.

Take about 1 tablespoon of the mixture and roll between your palms to form a ball, then place on the lined plate. Repeat to make 25–30 balls.

Store the balls in an airtight container, with layers of parchment beneath and between. Although they will keep in an airtight container at room temperature for a couple of weeks, I recommend storing them in the refrigerator. They taste just as delicious when firmer and cooler.

Note: Date paste can be found in any Middle Eastern grocery shop. You could also buy very soft Medjool dates and work them into a paste with your hands. If you do, I recommend wearing gloves and using some oil, otherwise, it can get quite sticky. To get 14 ounces (400 g) of date paste, you will need roughly 25 large Medjool dates.

Aniseed and Sesame Qurshalleh

The history of rusks is complex, with some claims going back to the Byzantine Empire, others to the Persian, and some to the more recent Elizabethan era. To complicate matters even more, some references are to hard, twice-baked bread that sustained sailors on long journeys, while others are to sweetened cookies. The only thing easy to ascertain is that most cultures across the world today enjoy some version of rusk, most often dipped in a hot beverage like tea or coffee. In the Middle East, these cookies are usually flavored with aniseed, sometimes also sesame seeds, with sugar content varying from none to quite sweet. Generally, they are made out of a kneaded dough that is shaped and baked until dry, but I find the twice-baking method to be much easier. It is worth it to seek out aniseed specifically for this cookie, and I wouldn't attempt to make it with anise extract—it's just not the same. We are rarely without these rusks at home because my four-year-old makes sure to inform me every time the box is low. They are very easy to make and perfect on their own or with a cup of sage tea or cardamom coffee—try these once and I am sure they will become a staple in your home as well.

Makes about 30 rusks

- 3 cups (13 oz/375 g) all-purpose (plain) flour
- 2 tablespoons ground aniseed
- 2 tablespoons nigella seeds
- 2 tablespoons unhulled sesame seeds
- 1½ teaspoons baking powder
- ½ teaspoon salt
- 3 eggs
- ½ cup (4 fl oz/120 ml) vegetable oil
- ¾ cup (5⅓ oz/150 g) sugar
- ½ cup (4 fl oz/120 ml) whole milk

Preheat the oven to 350°F (180°C/Gas Mark 4). Line a 9-inch (23 cm) square cake pan with parchment paper. (If you don't have this size pan, you could use your hands to form a square of dough this size directly on a parchment-lined baking sheet.)

In a small bowl, stir together the flour, aniseed, nigella seeds, sesame seeds, baking powder, and salt until evenly incorporated.

In a large bowl, combine the eggs, oil, sugar, and milk and whisk until very well combined. Add the flour mixture to the egg mixture and stir until combined. It will be quite stiff and sticky, so you may find it easier at some point to mix with gloved hands to incorporate.

Spoon the mixture into the prepared pan and, with wet palms, spread evenly to the edges. Bake until firm to the touch, 20–30 minutes.

Meanwhile, line a large baking sheet with parchment paper.

Remove the cake from oven and leave the oven on. Allow the cake to cool in the pan for a few minutes, then invert onto a cutting board. Using a sharp serrated knife, cut the cake in half, then cut each half crosswise into slices ½ inch (1.5 cm) wide.

Arrange the slices cut-side down on the baking sheet and return to the oven to cook until completely dried out and golden brown, 35–45 minutes. Turn the rusks over once halfway through. Transfer to a wire rack to cool.

Once cooled, the rusks can be stored in an airtight container at room temperature for 1–2 weeks.

Aniseed and Sesame Qurshalleh (1); Quick and Easy Bseeseh (2) p. 201

Nut and Sesame Seed Stuffed Pancakes

My daughter's best friend in preschool is Korean and their playdates were my first foray into the delicious world of Korean food. One particular snack I found fascinating was *hotteok*, a brown sugar and peanut filled pancake brought to Korea by Chinese immigrants in the early 1900s. The dough is exceptionally soft and chewy, which was part of the appeal, but it also reminded me of a similar pancake, *atayef*, my grandmother always prepared during Ramadan, which she filled with sugar, walnuts, and cinnamon. I was intrigued with how so many cultures, in spite of being very different in geography, landscape, and history, still shared similar concepts in food. I experimented with the filling to make something that was as nutritious as it was delicious. This version relies on a mixture of nuts and sesame seeds, as well as tahini and grape molasses, not only to lend it an Arab flair, but also to help bind the filling together and make it easier to work with. These pancakes are especially delicious fresh out of the pan, but can also be enjoyed when cool. Leftovers can be frozen for up to one month and reheated in an oven for a freshly made taste.

---

p. 206

Makes 12 pancakes

For the dough:
2 ½ cups (10 ½ oz/300 g) all-purpose (plain) flour
½ cup (2 oz/60 g) sweet rice flour
2 teaspoons action dry (fast-acting) yeast
1 tablespoon sugar
1 teaspoon salt
1 tablespoon vegetable oil
1 cup (8 fl oz/250 ml) whole milk or nondairy milk, warmed

For the filling:
Scant 1 cup (3 ½ oz/100 g) mixed nuts (any combination of pine nuts, slivered almonds, pistachios, walnuts, pecans, or peanuts), lightly toasted
2 tablespoons unhulled sesame seeds, lightly toasted
¼ cup (1 ¾ oz/50 g) granulated sugar
¼ cup (1 ¾ oz/50 g) packed light brown sugar
1 tablespoon tahini
1 tablespoon date molasses, grape molasses, maple syrup, or honey
1 teaspoon rose water
¼ teaspoon ground cinnamon
Pinch of salt

To finish:
Vegetable oil, for shaping and frying

Make the dough:
In a large bowl, combine both flours, the yeast, sugar, salt, oil, warm milk, and ¼ cup (2 fl oz/60 ml) water. Knead or mix with a spatula until everything comes together in a sticky dough. Cover and set aside to rise until doubled in size, 1–2 hours.

Meanwhile, make the filling:
In a food processor, combine the nuts and sesame seeds and pulse until coarsely chopped. Transfer to a small bowl, add the granulated sugar, brown sugar, tahini, date molasses, rose water, cinnamon, and salt and mix until everything comes together in a coarse paste.

To finish:
Oil your hands and divide the dough into 12 equal portions (about the size of golf balls) and place on an oiled tray. One at a time, flatten each ball until it's slightly larger than your palm and spoon a generous tablespoon of the filling into the center. Bring the edges together to seal each parcel into a ball.

Pour a very thin layer of vegetable oil into a large frying pan and place over medium heat. When hot, place one ball and flatten it to a wide disc with an oiled spatula. Repeat until the pan is full. Cook until the bottom is golden brown, about 1 minute, then flip and continue to cook until the other side is a golden brown as well. Remove from the heat and serve while still warm.

Almond and Pine Nut Cake with Rose Water and Dates

Italians have their *pignolata* with pine nuts and Spaniards their *tarta de Santiago* with almonds. Even though the almond was introduced to Spain by the Moors and has since become ubiquitous in their desserts, we Arabs mostly use pine nuts and almonds, in rather generous proportions I might add, to top our savory rice dishes. They're always my favorite part, and yet, we never use them as the stars. So, I thought, why not combine the two but into something sweet? I tried different options, from custard tarts to yeasted rolls to cream desserts, but in the end, the simplest turned out to be the best. Decadent yet light, satisfying but not sickly sweet, crunchy in places and soft in others, this is a case of opposites that balance seamlessly into a cake that is as perfect next to a morning cup of coffee as it is for a post-dinner treat.

---

p. 207

Makes one 9-inch (23 cm) round or loaf cake

For the cake:
Butter and flour, for the pan
½ cup (about 2½ oz/75 g) almonds, toasted and cooled
¼ cup (about 1½ oz/40 g) pine nuts, toasted and cooled
1⅓ cups (5½ oz/160 g) all-purpose (plain) flour
1 teaspoon baking powder
¼ teaspoon baking soda (bicarbonate of soda)
¼ teaspoon salt
½ cup (3½ oz/100 g) pitted Medjool dates (about 5 pieces)
3 eggs
1 cup (7 oz/200 g) sugar
⅔ cup (5⅓ fl oz/160 ml) vegetable oil
⅓ cup (3½ oz/100 g) Greek yogurt
1 teaspoon rose water

For the topping:
2 tablespoons pine nuts
3 tablespoons slivered almonds

Make the cake:
Preheat the oven to 350°F (180°C/Gas Mark 4). Butter and flour a 9-inch (23 cm) round or loaf pan or line with parchment paper.

In a food processor, combine the toasted almonds, toasted pine nuts, and flour and pulse until finely ground. Transfer to a medium bowl and stir in the baking powder, baking soda (bicarb), and salt. Set aside.

In the same food processor, combine the dates, eggs, and sugar and process until the mixture becomes thick and pale yellow and the dates are all processed and in small flecks. Add the oil, yogurt, and rose water and pulse a few more times to combine.

Pour the date mixture over the flour mixture and gently fold just until no streaks of flour remain. Scrape the batter into the prepared cake or loaf pan and sprinkle the top with the untoasted pine nuts and slivered almonds.

Bake until the top is a light golden brown and a toothpick (cocktail stick) comes out clean, 40 minutes to 1 hour. A round cake will take less time than a loaf pan.

Remove and allow to cool in the pan for 10 minutes before transferring to a wire rack to cool completely. The cake will keep in an airtight container for several days at room temperature.

Note: Rose water and almonds are a classic combination, but rose can be a love-it-or-hate-it flavor. If you're in the hate-it camp, replace the rose water with 1 teaspoon vanilla extract, or ½ teaspoon cinnamon and 1 teaspoon vanilla extract, or 1 teaspoon grated lemon zest and 1 teaspoon vanilla extract for equally delicious outcomes.

Almond and Pine Nut Cake with Rose Water and Dates

Pistachio Cake with Orange Blossom Ganache

In Arabic, the term for pistachio is *fistuk halabi* or literally "nut of Aleppo." Indeed, the pistachio is believed to have originated in Syria and from there made its way across the region and the world. In the Arab world, it is largely consumed roasted and salted as a snack, or used as a filling for sweets like *baklawa*. Here I let the nut shine in a simple cake where the flavor is pronounced because of the amount of pistachios used. Pistachios are often combined with orange blossom water in Arabic desserts. I soften the contrast by flavoring a chocolate ganache glaze with orange blossom instead of the cake. It's a winning combination that's moist and tender with ample flavor. You can serve it with yogurt, crème fraîche, or ice cream to cut through the rich, deep flavors.

Makes one 9-inch (23 cm) round cake

For the cake:

- Butter, for the pan
- 1½ cups (7 oz/200 g) pistachios
- ¾ cup (3¾ oz/110 g) all-purpose (plain) flour
- ½ teaspoon salt
- 1 teaspoon baking powder
- ¼ teaspoon baking soda (bicarbonate of soda)
- 3 eggs
- 1¼ cups (8¾ oz/250 g) sugar
- ¼ cup (2 oz/60 g) yogurt
- 1 teaspoon vanilla extract
- ½ cup (4 fl oz/120 ml) vegetable oil (substitute up to half with good-quality roasted pistachio oil)

For the ganache:

- Scant ½ cup (4 fl oz/100 ml) heavy (double) cream
- 3½ oz (100 g) dark chocolate (at least 55% cacao), broken into small pieces
- 2 tablespoons orange blossom water
- 2 tablespoons pistachios, finely ground

Make the cake:

Preheat the oven to 325°F (160°C/ Gas Mark 3). Grease a 9-inch (23 cm) round cake pan and line with a round of parchment paper.

In a food processor, combine the pistachios, flour, salt, baking powder, and baking soda (bicarb) and pulse until the pistachios are finely ground. Transfer to a bowl.

In the same food processor bowl, combine the eggs, sugar, yogurt, and vanilla and process until combined and pale yellow in color. Add the oil and continue to process until incorporated. Add the pistachio flour mixture and pulse a few times to combine. Scrape the batter into the prepared pan.

Bake until the top is an even, light golden color and a skewer inserted in the center comes out with moist crumbs or clean, 45 minutes to 1 hour. The time will vary based on the oven, climate, and variety of pistachio, so start checking at 45 minutes.

Allow the cake to cool completely in the pan, then transfer to a wire rack.

Make the ganache:

In a small saucepan, heat the cream until it's about to boil. Remove from the heat, add the chocolate pieces, and let stand for a couple of minutes. Add the orange blossom water and, with a spatula, stir the cream until all the chocolate has melted and the mixture is smooth and shiny. Cover the ganache with plastic wrap (clingfilm) touching the surface and allow to cool until it is of a spreading consistency, about 2 hours at room temperature.

Using a spatula, spread the ganache on top of the cake. Sprinkle the pistachios in a pattern over the ganache and set aside to cool completely. The cake will keep at room temperature, tightly covered, for a couple of days.

Variation: Another winning combination is topping the cake with tahini-flavored icing instead of ganache. It becomes reminiscent of really good-quality pistachio halaweh (halva). If you go down that route, simply beat 4 tablespoons (60 g) room-temperature butter in a hand mixer until smooth. Add ⅓ cup (80 g) tahini and continue to beat until incorporated, then add ¼ cup (30 g) powdered (icing) sugar and a pinch of salt and continue to beat until light and fluffy. Ice the cake as above.

Pistachio Cake with Orange Blossom Ganache

Tahini

If you've ever been to a tahini mill in the Middle East and seen the luxurious texture spilling out; if you've ever dipped a finger and tasted the nutty, creamy elixir; and if you've ever eaten it with a spoon and then come back for more, you know just how magical good tahini can be. For me, and probably anyone else who grew up in the Middle East, tahini is one of our most beloved staples. Incredibly versatile, it is a harmonious complement to herbs, fruits, meats, and even sweets.

Tahini is a paste made of ground sesame seeds. Nothing else. Sesame seeds, the oldest oil-crop known to man, are native to Africa and possibly India as well. Some claim that Ethiopian sesame seeds are the best kind because of the soil they are grown in. The thinking is that terroir affects sesame seeds, and by extension tahini, the same way it affects grapes and wine. I have tasted tahini made from Ethiopian seeds and others. From my experience, the importance of the seeds' origin is a little overblown. I think just as much as the seed, the process used for milling the tahini, the degree of roasting, and the freshness when you purchase it, all impact the flavor as much as, if not more than, the terroir.

As with most things food though, a lot of the preference for flavor is subjective. Tahini can be made from hulled sesame seeds that have not been roasted, which gives it the lightest and mildest flavor. It can also be made from seeds that have been hulled and then roasted, and the degree of roasting impacts the final flavor and color, making it darker and nuttier, but also increasing its subtle bitter notes. A whole-grain version of tahini can also be made with unhulled seeds. The only way to really know what you like is to taste and experiment.

The first mention I found of tahini in my research was in *Kìtab al-Tabìkh* (the tenth-century cookbook), where it was referred to not by that name but in a descriptive way as "*tahìn al sìmsìm*," or "paste of sesame." The word *tahìnì*, a colloquialism of the Arabic word *tahhìnìyya*, comes from the root Arabic verb *tahan*, which simply means "to grind" or "mill." Most references in the book use it as a spread on different breads. Some recipes state that having it with honey or date syrup might help it pass through the digestive system faster—probably where the dish *dìbs wa tahìnì* (tahini with date or grape molasses) originated from. It also features as an ingredient in baked goods and as a condiment to be spread on bread that is then topped with dried or cured meats.

Today, tahini's popularity is soaring across the world, propelled by its esteemed place in Middle Eastern cooking, specifically the Levant region, and its ensuing delicious recipes like hummus and *halaweh* (halva). The recipes in this chapter capitalize on tahini's deep, earthy flavor but apply them in new ways. A Tahini Cheesecake (page 226) is suddenly much more complex and less cloyingly sweet. Good-quality fresh *halaweh* (halva), usually difficult to find outside the Middle East, becomes an easy affair to make at home (page 222) with a few simple ingredients. Fish (page 218) and beef (page 220) are transformed into impressive meals with the inclusion of simple tahini-based sauces. Think of the recipes in this chapter as a blueprint for the different ways you can use tahini, and from there let your imagination take you on any culinary adventure you like.

Tomato Tahini Bread Salad

It was usually on hot summer evenings, when turning the stove on was unimaginable, that my mother made this dish for supper. She would take fleshy sun-ripened tomatoes, toss them with green chilies and torn pieces of bread, then drizzle everything with tahini and lemon juice and mix by hand to squeeze the juices and flavors together. It was so simple, yet it remains lodged in my memory as much as the sweltering heat of those nights. I later realized how common it was, across the entire Mediterranean region, to add stale bread to soups and salads to turn them into a substantial meal. Just take panzanella, fattoush, *dakos*, ribollita, *wodzionka*, *thareed*, and the countless *fatteh* dishes as examples. The origins of such dishes are twofold, I imagine. On the one hand, they bulk up ingredients to feed more people, and on the other hand, they make use of stale bread instead of tossing it. This salad is an elevated take on that humble summer supper.

Serves 4 as a side or part of a spread

- 1 cup (about 2 oz/60 g) pita bread, cut into bite size squares
- 1 teaspoon olive oil
- 10 oz (300 g) tomatoes, cut into bite-size pieces (or halved if using cherry tomatoes)
- ½ teaspoon salt
- 2 tablespoons fresh lemon juice
- 1 tablespoon plus 1 teaspoon tahini
- 2 scallions (spring onions), thinly sliced
- 1 green chili, thinly sliced
- 3 sprigs fresh mint, leaves picked and finely chopped

Preheat the oven to 350°F (180°C/Gas Mark 4).

Arrange the bread squares on a sheet pan, drizzle with the olive oil, and toss to combine. Bake until crisp but not browned, about 20 minutes. Remove from the oven and set aside. (This step can be done several days in advance and the croutons stored in a zipseal plastic food bag or an airtight container at room temperature.)

Place the tomatoes in a colander set over a bowl and sprinkle with the salt. Set aside for at least 20 minutes, tossing occasionally, to allow the juices to drain into the bowl.

Measure out 1 tablespoon of drained tomato juice and place into a small bowl. Stir in the lemon juice and tahini to combine.

To serve, transfer the tomatoes to a serving bowl and add the scallions (spring onions), chili, mint, and pita croutons. Drizzle with the tahini sauce and toss to combine. This can be enjoyed immediately, but is best if set aside for 5–10 minutes before serving to allow the bread to absorb most of the dressing.

Beet and Sweet Potato Mutabal

An ancient 800 BCE text mentioned beets growing in the Hanging Gardens of Babylon. True or not, the beet we know today has evolved substantially since its first recorded cultivation for consumption in 1542. From an original carrot-like shape to the round bulb we recognize today, garden beets are a staple in Eastern European cuisine and used for 20 percent of the world's sugar production. In the Arab world, however, they are most often relegated to the realm of salads. Generally, and this is a gross oversimplification, when an Arab person has a vegetable he wants to eat in a salad, he will either dress it in lemon and olive oil or mix it with tahini. This recipe is in the latter camp. The addition of sweet potatoes is not traditional and might sound odd, but it works wonderfully. The color of the dip remains bright pink and you do not taste the sweet potatoes at all, but they impart a unique sweetness that breaks through the earthiness of just beets and tahini.

Serves 4 as part of a spread

- 1 medium-small (4 oz/120 g) beet
- 1 very small (4 oz/120 g) sweet potato
- 4 tablespoons tahini
- 2 tablespoons regular or Greek yogurt
- 2 tablespoons fresh lemon juice
- 1 small clove garlic, crushed in a garlic press (optional)
- ½–¾ teaspoon salt, to taste
- Extra-virgin olive oil, for drizzling
- Blanched slivered pistachios, pumpkin seeds, or cashews (or sesame seeds and a sprinkling of finely chopped parsley leaves), for garnish

Preheat the oven to 450°F (230°C/Gas Mark 8).

Remove any leafy tops from the beet, keeping the stems intact so no flesh is exposed. Wash and scrub the beet and sweet potato thoroughly.

Wrap the beet and sweet potato separately in aluminum foil and bake until a skewer or sharp knife easily penetrates the flesh, 45–60 minutes. Remove and set aside until cool enough to handle.

Once cooled, peel the sweet potato by hand. To peel the beet, use a peeler or rub the skin off with your fingers. Use gloves to avoid staining your hands, or simply scrub your hands with lemon when done to remove stains.

In a food processor, combine the beet, sweet potato, tahini, yogurt, lemon juice, garlic (if using), and salt and pulse until you have a smooth paste. Transfer to a shallow bowl and, using the back of a spoon, make a small well in the center. Drizzle with olive oil, sprinkle with your chosen garnish, and serve.

Tahini, Walnut, and Aleppo Pepper Spread (1) p. 216; Lentil and Chickpea Msabaha (2) p. 217; Beet and Sweet Potato Mutabal (3)

Tahini, Walnut, and Aleppo Pepper Spread

Rumor has it that my Palestinian great-grandfather was a bon vivant of sorts who spent his days entertaining friends while my Syrian great-grandmother spent hers crafting unique mezze spreads to keep him and his company satisfied. Over the years, as these stories made their way through my family, different dishes were referred to and reminisced about. One that always stood out to me was this tahini and walnut spread. While no exact recipe was ever handed down in our family, I've reconstructed this one from the numerous descriptions I've heard over the years. The flavors are robust and earthy, so I find it works really well as a dip with fresh vegetables to brighten it up, but certainly nobody will complain if you serve this delicious concoction with bread.

---

p. 215

Serves 4 as part of a spread

4 tablespoons tahini
2 tablespoons yogurt
1 tablespoon fresh lemon juice
1–2 teaspoons Aleppo pepper, plus more for garnish
1 teaspoon paprika (optional, for bright color; add if using only 1 teaspoon Aleppo pepper)
1 small clove garlic, crushed in a garlic press
¼ teaspoon salt, plus more to taste
Generous ½ cup (2 oz/60 g) walnut pieces, lightly toasted and very coarsely ground or chopped by hand

In a bowl, stir together the tahini, yogurt, 3 tablespoons water, the lemon juice, Aleppo pepper, paprika (if using), garlic, and salt. Add the walnuts and stir until evenly incorporated. Taste and add more salt to your liking.

To serve, spoon into a shallow bowl and sprinkle with some Aleppo pepper.

Lentil and Chickpea Msabaha

The word *msabaha* means "swimming" or "floating" in Arabic, and refers to a dish of chickpeas swimming in tahini sauce—a lazy man's hummus, if you will. It's eaten warm and is one of my favorite breakfast dishes, not only for how easy it is to prepare, but also for how alive the flavors are. In my haste one day, I picked up the wrong beans in the supermarket and ended up with cans of white beans instead of chickpeas. So we had cannellini bean *msabaha* for breakfast the next day. I was initially worried that it would feel like an inferior sub-in for the classic dish, but it carried its own weight and left me wondering why we shouldn't experiment with other beans as well. I have since made it with black beans, kidney beans, and even with lentils. They all work well, but the flavor profile is different for each. My favorites are the white beans or a combination of lentils and chickpeas.

---

p. 215

Serves 4–6

For the lentils and chickpeas:
¾ cup (5 oz/150 g) French green (Puy) or beluga lentils
1 can (14 oz/400 g) chickpeas, rinsed and drained
1 teaspoon ground cumin

For the dressing:
1 large clove garlic, minced
1 green chili, minced
2 tablespoons extra-virgin olive oil
2 tablespoons fresh lemon juice

For the msabaha:
Scant 1 cup (225 g) tahini
1 large clove garlic, crushed in a garlic press
1 teaspoon salt
½ cup (4 oz/120 g) yogurt
4 tablespoons fresh lemon juice

For serving:
2 tablespoons chopped fresh flat-leaf parsley
Ground cumin
Paprika
Flatbread, store-bought or homemade (page 30)

Prepare the lentils and chickpeas:
In a small pot, combine the lentils and 2 cups (16 fl oz/475 ml) cold water. Bring to a simmer over medium heat and cook until tender but not falling apart, 15–30 minutes. Timing will vary by brand and variety. Drain well. Measure out a couple of tablespoons and set aside for garnish.

Meanwhile, in a saucepan, combine the drained chickpeas, cumin, and water to generously cover. Bring to a bare simmer, covered, just to keep warm as you prepare the rest of the dish.

Make the dressing:
In a small bowl, stir together the garlic, chili, olive oil, and lemon juice. Set aside.

Prepare the msabaha:
In a large bowl, stir together the tahini, garlic, salt, yogurt, and lemon juice; the sauce will be very thick and sticky at this point. Add ½ cup (4 fl oz/120 ml) of the hot chickpea cooking water to the tahini sauce and mix well. Scoop out roughly one-quarter of the chickpeas, add to the tahini sauce, and mix well, using the back of a spoon to mash lightly.

Drain the rest of the chickpeas, reserving a couple of tablespoons for garnish. Add the chickpeas and lentils to the tahini sauce and mix with a spoon to evenly combine.

To serve:
Transfer to a shallow serving bowl. Spoon the lemon and garlic dressing on top, then sprinkle with the parsley, cumin, and paprika, and add the reserved chickpeas and lentils for garnish.

Serve immediately with bread.

Note: If using beans, you will need two 14 oz (400 g) cans of your chosen bean in place of the chickpeas and lentils.

Pan-Fried Branzino with Tahini-Onion Sauce

Samak bì tahìnì is a very common dish across the Levant, especially in coastal towns, where fish fillets are placed in an onion and tahini sauce and baked in the oven. It's a great way to use up leftover fish, but is equally impressive made with a whole roast fish for company. As delicious as it is, the texture and color are often one-dimensional, and the two-step process of first cooking the fish and then setting it in the sauce and baking it can be tedious. So on weeknights, when I am anxious to put a quick and healthy meal on the dinner table, I've taken to making this easier and somewhat deconstructed version of that classic dish. Here I also brighten the tahini sauce in flavor and color by adding some paprika, chili, and a hint of tomato paste (purée), but you can forgo those for the traditional white sauce. It's wonderful on its own, next to rice or potatoes, or with a simple loaf of bread to mop up the sauce.

Serves 4

2 lb (900 g) skin-on branzino, sea bass/bream, flounder, or snapper fillets (4–8 fillets depending on fish size)

For the sauce:
- 4 tablespoons olive oil
- 2 onions, sliced into half-moons
- 1 cup (8 oz/240 g) tahini
- ½ cup (4 oz/120 g) yogurt
- 4–5 tablespoons fresh lemon juice, to taste
- ¾ teaspoon salt
- ½ teaspoon paprika
- ½ teaspoon cayenne pepper (substitute paprika for some or all for a less spicy variation)
- ½ teaspoon tomato paste (purée)

For finishing:
- 4 tablespoons olive oil
- Salt
- 1 tablespoon pine nuts, lightly toasted
- 1 tablespoon finely chopped fresh parsley
- Finely diced red chilies (optional)

Pat the fish fillets dry and place in a single layer on a plate, skin-side up. Chill in the refrigerator, uncovered, as you prepare the rest of the dish or for up to 3 hours. This allows the skin to dry out and crisp up when pan-fried. If you are using skinless fillets, you can skip the chilling step.

Make the sauce:
In a saucepan, heat the olive oil over medium heat. Add the onions and cook, stirring regularly, until the onions have completely softened but are not yet crisp, about 10 minutes.

Meanwhile, in a bowl, combine the tahini, ¾ cup (6 fl oz/180 ml) water, the yogurt, lemon juice, and salt and mix well. Add the paprika, cayenne, and tomato paste (purée) and mix to combine.

When the onions are ready, pour the tahini sauce over them, stir to combine, then cook just until warmed through but not boiling. If you allow it to boil, the yogurt will curdle. Keep warm until you fry the fish. If the sauce appears too thick, you can add a tablespoon of water at a time and stir.

To finish:
In a large heavy-bottomed frying pan, heat the oil until shimmering. Sprinkle the fillets with salt on both sides and place in the pan, skin-side down, pressing gently on each fillet for 15–30 seconds to make sure the skin has full contact with the hot pan so the fillet doesn't curl up. Cook the fish undisturbed for 3–4 minutes, until the edge is a nice golden-brown color and the fish is almost opaque on top. Using a fish spatula, gently flip each fillet and cook for another 30–60 seconds on the flesh side. Transfer to a plate lined with paper towels to drain.

Spread the tahini/onion sauce on a platter and top with the fried fish fillets. Sprinkle with toasted pine nuts, parsley, and red chilies (if using) and serve.

Pan-Fried Branzino with Tahini-Onion Sauce

Crispy Beef Tongue with Watercress Tahini and Walnuts

Offal is commonly eaten throughout the Arab world, but mostly from sheep. Some cuts are braised, others grilled, and some, like tongue, even used to line the bottom of a pot of stuffed grape leaves. Beef offal is rarely used, but beef tongue happens to be one of my favorite cuts of meat and I think one of the most underrated parts by far. It has a concentrated taste of meat without any of the gaminess. The texture is sublimely soft, which lends itself wonderfully to being seared crisp after cooking. While tongue is not usually prepared this way in the Middle East, this dish is inspired by how Arabs serve tahini with most grilled meats and how abroad meats are often served with greens (e.g., *tagliata* in Italy). The sharp and bright tahini sauce is a wonderful contrast to the rich mellow flavor of the tongue, while walnuts add a perfect texture to the dish.

Serves 4–6

For the tongue:
- 1 beef tongue (2–3 lb/1–1.5 kg)
- 2 bay leaves
- 2 cloves garlic, peeled
- 1 onion, peeled but left whole
- ½ cup (2½ oz/70 g) coarse salt
- 1 tablespoon Nine-Spice Mix (page 27), baharat, or Lebanese 7-spice blend

For the tahini sauce:
- ½ cup (4 oz/120 g) tahini
- 4 tablespoons fresh lemon juice
- 4 tablespoons yogurt
- 3½ oz (100 g) mix of watercress and cilantro (coriander), or any combination of fresh herbs, including parsley and dill
- 1 small clove garlic, peeled
- ½ teaspoon salt

To finish:
- Vegetable oil, for frying
- ½ cup (50 g) walnut pieces, lightly toasted
- Maldon sea salt

Prepare the tongue:
Place the tongue in a large pot with enough fresh water to cover. Add the bay leaves, garlic, onion, salt, and spice blend and bring to a boil. Reduce the heat to maintain a low simmer and cook until the tongue is tender, 1 hour 30 minutes to 2 hours.

Drain, discarding the broth, and when the tongue is cool enough to handle, peel away the outer layer. (This step can be done a day or two in advance and the tongue kept refrigerated until ready to use.)

Make the tahini sauce:
In a mini food processor, combine the tahini, lemon juice, yogurt, herbs, garlic, and salt and process until the mixture is smooth and bright green in color.

To finish:
When ready to serve, cut the tongue into bite-size cubes or slice into rounds.

In a frying pan, heat enough oil to generously cover the bottom over medium-high heat until shimmering but not smoking. Add the tongue and cook until crisp, about 15 seconds on each side if cubes, or 30–45 seconds on each side if sliced into rounds. Remove with a slotted spoon and set on a plate lined with paper towels to drain.

Spoon the tahini sauce onto a serving platter and spread evenly with the back of a spoon. Arrange the tongue over the tahini and sprinkle with the toasted walnuts and some flaky salt. Serve immediately.

 Crispy Beef Tongue with Watercress Tahini and Walnuts

Halaweh

Halaweh (halva) and all derivatives of that globally used word are rooted in the Arabic word *halw*, which means "sweet." The first known written recipe for *halaweh* appeared in the early tenth-century Arabic *Kitab al-Tabìkh*, but it has since spread across the world, from India to the Balkans, where each culture has its own unique version. When Arabs use the word, however, it refers to the confection made from tahini milled from sesame seeds. Originally, it was made from tahini and the root of the soapwort plant. Today, however, few commercial varieties are made in the traditional way, with many using artificial flavorings and sugar instead. But if you've had the original kind, you know there is a huge difference between good *halaweh*, which is smooth and dense with a deep nutty flavor, and the commercial variety, which is often powdery and sticky with a single note of sweetness. This recipe is the best solution I have found for making it at home, which gives the wonderful flavor of original *halaweh* but with only a few simple ingredients. It can be sliced or crumbled and eaten with bread or crackers, or simply as is.

Makes about 1 pound (450 g)

- 1 cup (4½ oz/120 g) powdered (icing) sugar
- 1 heaping cup (120 g) whole milk powder
- ¾ cup plus 1 tablespoon tahini (200 g), stirred well before using
- 1 teaspoon vanilla extract
- 1 tablespoon coarsely crushed pistachios

In a medium bowl, combine the powdered (icing) sugar and milk powder and stir to combine. Add the tahini and vanilla and mix until starting to come together, then use your hands to knead into a paste. It will take a couple of minutes, but the mixture should come together into a smooth ball and not be sticky, like shiny Play-Doh. Depending on the brand of milk powder and tahini you are using, you may need to adjust very slightly. If you still find it too dry and crumbly after kneading for a couple of minutes, add a teaspoon of tahini at a time until you reach the right consistency. If it is too sticky, sprinkle a teaspoon of powdered milk until it comes together more smoothly.

Line a 3-cup (710 ml) round, square, or rectangular glass container with plastic wrap (clingfilm), leaving an overhang around the edges.

Sprinkle the crushed pistachios evenly at the bottom and tip the tahini mixture on top. Press the mixture down to pack tightly, then bring the plastic overhang over the top to cover it. Cover with a lid and put in the refrigerator for several hours or overnight.

To serve, remove the lid, open the plastic wrap, then place an inverted plate over the container and flip. Unmold the *halaweh* (halva) and remove the plastic wrap to reveal a beautiful pistachio-studded top.

Variations: The above recipe is the most basic flavor for *halaweh*, but you can experiment with other combinations. These are just a few suggestions:

— Add 1 tablespoons crushed pistachios and ¼ teaspoon ground cardamom to the powdered sugar/milk powder mix.

— Add 1 tablespoon unsweetened cocoa powder and 1 more tablespoon powdered sugar to the powdered sugar/milk powder mix. Line the mold with crushed roasted peanuts instead of pistachios.

— Add 1 teaspoon rose water when you add the tahini. Line the mold with freeze-dried raspberries or dried rose buds instead of (or along with) the pistachios.

Chocolate-Covered Tahini Truffles

While I encourage you to make these truffles, I warn you to do so at your own risk, for once you take a bite you will not be able to stop at just one. The nutty, mild bitterness of tahini stands up well to the understated sweetness of dark chocolate, making it one of the best truffles I have ever had. Chocolate truffles—balls of ganache coated in cocoa powder—are a fairly recent French confectionary invention named for their visual resemblance to actual truffles. The word has since taken on different meanings in different countries depending on the chocolate's unique composition. This recipe is fairly straightforward with the same concept as the original truffle but uses homemade Halaweh (page 222) instead of ganache and coats it with chocolate instead of cocoa powder. Although these truffles are supposed to last for several weeks in the refrigerator, I have yet to make any that aren't devoured within a couple of days.

Makes 40 small or 20 large truffles

- Halaweh (page 222), made without pistachios
- 7 oz (200 g) dark chocolate (70% cacao)
- ½ teaspoon vegetable oil
- Crushed or slivered pistachios or dried rose petals, for garnish

Line a plate with parchment paper and set aside. Prepare the *halaweh* mixture as directed, but do not place in a container or mold.

Using a measuring spoon or ice cream scoop, measure out 1 heaping tablespoon of the tahini mixture and roll between your hands into a ball. Set on the parchment-lined plate. Repeat until the mixture is done. You should have about 20 truffles. (Use a smaller size of ice cream scoop or measuring spoon for smaller truffles.) Put the truffles in the freezer until completely firm, about 1 hour.

When ready to coat, in a small heatproof bowl set over a pan of simmering water (but not touching the water), combine the chocolate and vegetable oil. Stir occasionally until the chocolate is completely melted. Remove the pan from the heat, but keep the bowl over the steaming water to stay warm.

Take the truffles out of the freezer. One by one, place a truffle into the melted chocolate and gently roll it around with a fork until fully covered. Lift with the fork, allowing excess coating to drop, then return to the parchment-lined plate. Immediately top with crushed pistachios. The chocolate starts to set very quickly because the truffles are cold, so the pistachios will not stick if not sprinkled immediately. Chill the truffles in the refrigerator until the chocolate is fully set.

To serve, peel from the parchment paper and place in mini cupcake liners. The truffles will keep in an airtight container in the refrigerator for 2–3 weeks.

Tahini Cheesecake with Chocolate Glaze and Sesame Seeds

Cheesecakes are thought to date back to Greco-Roman times, but the consumption of cheese in sweet form is as old as cheese itself. Arabs use cheese in famous desserts like *knafeh* (see Coconut Knafeh with Lemongrass Syrup, page 246), *kulaj*, *mutabaq*, and *atayef*, which are all different kinds of pastry filled with cheese and soaked in syrup. The European and American versions of cheesecake with a crust are a far cry from those desserts, but the combination of a crunchy base with a creamy filling, seen across the world, is evidently a winning one. Here I make a classic baked Western cheesecake, but flavor it with tahini and top with chocolate and sesame seeds. This East meets West dessert balances sweet with savory and creamy with crunchy to create a decadent cake with pleasantly complex layers of flavors.

Serves 12

For the crust:
- 1½ cups (5⅓ oz/150 g) graham cracker crumbs (or a mix of speculoos, digestive cookies/biscuits, and/or petit beurre cookies)
- 1 cup (3½ oz/100 g) pistachios or pecans, finely chopped
- ¾ cup (5⅓ oz/150 g) sugar
- 1 stick (4 oz/113 g) unsalted butter, melted

For the filling:
- 3 packages (8 oz/225 g each) cream cheese, at room temperature (this is very important to avoid lumps in your cake)
- 1 cup (7 oz/200 g) sugar
- 3 eggs
- ⅓ cup (2¾oz/80 g) good-quality tahini
- 3 tablespoons grape molasses, honey, or maple syrup
- 2 tablespoons heavy (double) cream
- 2 teaspoons cornstarch (cornflour)
- 1 teaspoon vanilla extract
- ½ teaspoon salt

For the topping:
- Scant ½ cup (4 fl oz/100 ml) heavy (double) cream
- 3½ oz (100 g) dark chocolate (at least 55% cacao), broken into small pieces
- 2 tablespoons unhulled sesame seeds, lightly toasted

Preheat the oven to 350°F (180°C/Gas Mark 4). Line a 9-inch (23 cm) springform pan with a round of parchment paper.

Make the crust:
In a bowl, combine the crumbs, nuts, sugar, and melted butter and mix until evenly incorporated. Press the crumb mixture evenly into the bottom of the pan, pushing it halfway up the sides (a flat measuring cup/jug helps with this). Bake the crust for 10 minutes, then set aside to cool. Leave the oven on. (This crust can be prebaked up to 1 day ahead and left covered at room temperature once cooled.)

Make the filling:
In a stand mixer with the paddle (or in a bowl with an electric mixer or even in a food processor), beat the cream cheese and sugar together at medium-high speed until creamy and smooth, about 1 minute. Add the eggs, tahini, grape molasses, cream, cornstarch (cornflour), vanilla, and salt and continue to beat at medium speed until incorporated and smooth, 1–3 minutes. (A food processor will be much quicker than a stand mixer, so adjust accordingly.)

Pour the filling into the crust, smoothing the top. Transfer the pan to the oven and bake until the cake is set but the center has a light jiggle, about 50 minutes. Turn the oven off, prop the door open with a wooden spoon, and allow the cake to cool inside for another hour. Remove the cake from the oven and set on the counter to cool completely.

Make the topping:
In a small saucepan, heat the cream until it's about to boil. Remove from the heat, add the chocolate pieces, and let rest for a couple of minutes. With a heat-resistant spatula, stir the cream until all the chocolate has melted and the ganache is smooth and shiny. Allow to cool for a few minutes.

Pour the chocolate ganache over the cheesecake and smooth the top. Sprinkle the sesame seeds in a pattern over the ganache and set aside to cool completely. Once cooled, refrigerate for a few hours or overnight. To serve, remove the sides of the springform pan and slide the cake onto a platter.

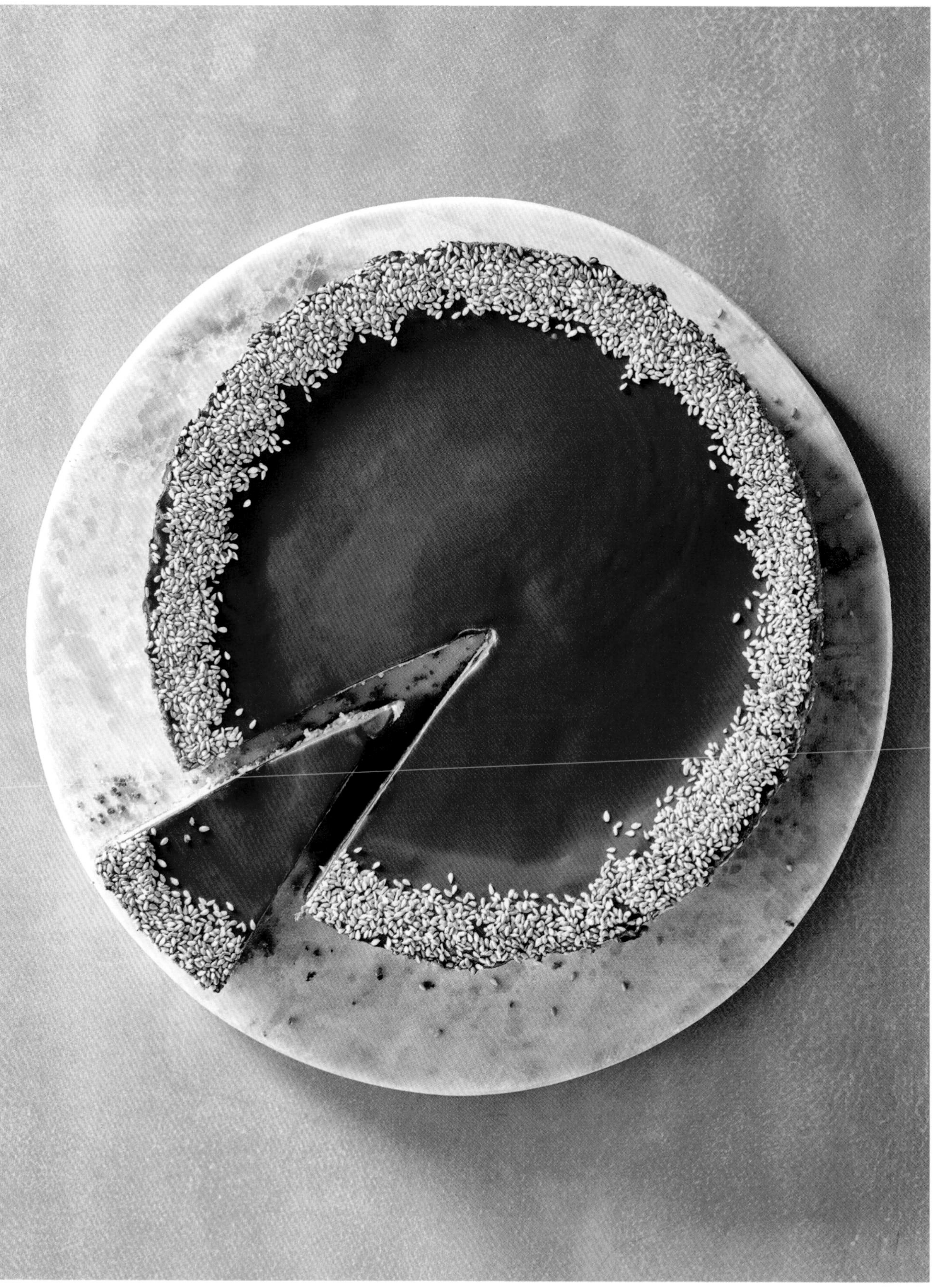

Tahini Cheesecake with Chocolate Glaze and Sesame Seeds

Tahini Toffee Pudding

My feet were sore and my heart was heavy after a long day of walking. I had left Jerusalem again and was going to make London my home for the foreseeable future. After a day spent sorting out living arrangements, I stumbled into a pub I had read about once in a novel. I ordered fish and chips and I splurged on a dessert the waiter told me was not to be missed. It was my first experience with sticky toffee pudding. It wrapped me in such warm comfort that night and remained my favorite dessert until I left London with a family in tow, five years later, to make Philadelphia my new home. At first, I felt a sense of betrayal at tinkering with this dessert that had been so good to me, but this version with tahini is so sublime that the transgression can only be forgiven.

Serves 9–12

For the cake:

- Butter and flour, for the pan
- 9 oz (250 g) pitted Medjool dates
- 1 cup (8 fl oz/250 ml) boiling water
- 1 teaspoon vanilla extract
- 4 ½ tablespoons (2 ½ oz/70 g) unsalted butter
- ¾ cup (5 ⅓ oz/150 g) granulated sugar
- 2 eggs
- 5 tablespoons tahini
- 1 ½ cups (7 oz/200 g) all-purpose (plain) flour
- 2 teaspoons baking soda (bicarbonate of soda)
- 1 teaspoon baking powder

For the toffee sauce:

- ¾ cup (6 fl oz/175 ml) heavy (double) cream
- 6 tablespoons (3 oz/85 g) unsalted butter
- Scant ½ cup (3 oz/85 g) light brown sugar
- 3 tablespoons date molasses
- 1 tablespoon tahini
- Pinch of salt

Vanilla ice cream or Greek yogurt, for serving

Make the cake:
Preheat the oven to 350°F (180°C/Gas Mark 4). Butter and flour a 9-inch (23 cm) round or 9 x 13-inch (23 x 33 cm) rectangular cake pan.

In a food processor, combine the dates, boiling water, and vanilla and blend into a smooth purée. Transfer to a bowl and set aside.

In the same food processor bowl, combine the butter and granulated sugar and cream until pale and well combined. It won't fluff up as it would in a mixer, but that's fine. Add the eggs and tahini and process until you have a pale smooth purée.

Tip the flour, baking soda (bicarb), and baking powder into the food processor and process until combined. Fold the date mixture back in and process just until combined, taking care not to overbeat the batter.

Scrape the batter into the prepared cake pan and transfer to the oven. Bake until a skewer inserted into the center comes out clean, about 45 minutes. You can start testing at 35 minutes.

Meanwhile, make the toffee sauce:
In a small saucepan, combine the cream, butter, brown sugar, and date molasses and cook over low heat until the butter melts. Increase the heat to medium and bring the mixture to a boil. Simmer for 2–3 minutes, stirring occasionally, until slightly thickened. Remove from the heat, add the tahini and salt, and give one final stir. The tahini toffee sauce should be warm when served and can be reheated on the stovetop if necessary.

To serve, place an individual slice on a serving plate, top with ice cream or yogurt, and drizzle with the warm sauce.

Fruits + Floral Waters

When I was a child and we were about to drive back to Jerusalem from my grandparents' home in the Galilean hills, I would complain about my impending carsickness. My mother would pick a lemon off one of the trees or, in season, a blossom off one of the citrus trees. "Smell this on the ride back and you'll be fine," she always assured me. If any of us had a stomachache, she poured a few drops of orange flower water into a warm cup of water and we found immediate relief. To this day, when life is stressful, when I am not feeling well, or when I simply need a break, the smell of citrus and its blossoms calms me down.

Nothing evokes memories and a sense of place as much as scent, and nothing compares to the scent of a ripe fruit picked in season, other than, perhaps, floral waters, which give Arab cooking a certain lingering, indefinable essence of its own. A quick look through historic Arabic cookbooks like *Kitab al-Tabìkh* (a tenth-century cookbook) or *Kitab al-Wusla ila al-Habìb* (a thirteenth-century cookbook) shows entire chapters dedicated to perfumes and distilled floral waters. In many cases, they were seen to have medicinal properties, and since cookbooks were compiled as much for the humoral qualities of the food as for the recipes, it is not surprising to see their prevalence throughout.

Historically, Arabs ate with their hands and thus paid great attention to cleanliness. Perfumed soaps were used to wash hands before and after meals and floral waters to perfume oneself before and after dining. Reading through many medieval Arabic cookbook texts, I couldn't help but imagine the seductive splendor of medieval banquets, where perfume set the ambience but also was featured throughout the many luxurious dishes cooked at the time. It was a time when nuts and dried fruits were scattered like jewels throughout dishes, where fresh herbs painted a lively landscape around platters, and where the scent of a dish was as transportive as its taste.

Throughout medieval times, and over the course of the Persian and Muslim empires, sprinkling rose water on a pot of food was the customary final step in cooking a dish. Today, it seems floral waters tend to feature more in desserts and sweet dishes. In this chapter, I have grouped fruits with floral waters because fruits, when picked in season, also have the most enticing aromas. A succulent watermelon has hints of blossoming citrus, pears can have sweet floral notes verging on vanilla, while hibiscus flowers tend to have hints of cranberry when steeped or used in desserts.

It's not difficult to see how fruits and floral waters play a tandem tune. Adding orange blossom water to a fruit salad (page 234) transforms a basic dish into a luxurious one. Poaching pears with warm spices for Baharat Poached Pear with Radicchio White Cheese Slaw a (page 237) highlights their floral flavor, making them a perfect companion to the sharp slaw served alongside. Using hibiscus and rose offers much needed contrast to the mellow *muhallabìyeh* tart (page 240). The following recipes are a testament to the fact that the biggest flavor impact can come from the smallest and most unexpected usage or combination of ingredients.

Watermelon and Burrata with Pistachios, Mint, and Lime

Contrary to what has been popularized by those who write about Middle Eastern food, nobody eats watermelon salad in the Arab world. We don't chop or mix, we don't dress or season. We eat watermelon and cheese. Period. Sometimes we'll put the cheese in a piece of bread and eat the watermelon on the side, but that's the extent of it. So this simple platter is an ode to my memory of carefree childhood days, running with cousins around mountains or on beaches, with watermelon juice dripping down our chins and fingers. I use burrata or mozzarella in place of the traditional white Arabic cheese because it's more consistent abroad. At first bite this might leave you wondering, "Where is the salty cheese?," but the subtle layers of flavor—from fragrant mint and lime zest to crunchy pistachios and salt flakes—will slowly hit your palate and leave you more than satisfied.

Serves 2–4

3 cups (1 lb/450 g) bite-size cubes of watermelon
8 oz (225 g) burrata or fresh buffalo mozzarella
2 heaping tablespoons pistachios, finely chopped
2 sprigs fresh mint, leaves picked and finely chopped
1 teaspoon grated lime zest from an unwaxed or organic lime
Maldon sea salt, for sprinkling
Very good-quality extra-virgin olive oil, for drizzling

Arrange the watermelon cubes on a serving platter. Tear the cheese into pieces and place on top of the watermelon. Scatter the pistachios, mint, and lime zest on top and sprinkle with flaky salt. Drizzle with some olive oil and serve immediately.

Watermelon and Burrata with Pistachios, Mint, and Lime

Fruit Salad with Orange Blossom Water and Pistachios

This salad is a far cry from the typical fruit salad passed around after many Arab dinners or picnics—the one made with apples, pears, and oranges, often not in peak season, soaked in sugar syrup as a way to add flavor to unexciting fruits. Today, I prepare this salad with a much more appealing selection of fruits, and only when they are at their peak. The floral waters bring out notes of sweetness from the fruits while the pistachios and mint turn what could become a monotonous dish into a perfect balance of sweet, bright, and crunchy. The fruit suggestions below are exactly that: suggestions. Feel free to use whatever seasonal combinations you prefer or have on hand.

Serves 4–6

- ¼ cup (1¾ oz/50 g) sugar
- 1 tablespoon fresh lime or lemon juice
- 1 tablespoon orange blossom water
- 1 tablespoon rose water (optional)
- ¼ cup (1 oz/25 g) Sicilian or Turkish pistachios (see Note)
- Boiling water
- 2 fuyu persimmons or 1 mango, cut into ½-inch (1.25 cm) dice
- 1½ cups (8 oz/225 g) berries or summer stone fruits, cut into ½-inch (1.25 cm) dice
- 1½ cups (5 oz/150 g) grapes, kept whole if small or halved if big
- ¾ cup (4 oz/120 g) cubed (½ inch/ 1.25 cm) cantaloupe or honeydew melon
- ½ cup (3 oz/85 g) pomegranate seeds or pitted cherries
- A few sprigs fresh mint, leaves picked

In a small saucepan, combine the sugar, lemon juice, and ¼ cup (2 fl oz/ 60 ml) water. Bring to a boil over medium heat, stirring a couple of times, until the sugar has melted. Remove from the heat and add the orange blossom water and rose water (if using). Set aside to cool. (This step can be done several days in advance.)

In a small bowl, combine the pistachios with boiling water to cover. Set aside until cool enough to handle and the skins peel away easily. Peel the skins by rubbing between your fingers (or rub back and forth between two paper towels a few times to loosen the skins) and discard the skins. Put the peeled pistachios in a small bowl and keep covered in cool water while you finish the rest of the salad.

In a large bowl, combine all the fruit. Drain the pistachios, add to the salad, and pour the cooled sugar syrup over the fruits. Very gently toss to combine. Sprinkle with the mint leaves and serve immediately. The salad will keep in the refrigerator for 1–2 days, but is best enjoyed soon after preparation.

Note: Sicilian and Turkish pistachios are different from the Iranian varieties commonly grown in the United States. The Sicilian/Turkish varieties are descendants of the original Syrian variety and tend to be pink on the outside and a very distinct bright green on the inside. For this salad it makes a big difference to see the bright green color, which is why I recommend using them and removing the skin. In terms of flavor, the difference might not be very noticeable, but the Sicilian/ Turkish kind are marginally sweeter.

Fruit Salad with Orange Blossom Water and Pistachios

Cantaloupe in Honeydew Almond Soup

During Ramadan, there are two drinks always sold in the Old City of Jerusalem: a tamarind/orange blossom juice and a sweet almond juice. Families buy them in bottles to take home and mix with water for a refreshing drink after breaking the fast. Almond was the choice for my family. Native to the Mediterranean region and used in Arabic cuisine since it was first recorded, almond is consumed in all its forms across the Middle East. In spring, green almonds are picked and eaten whole, oftentimes dipped in salt. Later in the season, they are shelled, roasted, blanched, ground, or juiced and also eaten raw or used in cooking. Rare is the family that does not have almonds at home. One of my favorite things to eat as a child was slices of melon washed down with almond juice. This dessert is my take on that beloved snack. Not only is it delicious, but the contrast of orange against green is also visually stunning. Just make sure the almond milk you use is unsweetened and unflavored and has as few additives as possible and that everything is very cold when served.

---

p. 238

Serves 4

- 9 oz (250 g) honeydew melon (about one-quarter of a large melon), cut into chunks
- 1½ tablespoons sugar
- 1¼ teaspoons almond extract
- 1 cup (8 fl oz/250 ml) unsweetened almond milk
- 9 oz (250 g) cantaloupe (about one-quarter of a large melon)

In a blender, combine the honeydew, sugar, almond extract, and almond milk and blend until very smooth. Chill until cold.

Use a melon baller to scoop out balls of cantaloupe, or simply cut into small bite-size cubes. Keep chilled until ready to serve.

To serve, pour ½ cup (4 fl oz/120 ml) of the honeydew almond soup into a shallow bowl and top with pieces of cantaloupe.

Baharat Poached Pear with Radicchio White Cheese Slaw and Candied Pecans

I waved my hand across the street at a gentleman in a black cap with a salt-and-pepper beard and a backpack. Somehow, at the bustling intersection of Rittenhouse Square in Philadelphia, I sensed he was the Arab chef I was supposed to meet for lunch. "What gave it away? Was it the beard?" he asked. I laughed. No, it wasn't, but there was something—perhaps in the blood, perhaps just having grown up in an Arab country—that I could recognize an Arab person even amidst a crowd. As we ate a burger and a cheesesteak, Moeen Abuzaid told me about the inspiration behind his avant-garde Arabic cooking and the exciting ways he was transforming traditional Arabic dishes. Having trained by the sides of numerous Michelin three-starred chefs who had retired to his native Amman, Moeen had a wealth of ideas and information about transforming ingredients into magic on a plate and a celebration on the palate. In this dish, he takes a traditional French dessert cooked in wine, and to make it suitable for non-alcohol drinkers in the Arab and Muslim world, poaches it in a juice transformed with Arab spices, then serves it with a few other complementary elements.

---

p. 239

Serves 6

For the pears:
- 6 firm-ripe Bosc or Conference pears
- 5 cups (40 fl oz/1.2 liters) apple juice
- ½ cup (3½ oz/100 g) sugar
- 10 black peppercorns
- 5 cardamom pods
- 5 allspice berries
- 4 whole cloves
- 1 cinnamon stick

For the slaw:
- 3 cups (7 oz/200 g) shredded radicchio
- 6 oz (170 g) Akkawi or halloumi cheese, coarsely grated
- ½ cup (1¾ oz/50 g) candied pecans, very coarsely chopped
- 2 tablespoons fresh lemon juice
- 1 teaspoon nigella seeds
- A few sprigs fresh mint, leaves picked and roughly torn

Prepare the pears:
Peel the pears, halved lengthwise, and use a measuring spoon to scoop out the seeds. (You could also keep the pears whole and use a corer to remove the seeds.) Place the pears in a large saucepan and add the apple juice, sugar, and whole spices. Cover with a round of parchment paper with a small hole cut in the center (or put a plate on top) to keep the pears submerged in the liquid.

Bring the saucepan to a boil, then reduce the heat and simmer until the pears are fully cooked through but not falling apart, 25–50 minutes. The timing will depend on the variety, size, strength of heat, and size of saucepan. A point of a knife should very easily pierce the pears when ready.

Remove the pears from the heat and allow to cool in the poaching syrup before refrigerating overnight. (This step can be done up to several days in advance as the pears continue to absorb and improve in flavor the longer they sit in the syrup.)

Make the slaw:
In a bowl, combine the radicchio, cheese, candied pecans, lemon juice, nigella seeds, and mint leaves. Add 4 tablespoons of the pear poaching liquid and toss to combine.

To serve, spoon some of the slaw into individual serving dishes and top with two pear halves (or a whole pear).

Cantaloupe in Honeydew Almond Soup

 Baharat Poached Pear with Radicchio White Cheese Slaw and Candied Pecans

Muhallabiyeh and Hibiscus Rose Tart

Contrasts work for a reason. Sweet and salty, soft and crunchy, the juxtaposition of opposing textures and flavors confuses the senses and makes us come back for more. *Muhallabìyeh*, a milk pudding, is a widespread dessert across the Arab world, yet I always found the texture too uniform for my liking. Looking at the historic origins of this dish (see Fresh Mint Muhallabiyeh, page 53), one sees it was originally a topping for a crunchy base of bread and meat (sweet and savory dishes were common in medieval times). So I decided to try something similar, but using a sweet base instead. This is the dessert that ensued. It looks deceptively similar to cheesecake, but that's where the similarities end. It is substantially lighter, and the floral and fruity flavors are reminiscent of the banquet descriptions in *One Thousand and One Nights*. So make this dessert and allow it to transport you.

Makes one 9-inch (23 cm) tart

For the crust:
- ¾ cup (2½ oz/75 g) graham cracker (digestive biscuit) crumbs (about 5 full sheets graham crackers)
- ¾ cup (2½ oz/75 g) pistachios
- ½ cup (3½ oz/100 g) sugar
- 6 tablespoons (3 oz/85 g) unsalted butter, melted
- Pinch of salt

For the muhallabiyeh filling:
- 1½ cups (12 fl oz/350 ml) whole milk
- 1 cup (8 fl oz/250 ml) heavy (double) cream
- Scant ½ cup (3oz/90 g) sugar
- ½ cup (1¾ oz/50 g) cornstarch (cornflour)
- 2 teaspoons rose water

For the hibiscus topping:
- ⅓ cup (10 g) dried hibiscus flowers
- 3 tablespoons sugar
- ½ cup (1¾ oz/50 g) cornstarch (cornflour)
- 1 teaspoon rose water

For optional garnish:
- Unsweetened shredded (desiccated) coconut
- Slivered or crushed pistachios

Preheat the oven to 350°F (180°C/Gas Mark 4). Line the bottom of a 9-inch (23 cm) springform pan with a round of parchment paper.

Make the crust:
In a food processor, combine the graham crackers, pistachios, and sugar and pulse until finely ground. Add the melted butter and salt and mix until evenly incorporated. Press the crumb mixture evenly into the bottom of the springform. (You do not need to take it up the sides.) Bake the crust for 10 minutes, then set aside to cool completely before you prepare the filling. Leave the oven on.

Make the muhallabiyeh:
In a saucepan, combine 1 cup (8 fl oz/250 ml) of the milk, the cream, and sugar and bring to a simmer over medium heat. Meanwhile, in a small bowl, stir the remaining ½ cup (4 fl oz/120 ml) milk into the cornstarch (cornflour) until fully dissolved. When the milk and cream are on the verge of coming to a boil, pour in the rose water and the cornstarch mixture and whisk constantly until the mixture thickens, 1–2 minutes. Remove from the heat and pour the mixture into the center of the tart shell and lightly tap the pan to even out the surface. Refrigerate to cool while you prepare the hibiscus topping.

Make the hibiscus topping:
In a saucepan, combine the hibiscus flowers with 2 cups (16 fl oz/475 ml) water and the sugar and bring to a boil. Simmer for 1–2 minutes, then strain the tea and return to the saucepan over low heat.

In a small cup, stir ½ cup (4 fl oz/120 ml) water into the cornstarch until dissolved. Add the cornstarch mixture and the rose water to the hibiscus tea, whisking constantly. The hibiscus will thicken almost immediately, so remove it from the heat and allow to cool for a minute or two, stirring constantly.

Pour the hibiscus mixture over the *muhallabìyeh* and lightly tap the cake pan to smooth out the surface. Refrigerate for at least 2 hours and preferably overnight. If desired, garnish with coconut and slivered pistachios.

To serve, remove the sides of the springform pan and slide the tart off the base onto a platter.

Pistachio and Rose Water Tart with Yogurt and Cherries

Few things are as interesting as experiencing Thanksgiving—the ultimate American holiday—in the homes of various ethnic minorities and seeing the same exact dish made in countless variations. A Pakistani friend of mine enjoys *mìrch masala* (hot spice) turkey that is bright red. My in-laws use the traditional Arab stuffing of rice and lamb instead of the American bread one. A Mexican friend makes tamales instead of bread stuffing. These blended culinary traditions often bring about unexpected and delicious change. A few years ago, I was responsible for dessert on Thanksgiving and so I made a pistachio rose pie in place of the pecan one, but countered all the richness with a topping of Greek yogurt. I garnished with red currants at the time, but I use different garnishes depending on the season, so feel free to experiment on your own. Some of my favorites are fresh rose petals or cherries.

Makes one 9-inch (23 cm) tart

For the pastry:

- 1½ cups (7 oz/200 g) all-purpose (plain) flour
- ½ cup (2 oz/60 g) powdered (icing) sugar
- Pinch of salt
- 9 tablespoons (4½ oz/125 g) very cold or frozen unsalted butter, cut into small cubes
- 1 egg
- ½ teaspoon vanilla extract

For the pistachio filling:

- ¾ cup (3½ oz/100 g) pistachios
- 1 tablespoon all-purpose (plain) flour
- 6 tablespoons (3 oz/85 g) cold unsalted butter, cut into small cubes
- 6¾ tablespoons (3 oz/85 g) granulated sugar
- Pinch of salt
- 2 tablespoons pistachio paste/butter
- 1 egg
- 2 tablespoons cold milk
- 2 tablespoons rose water

For the topping and garnish:

- ¾ cup (8 oz/225 g) Greek yogurt
- 4 tablespoons powdered (icing) sugar
- Grated zest of 1 unwaxed or organic lemon
- Cherries, halved and pitted, or other seasonal fruits, for garnish
- Crushed pistachios or rose petals, for garnish (optional)

Make the pastry:
In a food processor, combine the flour, powdered (icing) sugar, and salt and pulse to combine. Add the butter and continue to pulse until the mixture resembles coarse, uneven breadcrumbs. Add the egg and vanilla and process in a few long pulses until the dough starts to clump together. Turn the dough out onto a lightly floured work surface and gently knead until it comes together in a ball.

Gently press the dough into the bottom and up the sides of a 9-inch (23 cm) tart pan with a removable bottom. Trim off any overhang and use it to seal any cracks in the dough. Freeze the crust for at least 1 hour, or wrap tightly and freeze for up to 8 weeks.

When ready to make the tart, preheat the oven to 350°F (180°C/Gas Mark 4). Line the crust with parchment paper and top with pie weights (baking beans). Bake until the crust is a light golden color, about 20 minutes. Remove and set aside. Leave the oven on.

Meanwhile, make the pistachio filling:
In a food processor, combine the pistachios and flour and grind into a fine powder. Add the butter, granulated sugar, salt, and pistachio paste and blend until the mixture comes together. Add the egg, milk, and rose water and blend again until you get a thick spreadable cream.

Spread the cream evenly into the tart shell and return the pan to the oven. Bake until the cream is set at the edges and slightly soft in the center, 15–20 minutes. Remove from the oven and set aside to cool completely.

Prepare the yogurt topping:
In a bowl, combine the yogurt, powdered sugar, and lemon zest and whisk until smooth.

Once the tart is cooled completely, spoon the yogurt topping on top. Place the cherries in the center and garnish with rose petals or pistachios (if using).

The tart without the yogurt topping will keep in an airtight container at room temperature for up to 3 days, but once topped with the yogurt is best enjoyed on the same day.

 Pistachio and Rose Water Tart with Yogurt and Cherries

Lemon Rosemary Semolina Cake

A sweet Italian lady, her brown eyes framed by wrinkles from squinting in the sun, smiled and asked, "The usual?" I nodded and forked over change as she handed me a box wrapped in baker's twine. From her stall in the weekend farmers' market outside my flat in London, I bought my ultimate guilty pleasure: a lemon-rosemary polenta cake. Every time I have made the traditional Arab semolina cake *basbousa* (or *hareeseh/nammoura*) since then, I have thought back to that cake and wondered why no one ever flavors the semolina cake with a lemon and rosemary syrup instead of the usual orange blossom. This cake does exactly that and results in a truly decadent dessert that is as rich as it is fresh.

Makes one 11-inch (28 cm) round cake

For the lemon sugar syrup:

- 2 cups (14 oz/400 g) sugar
- 3 sprigs fresh rosemary
- ½ cup (4 fl oz/120 ml) fresh lemon juice
- 1 tablespoon butter
- 1 teaspoon orange blossom water

For the cake:

- Butter or ghee, for the pan, plus more for brushing
- 2¼ cups (13 oz/375 g) medium- or fine-grain semolina (not semolina flour)
- 1 teaspoon baking powder
- 6 tablespoons (3¼ oz/90 g) melted ghee or melted butter or vegetable oil
- ½ cup (4 fl oz/120 ml) whole milk
- ½ cup (3½ oz/100 g) sugar
- Grated zest of 1 unwaxed or organic lemon
- Pinch of salt

Make the lemon sugar syrup:
In small heavy-bottomed saucepan, combine the sugar, 1½ cups (12 fl oz/350 ml) water, and the rosemary sprig and bring to a boil over medium-high heat. Reduce the heat and simmer for 2–4 minutes to slightly thicken. Remove from the heat, discard the rosemary, and add the lemon juice, butter, and orange blossom water and stir. Allow to cool completely before using.

Make the cake:
Line the bottom of an 11-inch (28 cm) round cake pan (or 9 × 13-inch/23 × 33 cm rectangular cake pan) with parchment and grease with melted ghee or butter.

In a medium bowl, combine the semolina, baking powder, and ghee and mix well until the mixture resembles wet sand and the semolina grains are evenly coated in the fat. In a small bowl, whisk together the milk, sugar, lemon zest, salt, and 3 tablespoons of the previously prepared lemon syrup until combined. Add this to the semolina mixture and stir until combined, taking care not to overmix. The batter will be slightly thick and sticky. Pour into the prepared pan and spread evenly, tapping lightly on a hard surface to even out. Cover with plastic wrap (clingfilm) and set aside for at least 30 minutes, and up to several hours, until the batter solidifies slightly and the semolina has time to absorb the liquid in the batter.

When ready to bake, preheat the oven to 350°F (180°C/Gas Mark 4).

Brush the top of the cake with a very thin layer of melted ghee (this allows even browning) then slice into your desired shape. Bake until the top is a golden brown, 20–30 minutes. If after 25 minutes, the cake is still light in color, broil (grill) for 1–2 minutes until you have a nice golden-brown top.

Remove the cake from the oven and pour the cooled lemon syrup over the hot cake. It may look like a lot at first, but the cake will absorb it. Allow to sit for a few hours, and preferably overnight, before cutting and serving. The cake will keep, covered, for several days at room temperature.

Notes: This recipe yields a large cake, but can easily be halved to make an 8-inch (20 cm) round cake.

Coconut Knafeh with Lemongrass Syrup

We were driving through upstate New York one weekend when a program came on the radio discussing the best cakes in America. My husband heard about the top contender, a coconut cake served in a Charleston restaurant, when he turned to me excitedly, "Can you make a coconut *knafeh*?" My initial response was scepticism, why would I mess with a trusted classic?! But his excitement compelled me to try. Toasted coconut is such a satisfying flavor, it is nutty and naturally sweet and I figured it would work with the sweet/salty contrast of *knafeh*. It took months of experiments to finally get the balance right, but the result was well worth it for a dessert that is a perfect balance of sweet and salty, soft and crunchy, and refreshingly fragrant. The recipe can easily be doubled.

Makes one 8-inch (20 cm) cake (to serve 4)

For the syrup:
- 1 cup (7 oz/200 g) sugar
- Squeeze of fresh lime juice
- ½ stalk lemongrass, lightly crushed

For the cake:
- Ghee, for the pan
- Scant 1 cup (90 g) unsweetened shredded (desiccated) coconut, plus more for garnish
- 4 ½ oz (125 g) low-moisture mozzarella cheese, shredded
- 4 ½ oz (125 g) whole-milk ricotta cheese
- Grated zest of 1 unwaxed/organic lime, plus more for garnish
- 4 oz (115 g) shredded phyllo (filo) pastry (see Note)
- 5 ½ tablespoons (75 g) ghee or clarified butter, melted

Make the syrup:
In a small saucepan, combine the sugar, lime juice, lemongrass, and ¾ cup (6 fl oz/175 ml) water and bring to a boil over medium heat. Simmer for 5 minutes to thicken. Remove from the heat and allow to cool before using.

Make the cake:
Preheat the oven to 400°F (200°C/Gas Mark 6). Grease an 8-inch (20 cm) nonstick round baking pan with ghee.

In a dry frying pan, dry-roast the coconut over medium heat, stirring constantly, until aromatic and nutty, about 5 minutes. You do not want it to darken as it will cook in the oven; you just want to give it a head start. Transfer to a large bowl and set aside.

In a bowl, stir together the mozzarella, ricotta, and lime zest and set aside.

In a food processor, process the shredded phyllo (filo) until the shreds are roughly ¾ inch (2 cm) in length. Transfer to the bowl with the toasted coconut and mix to combine. Pour the melted ghee on top and work with your hands until it has been fully absorbed.

Transfer about two-thirds of the mixture to the greased baking dish, pressing it tightly with your hands to cover the bottom. Spread the cheese mixture evenly over the pastry. Spread the remaining pastry evenly on top of the cheese filling, making sure to fully cover the cheese, then firmly pat down with your hands.

Bake until the cheese has melted and the crust is a golden brown, 25–35 minutes.

Remove from the oven and allow to cool for 5 minutes. Loosen the edges with a knife, place an inverted serving platter over the cake pan, carefully flip it over, and lift the cake pan. Drizzle with enough sugar syrup to soak the cake. Garnish with coconut and lime zest and serve immediately.

Notes: Shredded phyllo pastry, or *kataïfi*, can be found in the frozen section at any Middle Eastern grocery store. It is much easier to shred the dough if it is partially frozen.

Spiced Pavlova with Orange Blossom Cream and Berries

There is a sizable Arab population in Australia and New Zealand, so it's no surprise that one of the most iconic Aussie desserts, the Pavlova, has been given an Arab twist. A dear friend of mine who married a Palestinian man from Australia first gave me the idea for this dessert, but I have since seen it adapted to a variety of Middle Eastern flavors from figs to dates, from saffron to rose water, and beyond. This is my Arab take on the Aussie classic.

Makes one 9-inch (23 cm) cake

For the meringue:
1 cup (7 oz/200 g) granulated sugar
1½ teaspoons cornstarch (cornflour)
¼ teaspoon ground cardamom
¼ teaspoon ground cinnamon
4 egg whites, at room temperature (see Note)
Pinch of salt
1 teaspoon distilled white vinegar
1 teaspoon vanilla extract

For the cream:
1 cup (8 fl oz/250 ml) heavy (double) cream
1 tablespoon powdered (icing) sugar
1 teaspoon orange blossom water

For the berries:
12 ounces (350 g) mixed berries (2–3 cups)
1 tablespoon granulated sugar
2 teaspoons orange blossom water
Crushed pistachios, for garnish

Make the meringue:
Preheat the oven to 250°F (120°C/Gas Mark ½). Using a pencil, trace around a 9-inch (23 cm) round cake pan on a piece of parchment paper. Flip the paper over so the pencil marks are down and place on a sheet pan.

In a small bowl, combine the granulated sugar, cornstarch (cornflour), cardamom, and cinnamon and stir to combine.

In a stand mixer with the whisk attachment (or in a large bowl with a hand mixer), combine the egg whites and salt. Starting on low and increasing incrementally to medium speed, whip until you see small uniform egg white bubbles, 2–3 minutes. Increase the speed to medium and gradually add the sugar mixture, a couple tablespoons at a time, until the sugar is incorporated and the egg whites begin to look white and glossy, about 5 minutes.

At this point, add the vinegar and vanilla, increase the speed to its highest setting, and beat until stiff peaks form, about 5 minutes. Peaks are stiff if, when you flip the bowl of the mixer upside down, the meringue stays in place.

Spoon the meringue into the circle on the prepared baking sheet and smooth out toward the edges, making them slightly higher than the center.

Bake for 1 hour 45 minutes, then turn the oven off and allow the meringue to cool inside for another 2 hours. Once cooled, remove from the oven and set aside.

Make the cream:
In a stand mixer with the whisk attachment (or in a bowl with a hand mixer), combine the cream, powdered (icing) sugar, and orange blossom water and whip until medium to stiff peaks form, about 4 minutes. Cover and chill until ready to use.

Meanwhile, prepare the berries:
In a bowl, sprinkle the berries with the granulated sugar and orange blossom water. Toss gently to coat, then cover and set aside for at least 30 minutes and up to 3 hours until ready to use.

To assemble, gently spread the cream over the meringue base, then spoon the soaked berries on top. Sprinkle with crushed pistachios and serve immediately; the dessert is best enjoyed within a few hours of assembly.

Note: It's best to separate the eggs while they are still cold, but the egg whites should be at room temperature for whipping, so let them sit out while you prepare the remaining ingredients for the meringue.

Spiced Pavlova with Orange Blossom Cream and Berries

Ma'amoul Suniyeh

Ka'ak o ma'amoul, bite-size semolina cakes stuffed with dates or nuts, are synonymous with the holidays for both Christians and Muslims in the Arab world. They are, however, quite labor-intensive and usually involve the whole family getting together and preparing them en masse, and in celebration, a few times a year. This dessert takes the finicky and time-consuming part of shaping individual cakes out of the process, and gives you a single cake that is much quicker to make, can easily be sliced, and tastes just as delicious.

Makes one 9 × 13-inch (23 × 33 cm) cake

For the pastry:
- 1½ cups (8¾ oz/250 g) fine semolina (not semolina flour)
- 2 cups (8¾ oz/250 g) all-purpose (plain) flour
- 14 tablespoons (7 oz/200 g) unsalted butter, at room temperature
- 2 tablespoons vegetable oil
- 2 tablespoons powdered (icing) sugar
- 1 tablespoon orange blossom water
- 1¼ teaspoons baking powder
- 1 teaspoon ground mahlab (if unavailable, substitute with vanilla or ground mastic)
- ¼ teaspoon salt

For the date filling:
- 1 lb 2 oz (500 g) date paste (see Note, page 201)
- 1 teaspoon ground cinnamon
- 1 tablespoon vegetable oil or ghee

For assembly:
- ½ cup (1¾ oz/50 g) finely chopped lightly toasted walnuts or pistachios
- Whole pistachios or walnuts, for decoration (optional)
- Powdered sugar, for dusting (optional)

Make the pastry:
In a large bowl, combine the semolina, all-purpose (plain) flour, butter, and oil and work with your hands until the mixture resembles wet sand, at least 10–15 minutes. Cover with plastic wrap (clingfilm) and leave for several hours, or overnight, at room temperature.

Add the powdered (icing) sugar, orange blossom water, baking powder, mahlab, and salt and mix to combine. Start to add 4 tablespoons water, a tablespoon at a time, and knead gently (do not overmix or the pastry will be too tough) until a clump of dough holds together without crumbling. Cover and leave to rest for 15–30 minutes, while you prepare the filling.

Preheat the oven to 400°F (200°C/Gas Mark 6). Prepare a 9 × 13 inch (23 × 33 cm) or an 11-inch/28 cm round metal baking pan (not glass).

Make the date filling:
In a small bowl, combine the date paste, cinnamon, and oil and mix.

To assemble:
Line a baking pan with plastic wrap, leaving an overhang on all sides. Take half of the semolina mixture and spread it evenly on the plastic wrap. Using the edges of the plastic wrap, lift the layer out of the pan and set aside. This will become your top layer. Take more plastic wrap and with oiled hands repeat with the entire date mixture. Lift it out of the pan and set aside. This will become your middle layer.

Brush your pan with ghee and spread the remaining semolina mixture evenly in the bottom of the pan. This is your bottom layer. Take the date layer and gently flip it onto the bottom layer in the pan. Remove the plastic wrap and discard.

Sprinkle the toasted nuts over the date mixture and lightly press with your hands. Take the remaining layer of semolina and gently flip it over the date filling and nuts. Remove the plastic wrap and discard. Lightly moisten your hands with water and smooth this top layer out.

With the tip of a sharp knife score the cake all the way through to form a diamond pattern. If you have ma'amoul metal mold tweezers, you can use them to create a design within each diamond.

Place a pistachio or walnut in the center of each diamond or on the intersections, if desired.

Bake until just starting to get a golden color around the edges, about 20 minutes. Keep an eye on it as you do not want it to brown at all.

Allow to cool completely at room temperature, for several hours at least, before attempting to cut it. Dust with powdered sugar (if using). Tightly covered or in an airtight container, the cake will keep for at least 10 days.

Index

Note: Page references in *italics* indicate photographs.

Sources:

Bavarchi Muhammad Ali, et al. *A Persian Cookbook: The Manual: A 16th Century Persian Cookbook*. Prospect Books, 2018.
Clarkson, Janet. *Food History Almanac: over 1,300 Years of World Culinary History, Culture, and Social Influence*. Rowman & Littlefield, 2014.
Dalby, Andrew. *Dangerous Tastes: The Story of Spices*. British Museum Press, 2004.
Dalby, Andrew. *Tastes Of Byzantium: the Cuisine of a Legendary Empire*. Tauris Parke I B Tauris, 2019.
Davidson, Alan. *The Oxford Companion to Food*. Oxford University Press, 2014.
Heine, Peter, and Peter Lewis. *The Culinary Crescent: A History of Middle Eastern Cuisine*. Gingko Library, 2018.
Heine, Peter. *Food Culture in the Near East, Middle East, and North Africa*. Greenwood Press, 2004.
Helou, Anissa. Feast: *Food of the Islamic World*. HarperCollins Publishers, 2018.
Khoury, Colin. "Where Our Food Crops Come From." CIAT Blog, International Center for Tropical Agriculture, 2016, blog.ciat.cgiar.org/origin-of-crops/.
Kiple, Kenneth F. *The Cambridge World History of Food*. Cambridge Univ. Press, 2001.
Laudan, Rachel. *Cuisine and Empire: Cooking in World History*. University of California Press, 2015.
Lewicka, Paulina B. *Food and Foodways of Medieval Cairenes: Aspects of Life in an Islamic Metropolis of the Eastern Mediterranean*. Brill, 2011.
Marks, Gil. *Encyclopedia of Jewish Food*. Wiley, 2010.
Nasrallah, Nawal. *Annals of the Caliphs' Kitchens (Kitab al-Tabikh) Ibn Sayyar Al-Warraq's Tenth-Century Baghdadi Cookbook*. BRILL, 2014.
Nasrallah, Nawal. *Delights from the Garden of Eden: A Cookbook and a History of the Iraqi Cuisine*. Equinox Publishing, 2019.
Perry, Charles, translator. *Scents and Flavors (Kitab al-Wusla ila al-Habib): A Syrian Cookbook*. Edited by Charles Perry, New York University Press, 2020.
Perry, Charles. "Chapter 5: Middle Eastern Food History." *Food in Time and Place: the American Historical Association Companion to Food History*, by Paul H. Freedman et al., University of California Press, 2014.
Pilcher, Jeffrey M. *Food in World History*. Taylor and Francis, 2017.
Salloum, Habeeb, et al. *Sweet Delights from a Thousand and One Nights: The Story of Traditional Arab Sweets*. I.B. Tauris, 2013.
Salloum, Habeeb. *Scheherazade's Feasts: Foods of the Medieval Arab World*. University of Pennsylvania Press, 2013.
Spengler, Robert N. *Fruit from the Sands: the Silk Road Origins of the Foods We Eat*. University of California Press, 2019.
Zaouali, Lilia, and M. B. DeBevoise. *Medieval Cuisine of the Islamic World: A Concise History with 174 Recipes*. University of California Press, 2009.

Recipe Notes:

Butter is unsalted, unless specified otherwise.
All milk is whole (full-fat) milk, unless specified otherwise.
Herbs are fresh, unless specified otherwise.
Eggs are assumed to be large (US extra large) and preferably organic and free-range.
Onions are medium yellow onions, unless specified otherwise.
Potatoes are floury, unless specified otherwise—try Rooster, Maris Piper, or russet varieties.
Individual fruits and vegetables, such as onions and pears, are assumed to be medium sized, unless specified otherwise, and should be peeled and/or washed.
When using the zest of citrus fruit, buy unwaxed or organic.
Fish are assumed cleaned and gutted.
Cooking and preparation times are for guidance only, as individual ovens vary.
If using a convection (fan) oven, follow the manufacturer's instructions concerning oven temperatures.
Exercise a high level of caution when following recipes involving any potentially hazardous activity including the use of high temperatures and open flames and when deep-frying. In particular, when deep-frying, add food carefully to avoid splashing, wear long sleeves, and never leave the pan unattended.
When deep-frying, heat the oil to the temperature specified, or until a cube of bread browns in 30 seconds. After frying, drain fried foods on paper towels.
Exercise caution when foraging for ingredients; any foraged ingredients should be eaten only if an expert has deemed them safe to eat, and should be cleaned well before use.
Some recipes include raw or very lightly cooked eggs, meat, or fish, and fermented products. These should be avoided by the elderly, infants, pregnant women, convalescents, and anyone with an impaired immune system.
When sterilizing jars for preserves, wash the jars in clean, hot water and rinse thoroughly. Heat the oven to 275°F/140°C/Gas Mark 1. Place the jars on a baking sheet and place in the oven to dry.
When no quantity is specified—for example of oils, salts, and herbs used for finishing dishes or for deep-frying—quantities are discretionary and flexible.
All spoon and cup measurements are level, unless otherwise stated. 1 teaspoon = 5 ml; 1 tablespoon = 15 ml. Australian standard tablespoons are 20 ml, so Australian readers are advised to use 3 teaspoons in place of 1 tablespoon when measuring small quantities.
Cup, metric, and imperial measurements are used in this book. Follow one set of measurements throughout, not a mixture, as they are not interchangeable.

Acknowledgements:

Writing this book was much scarier than writing the first one. With the first, I was recounting my family's history and culinary traditions as an invitation to a Palestinian table. With this book, I felt like I was trying to combine centuries' worth of some of the world's richest history into a 250-page book. It was no easy feat, and many were the nights I was up questioning what I was doing or trying to accomplish. But you have this book in your hands, which means that I finally accomplished what I set out to do, or at least some version of it. And that is largely thanks to the people who believed in my vision, who supported me in small ways and large, and who were companions on a path that is often lonely and laced with doubt.

Mama and Baba, you are an endless source of information, and I am so grateful that I could pick up the phone to you and learn more valuable things in a five-minute conversation than I did in hours of reading. Thank you for your love, generosity, and kindness, which have never known any bounds. Najib, I think part of the reason writing this book was harder is that you weren't living down the street and able to honestly (and harshly!) critique everything I cooked.

To my grandmothers, Teta Fatima and Teta Asma (may she rest in peace), and this time also to my great-grandmothers and their mothers before them, a debt of gratitude is owed. I never got to know many of you, but your stories were passed on and became a source of inspiration. You are the unsung heroes and the history behind the beautiful face of our evolving cuisine.

A special thank you to the other mothers in my life—Khalto Alice Amto Lamees, Auntie Juju, and Auntie Nadia—for your generosity with your time, stories, and love.

To the friends who across continents and life circumstances have remained an extension of who I am and what I do—Katie, Sruthi, Vickie A., Juliana S., Hannah V., Lama B., Vinita, Denise, Zaina, and Majdah—I am beyond grateful to you.

To the friends who let me overfeed them, who offered honest feedback, who inspired me and listened to me talk endlessly about crazy ideas, and who on a day-to-day basis kept me sane and were great companions—Leen, Mike, Kate, Mayukh, Asima, and Sa'ed—thank you.

Emily Takoudes and Emilia Terragni: It's always an honor and a privilege to work with you. I see now why there's nobody else I could have trusted with this book.

To the best photographer I know and now also a dear friend, Dan Perez, it is worth it to literally cross the world to work with you.

Above all, to Aboud, my best friend, whose tender calmness embraces my fieriness, whose moral compass is my source of guidance, and whose humor keeps our home filled with laughter: Thank you for being my rock in more ways than I can count. Finally, and most important, to the two little ones who inspire me and teach me every day (even as they make the process of manifesting that inspiration incredibly long!): Yasmeen and Hala, you make life worth living and are the reason I write. In writing, I'm hoping to capture a colorful past you never experienced and pave an even brighter future for you to explore. Thank you for showing me the greatest love and joy a person can know.

Phaidon Press Limited
2 Cooperage Yard
London E15 2QR

Phaidon Press Inc.
65 Bleecker Street
New York, NY 10012

phaidon.com

First published 2021

ISBN 978 1 83866 251 6

A CIP catalogue record for this book is available from the British Library and the Library of Congress.

Editor: Emily Takoudes
Production Controller: Nerissa Dominguez Vales

Designed by Hans Stofregen
Photographs by Dan Perez

Printed in China

The publisher would like to thank Linda Bouchard, Lesley Malkin, Elizabeth Parson, Gemma Robinson, Sarah Scott, and Kate Slate.